THEY JUST DON'T GET IT

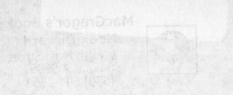

THEY
JUST DON'T
GET IT

How Washington Is Still Compromising
Your Safety—and What You Can Do About It

Colonel David Hunt (U.S. Army, Ret.)

THREE RIVERS PRESS

NEW YORK

All rights reserved.
Published in the United States by Three Rivers Press, an imprint of the
Crown Publishing Group, a division of Random House, Inc., New York.
www.crownpublishing.com

Three Rivers Press and the Tugboat design are registered
trademarks of Random House, Inc.

Originally published in hardcover in the United States in slightly different
form by Crown Forum, an imprint of the Crown Publishing Group,
a division of Random House, Inc., New York, in 2005.

Library of Congress Cataloging-in-Publication Data
Hunt, David, Colonel.
They just don't get it : how Washington is still compromising your safety—
and what you can do about it / David Hunt.—1st ed.
Includes index.
1. Terrorism—Government policy—United States.   2. National security—
United States.   3. War on Terrorism, 2001–   I. Title.
HV6432.H85   2005
363.32'0973—dc22   2004027168

ISBN-13: 978-1-4000-9742-5
ISBN-10: 1-4000-9742-8

Printed in the United States of America

Design by Leonard Henderson

10 9 8 7 6 5 4 3 2 1

First Paperback Edition

With humility and respect, this book is dedicated to all those great Americans who are putting their lives on the line every day in this War on Terror.

CONTENTS

THEY JUST DON'T GET IT

CHAPTER 1

Terror in Your Living Room

They came in low over the mountains doing about 190 miles per hour, two Task Force 160 UH 1 60 Black Hawk helicopters carrying an assault force of sixteen French Foreign Legion reconnaissance soldiers led by a British colonel. It was broad daylight. Not the best time for a tactical military operation, but we had little choice.

A NATO force of sixty thousand soldiers had just taken over the Bosnian peace mission from the United Nations. Now we were confronted with one of the most serious threats to peace in the bloody Balkans: a terrorist training camp was in full operation in Fojnica in northwest Bosnia.

The president of Bosnia claimed the terrorist camp did not exist, but we had all the evidence: satellite imagery, technical communications intercepts, and information that was being fed to us by the four two-man teams we had positioned in hidden "observation posts"—holes that were just yards from the terrorist compound. We knew that an Iranian branch of the terrorist organization Hezbollah had built the camp. And we knew Hezbollah means business; just to give you an idea, the number two man in the U.S. State Department later said publicly that "Hezbollah may be the A-team of terrorists and maybe al Qaeda is actually the B-team"—and he said this *after* the 9/11 attacks. During this long war in the Balkans, much of the Muslim world had rallied to the support of the Bosnian Muslims, who were outgunned and outmanned by the Serbs. But when you're dealing with Hezbollah and a terrorist camp—and with Hezbollah's main supporter, Iran, which the State Department puts on its list of state sponsors of terrorism for a reason—you know that helping people defend themselves isn't the only priority.

I was the tactical adviser to the commander in chief of NATO forces in Bosnia, Admiral Leighton "Snuffy" Smith, U.S. Navy. My job was to facilitate all U.S. national intelligence matters for him and to perform any other tasks he deemed necessary. Taking care of this terrorist training camp had become one of those "other" tasks. The mission became urgent when we learned that the Iranians were using hunters and dogs to guard the perimeter of the camp. They might soon discover our guys in the observation posts. We had to go in—*now.*

I had been in the Army for more than a quarter-century doing tours from Southeast Asia to South America. I had gone to every school the Army would let me go to, from Airborne to Ranger to Special Forces, and I had more years commanding soldiers than almost anyone still in uniform. But I still felt lucky to have been picked for this mission. Sure, I had years of experience, but I was a colonel. Colonels don't do raids. Now here I was, hanging and banging with the best Special Operations forces in the world. We were going to take down some very bad men and make Bosnia, and possibly the world, a safer place. I loved every minute of it.

My mission was twofold: link up with the assault force and establish an intelligence link to arrange for the Bosnian president to be shown the camp he said did not exist. As the Black Hawks carried the assault force to the terrorist camp, we made our way in an unarmored Chevrolet Suburban truck through Serb and Muslim territory that was known to be hostile to NATO forces.

We knew we would have to deal with roadblocks, which were everywhere, even though they had been illegal ever since NATO began its occupation in 1996. In this case, though, we weren't going to stop at any of the roadblocks. If need be, we'd shoot our way through. I would take all targets from the center of the car window to my right, while my colleague, Fran the Navy SEAL, would take all targets from the center to his left. The first shot would shatter the window and make our visibility difficult, but oh well—nothing was going to stop us from linking up with the assault force.

Our Chevy Suburban reached the camp just after the two Black Hawks landed within inches of the main house. The French Legionnaires, with their blackened, grim, and alert faces, took the house in a mere eleven seconds. They surprised and captured twenty-one men. We linked up with the assault force in time to see three Iranian diplomats get busted.

In the raid we recovered more than 10,000 valuable pieces of information, 200 separate explosive devices, 150 weapons, ammunition, cameras, and planning documents—documents that provided shocking evidence of the terrorists' deadly intentions. It quickly became clear that the terrorists had been planning to target the U.S. Embassy or the NATO headquarters next door, which served as barracks for Turkish and French soldiers. The terrorists knew that the approaches to the embassy and the barracks remained unguarded, and they planned to move over the unprotected walls, toward the barracks' side doors, and up the stairs that their spies had already photographed and checked out. They would have run down the long corridor, throwing bombs into the rooms and killing as they went. When they reached the main room of the enlisted barracks, where hundreds of men were bunked, the terrorists would have blown themselves up, leaving death and destruction everywhere.

Fortunately, we didn't let that happen, because our raid was a total success. It was, in fact, the first successful U.S. or NATO raid on an active terrorist training camp anywhere in the world.

But one can imagine the reaction within NATO and within the United States if at the beginning of the reluctant and controversial

NATO-led occupation in Bosnia terrorists had killed a substantial number of Americans or NATO soldiers or destroyed the recently reopened U.S. Embassy. I was there, and I assure you that if all of this had happened, we would have done what we did in Somalia, what we did in Lebanon—we would have turned tail and run.

Four years after the raid I was back in Bosnia, testifying in front of the Bosnian Supreme Court to try to prevent the release of the Bosnian government official who had been responsible for the terrorist camp. I testified for twelve hours with armed guards protecting me. I was allowed to have a loaded weapon with me while I testified. It was a good thing I was, because the Bosnian government was about to release this terrorist/government official. It turned out there was a price on my head.

Being involved in the only takedown of an active terrorist camp was just part of a long career spent fighting terrorists. I have trained Special Forces units, SWAT teams, the FBI, even the local police in counterterrorism tactics. I advised authorities on how to prevent terrorist attacks in the 1980, 1984, 1988, 2000, and 2002 Olympic Games. I am a designated terrorism expert in federal court, and I have testified at many of the major terrorist trials concerning everything from Pakistan to the World Trade Center. So although some people were surprised when terrorists attacked the United States by flying airplanes into the World Trade Center, the Pentagon, and a field in Pennsylvania, I was not. A handful of us had been sounding the call for years. But nobody listened.

I guess it's not all that surprising that our country was caught off guard on September 11, 2001. "We the people" have short memories. The fact is, Islamic terrorists killed nearly eight hundred Americans in the three decades leading up to 9/11. But as this book will detail, the United States did almost nothing to counter all the terrorist attacks we saw, except occasionally lob a few missiles and call it a day. No effective response. No willingness to deal with or even acknowledge the growing threat. For years we refused to face reality. Had we had leaders with foresight and courage, had we as a nation been paying attention, had we done anything to counter the rising threat of terrorism, we would not have been surprised on 9/11. But our mentality remained "Ain't gonna happen—not here. No way."

Well, it happened. And what's really scary is that the terrorist threat isn't going away. Look around. In Madrid, Islamic militants drop off ten backpack bombs on commuter trains and blow them up using cell phone technology, killing 191 people and injuring more than 1,600; the attack turns an election on its ear. In Indonesia, hundreds of people are murdered in a nightclub bombing. Outside of Singapore, terrorists seize a super oil tanker, killing all hands and destroying the ship. In the Middle East, Muslim radicals kidnap and behead Nicholas Berg, Paul Johnson, and other Americans. In Iraq, Hezbollah and other terrorist organizations kill American soldiers as part of the insurgency. Iran keeps giving the world the finger while it builds nuclear bombs. Syria is still an acknowledged supporter of terrorism. Al Qaeda cells are being uncovered in South and Central America, and the terrorist organization's top leaders remain at large. It is estimated that more than 10,000 terrorists were trained in al Qaeda camps in Afghanistan before we invaded.

Do you get that the bad guys aren't going anywhere?

Unfortunately, it seems that many of us are already starting to hide from this reality. Do you remember the horrors of 9/11? Do you remember how you felt on that terrible day and in the days and weeks that followed? Do you remember how our children cried? Do you remember the pictures of burning buildings and the calls for revenge? Well, you *must* remember. Winning the War on Terror—at home and abroad—is the most difficult and important task facing us as a nation, and that task can't be accomplished without all of us feeling a bit uneasy, a bit afraid, and a whole lot angry. These emotions shouldn't paralyze us. Not at all. They steel our resolve and spur us to take the actions necessary to win the War on Terror. We can't fall into the trap of saying—again—"No way. Ain't gonna happen here" or "They haven't hit us since 9/11." Those who attacked us on 9/11 took close to five years to get it done. They *will* attempt to hit us again. If we keep on the slippery slope of thinking "We're okay," "We're safe," "They wouldn't dare do it again," we're guaranteeing the bastards success.

Since we're fighting a war for our very survival, we had better figure out how to win. That's why I'm writing this book—to show us how we can win the war, how we can protect ourselves. As a military analyst for the Fox News Channel, I'm paid to offer insight into how our armed forces are conducting the fight against our enemies, and of course our military represents a key weapon in this fight. But this book shows that to win the War on Terror we need to concern ourselves with more than just military tactics. For one thing, we need to look at what our political leaders are doing.

The sad truth is, our leaders in Washington are screwing up in many ways. They still don't get it. It's as if they've forgotten what is important and how to wage war. Incompetence and bureaucratic bungling are everywhere. Turf wars are the rule, not the exception. Most people in our nation's capital are so busy pointing fingers that they're not dealing with the ongoing threats. (Just look at the former White House coordinator for counterterrorism, Richard "It-Ain't-My-Fault" Clarke. He wrote a book charging that the Bush administration did nothing for its 232 days in office before 9/11—even though Clarke himself worked on national security and terrorism issues in the Clinton White House for more than 2,900 days, during which time he did next to nothing. Sure, when he testified before Congress, Clarke did the apology thing, but it came years too late.)

I'm sure you've heard that we suffer from intelligence failures, our talking heads and politicians having a knack for stating what is fairly self-evident. But I doubt you know how bad it really is. I'm going to tell you. It's ugly and you might be tempted to look away, but I won't let you. We need to learn to face the darkness. Our intelligence community is underpaid, oversupervised, and overpoliticized. Somehow we have allowed this to happen to what is, along with the military, the most essential tool in the fight against terrorism.

Do you know who is running this war? I know, you think "they" are in charge. Answer this for me. Who the hell is "they"? Well, I'm going to show you that too. And if you think you're scared now, just wait and see how you feel once you find out who is running this show. I'll give you a hint. No one is in charge! No one is accountable. No one is leading. We are flying blind.

Things have to change. The incompetence, the excuse making, and the lack of accountability have to end, because we're facing an enemy intent on killing us. The nature of this beast we're fighting is butt-ugly. Every day we see more monstrous and barbaric acts perpetrated against us. The perpetrators are using religion, trumped-up political charges, and our freedom as reasons to kill us. Worse, our political leaders continue to tell us that some of the countries that feed, clothe, arm, and hide these killers are our friends. It is not just the rest of the world that is trying to kill us. Sometimes it seems as though we are set on doing it ourselves or at least making it easier for the bad guys to succeed. That's maybe the biggest change we have to make: our leaders have to stop worrying about being "sensitive" to other countries and start getting in the face of all those who would support terrorists and all those who would do us harm.

There's another critical dimension to this story. People who recognize me from Fox News come up to me all the time and ask, "Colonel Hunt, what can I do about any of this? What can I do to protect my family?" You probably want to know the same thing. The answer is, You can do a lot. Hell, you *must* do a lot. If we are to win this war, everybody must help, each in his own way. If you want to hoard canned goods, keep bottled water, and buy duct tape, go for it if it makes you feel better. But after you do that, just be ready to do something that will *really* affect this war. I will tell you how.

Some people won't like this book; actually, many won't. If you're sitting in your barber chair in the basement of the Senate office building getting a thirty-dollar haircut for three bucks, you won't like this book. If you're sitting in your ivory tower at some university looking for theory, you won't like this book. If you're looking for complicated, politically correct solutions that involve a trainload of lawyers to figure them out, and then a boatload of lawyers to decipher what the first bunch of lawyers said, you won't like this book—not for one second. If you're an indecisive, give-them-a-hug bureaucrat, you will definitely not like this book. But if you're tired of double talk and spin, then you just might like this book. This book is for those who care only about getting the job done without any regard for who gets the credit. If you could put together an organization of men and women who cared only about defeating terrorists, this fight would already be over.

The people in charge have now had more than three years to conduct this war, and in most instances they're still not getting it right. Sure, we've had some successes, and in some matters we're making progress. But as we'll see in this book, in some of the most critical areas we're failing to do what is absolutely essential to achieve victory. We have tried the politicians' and bureaucrats' way, the have-a-meeting, obscure-the-facts, figure-out-the-political-fallout, take-a-poll, ask-how-can-we-all-get-along, and how-can-we-create-a-"win-win" approach—which is *crap*! That way brought us 9/11. Now it's my turn. It is time for a new type of thinking and doing: "Go out and find and kill the bad guy."

Listen, fighting bad guys isn't brain surgery. You either do it or you don't. But that's not what you'd think based on what we've seen out of Washington and in the hundreds of books already written about terrorism. I've read literally hundreds of books on the subject, and none has ever talked about what we as a people can do in this war, as well as what our government needs to do and our military needs to do.

I have written this book because it is time that someone who has actually fought in this battle offers a solution. I am a soldier, trained to be a manager of violence; I'm a killer with two college degrees and a year at Harvard. I am a Ranger, Paratrooper, and Mechanized and Special Forces qualified officer with more than twenty-nine years of service to his country. I have been sent all over the world. I've led men and women in peace and in war. I have worked with our national intelligence services and such amazing men as Navy SEALs, Rangers, and Special Forces. I am one of them and proud of it. We are the ones charged with killing the bad guys. We have lain in wait for days and killed them. We have hunted them down and killed them. We have dropped bombs on them and killed them. That's what we do: we kill bad guys. In our careers, we have watched our military and political bosses fold when it counted, but we've fought anyway. We have listened to all the politically correct nonsense in briefings and meetings and still fought. We have tolerated incompetence and still fought.

So I write from my perspective, from my expertise, from my service, from my fear, and yes, from my hope. This book is my attempt to show you that there is another way besides the one we have chosen. It is a simple, no-BS, direct, and efficient way of getting at and solving the problem. It acknowledges, above all, that there is only one thing to do in a war, and that is to win. You win a war by killing every mother's son who would kill you first.

Given the stakes of the War on Terror—our very survival—don't you think it's time we took a look to see if we are ready? Are we ready as a nation, as a military, and as a government? I'll tell you right now, we're not. But we can be. We can be and I'll tell you how. You will be surprised at how simple it is. I am not saying that the changes we need to make are easy; they're not. But if you know what needs to be done, then you can get out there and make it happen.

First we'll look at the problems. How did we get in this mess in the first place? And who out there is trying to kill us? In some cases you'll be surprised and frightened to hear the answer. Then we'll examine the mistakes our leaders continue to make—and how we can fix these problems. We need to look at everything from our intelligence community to our bureaucratic structure in Washington to our relationships with our supposed allies to the state of our military to the kinds of military tactics we need to start using in order to defeat the terrorists. And finally we'll look at what all of us can and must do, as individuals, to help win this fight.

Some of the solutions to our problems will take a long time to implement and will require political pressure from the American people to force politicians to make the changes happen. That's okay, because whether we like it or not, and whether our politicians want to admit it or not, we're engaged in a fight that is going to take decades—thirty to fifty years, at least. Besides, there are many more changes we can implement immediately—changes that you and I can make, changes our leaders in Washington can make, and changes that our military commanders can make.

I'll have plenty to say in the course of the book, but let me just give you a preview of the kind of changes I'm talking about. We have political leaders publicly saying we need to be more "sensitive" to our allies. You think sensitivity wins a global War on Terror? Think again. No, we need to demand that our political leaders confront the leaders of places like Russia, Germany, and France. As I write this, we have these three hanging by their short hairs over the United Nations "Oil for Food" program, in which Saddam Hussein collected more than $20 billion in kickbacks. Hell, we can at least put some pressure on the bastards. We can organize boycotts against their goods like cars and wine. It will get everyone's attention and it hurts. We can pull all military bases out of Germany right now. We can openly say to the Russians, "Stop what you are doing and get the Russian mafia under control." We can stop applauding the arrest of Dr. Abdul Qadeer Khan in Pakistan, a man who has openly sold nuclear weapons and secrets, and demand that he first be tried and then publicly executed. We can do all these things and more. We just have to find the will.

This won't be pretty, but it will be an honest book. I have no agenda. I am not seeking political office or a career in the movies. I care only about my family's safety and about winning this war. Some say that in order to dramatically alter the way we think, in order to change the status quo, it is necessary to have a major wake-up call. Well okay, we've had that wake-up call. September 11 was that wake-up call. Now it is time to change how we look at the world.

Now it is time to get it right. We really don't want to wait for a second wake-up call; we need to understand that the threat we now face is very real, before we get whacked again. Terror is in your living room.

So hang on to your ball caps and hairpieces, this is going to be monkey-butt ugly. But it's not going to be boring. And you need to know the truth. You need to be prepared for the long fight ahead.

CHAPTER 2

How in the Name of God Did We Get Here?

I know you want to get right to it—fixing this deadly problem. We are Americans. We fix things. We make things better. We protect the world. So who gives a flying duck about our history with terrorism? Who cares about the who and the why of it? *Just fix it!*

Uh . . . excuse me, I have a question. What exactly is it you'd like fixed? What is the threat?

The threat we face is not just a few men who hide in caves and plot our death. It is the deadly combination of those killers in caves and the countries that support them with money, safe havens, and training. In terrorism, you cannot have one without the other. The simple fact is that terrorists have to eat, sleep, train, buy explosives, learn how to fly planes into buildings, build bombs to leave at the side of the road, and use computers to talk to one another. Without the support or at least tacit approval of these activities by a country/ benefactor, the terrorist cannot operate effectively.

A country that doesn't support terrorism will not allow terrorist activities to go on within its borders, period, no questions. That government will go after the terrorists and make moves to put a stop to their activities. It will drive the terrorists from their hiding places, capture them, give them up, or in a perfect world, kill them. When dealing with terrorism, we have to remember that both the cave dwellers and the countries in which they dwell are evil and must be dealt with as such.

Before we demand action from our government to deal with the terrorist threat, we should ask the question "Is our government up to the task?" It wasn't before 9/11. Unfortunately, it appears our government still isn't.

Don't misunderstand me; the terrorists are to be blamed for the evil they have wrought upon us. But it is also true that we as a people have been participating in our own demise. The reason we have been losing this fight is our unwillingness to face reality, attack our enemies, or even seriously threaten the terrorists. We have been led like sheep to the slaughter. September 11 made us all take notice that terrorists were trying to kill us, trying to destroy our civilization, but the fact is, we had plenty of warnings before that. More than 780 U.S. citizens were killed by terrorists in the twenty-nine years before 2001 (and that's *not* including the 168 who were killed in the 1995 Oklahoma City bombing), and our only response during all that time was to launch a few missiles from a safe distance at an aspirin factory, an empty terrorist training camp, and some hilltops in Lebanon. We were part of the problem, not the solution. By our inaction, we guaranteed that the terrorists would attack again and again.

How did we make such a mess of this fight? We need to know, because it really is true that "those who do not learn from history are doomed to repeat it." And repeating 9/11 is *not* an option.

Before we begin this brief history lesson, I suggest you get a bucket to throw up in, or at least have something on hand that you can hit or throw.

It all began at the 1972 Olympics. We were glued to our televisions anticipating the great and flamboyant Oregonian Steve Prefontaine's record-breaking runs. We wanted to see if we could win more medals than the Russians. But instead of bringing glory and national pride, the 1972 Olympic Games brought terror into our living rooms.

At 4:30 A.M. on September 5, 1972, five Arab terrorists climbed the 6½-foot fence surrounding the Olympic Village in Munich, Germany. They were members of Black September, a splinter group of Fatah—Yasser Arafat's faction of the Palestine Liberation Organization (PLO). These five terrorists met three others inside the fence, and together they broke into the rooms of some of the Israeli athletes, killing two and kidnapping nine others.

Later that same morning, the terrorists announced that they were Palestinian Arabs. They demanded the release of 234 Arab prisoners being held in Israeli jails and two German terrorist leaders imprisoned in Frankfurt. These were the first Olympic Games held in Germany since 1936, and the world press was out in full force. Therefore, the world had a front-row seat to every deadly event.

The German government showed its arrogance and stupidity by deciding to go this one alone. Many nations offered to help, but in reality, only the British Special Air Service (SAS) and the Israeli intelligence service, Mossad, could have done much. The Israelis and the British had been dealing with terrorists for twenty years or more. Because of this experience, both countries had developed sophisticated counterterrorist capabilities and intelligence services. The rest of the world, including the United States, was asleep when it came to terrorism. How the Munich incident was handled stands as testament to our ineptitude.

After hours of negotiations, the terrorists struck a deal with the Germans and were allowed to leave the Olympic Village. They traveled by bus to two waiting helicopters, which flew them to the NATO air base at Furstenfeldbruck. There they were to board a plane for Cairo.

German sharpshooters were standing by with orders to kill the terrorists (without harming the hostages, of course). But the Germans were expecting five terrorists, not eight terrorists. So when the eight members of Black September left the Olympic compound, the Germans did not have enough marksmen to successfully carry out the plan. Instead of the clean kill of the terrorists, a firefight between the Germans and the Palestinians followed. It ended at 3 A.M., when the Palestinians threw a grenade into one of the helicopters and killed all aboard. The terrorists in the second helicopter shot the remaining Israelis. When it was all over, eleven of the Israeli athletes, five terrorists, and one German policeman were dead. Three terrorists were captured.

If screwing up in front of 500 million people was all the German government did, that might be sufficient to place the Germans on the *Gong Show*. But no, they went and screwed up again and in an even bigger way. On October 29, less than two months after the assault on the Israeli athletes, Palestinian terrorists hijacked a Lufthansa jet and demanded that the Munich killers be released. No one seemed to notice at the time that the "hijacked" plane didn't have any passengers on board; the Germans gave in and set the imprisoned Munich terrorists free.

No passengers on a hijacked plane, a sovereign nation capitulating to terrorists who killed people and ruined the Olympics—anyone see anything funny going on here? All those who believe this was just a coincidence and that a deal was not struck before this "made for TV event" occurred, get in line—I have a bridge in Brooklyn for sale. It looked like a deal, plain and simple: in exchange for the release of terrorists being held in German jails, Black September would agree to no further attacks on German soil. It looked like the Germans choreographed this deal to spare their nation the embarrassment of a trial that would bring up how incompetent they were during the Olympics. And you don't have to take my word on all this: In 1985, terrorist mastermind Abu Abbas confirmed it to *al-Arabia* journalists while he was a guest of Saddam Hussein's in Iraq. Abbas said the German government made the deal with Black September. How would Abbas know? He claimed to have been the go-between.

This was insanity. Surely we in the United States of America, who saw all of this happen, who watched the reality of terrorism on our TVs, did something. Right? We must have mobilized, coordinated, planned, joined forces with other nations, and gotten ready for the day it would happen here. Except—we didn't. We did nothing and continued to do nothing or next to nothing for another twenty-nine damn years.

On March 9, 1977, twelve Hanafi Muslim terrorists armed with rifles, pistols, machetes, swords, and knives took over the B'nai B'rith International Center, the Islamic Center, and the District Building in Washington, D.C. They killed a reporter, paralyzed a city employee, and wounded several citizens, including a city councilman. They held 123 hostages on the eighth floor of one of the buildings for thirty-nine terror-filled hours. Terrorism in all its ugliness had paid us a visit four years after the 1972 Olympic Games in Munich. This time it was in our nation's capital. The similarities in governmental incompetence demonstrated by Munich and Washington are staggering.

This is the first incident in the United States that we officially called terrorism. How did the U.S. government handle this incident? The answer foretells the way we would handle terrorism in the future. We didn't send the FBI—the bureau didn't have a counterterrorist capability. We didn't send the CIA—this was a domestic incident and therefore not the agency's job. We didn't send the National Guard—for some reason, we never even asked the Guard to help. No, our government in its infinite wisdom turned to the Park Police. The Park Police are good men and women who do a terrific job . . . *guarding our parks*. But Park Ranger Bob is no way, nohow, going to know how to go into a high-rise and take back that building from men with guns and knives. Why didn't the U.S. government just send in the Boy Scouts?

When a standoff resulted, our government leaders had to turn to diplomats from three Muslim countries to end this fiasco. Why, you ask? Because we did not have the background or training to deal with this sort of terror. After thirty-nine hours, the Hanafis surrendered to police. They were duly tried, convicted, and sentenced to long terms in U.S. prisons, but we had been embarrassed. We were found wanting. The United States of America's capital was brought to a standstill by eight terrorist dipsticks.

So did we learn anything? No! For the next twenty-four years we did almost the same thing as we had done the previous five— *nothing*.

The incidents at the Olympic Games and in D.C. should have been a wake-up call and should have galvanized the West, especially the United States, into action. There were terrorists in our nation's capital, for Christ's sake! That should have snapped us up from our recliners and torn us away from *Monday Night Football.* But we did nothing of substance—making only cursory moves, nothing that really mattered. We are a nation of great people: caring, hardworking, moral, and kind. But I swear we need to be hit with a sledgehammer right between our eyes in order for us to pay attention. Not until 9/11 did we develop the political guts or resolve to even start thinking of what might be necessary to fight these guys. It seems that we have to be attacked, brutalized, and murdered in our own streets before we react. It drives me nuts—screaming-into-the-night nuts!

Yet another smack in the face came on November 4, 1979, when fifty-two American citizens were taken hostage by a radical group of militant Islamic students who stormed the U.S. Embassy in Tehran. President Jimmy Carter fought back by ordering a complete embargo of Iranian oil. Stronger economic embargoes followed. Five months later, on April 8, 1980, after negotiations for the hostages' release failed, Carter severed diplomatic relations with Iran. Why would we assume that this group of terrorists would care that diplomatic relations were severed? In case you are wondering, they didn't care.

Later in April, Carter authorized a top-secret mission named Operation Eagle Claw to free the hostages. The mission failed miserably. It had to be aborted on April 25 after three of the eight helicopters suffered mechanical failure and eight U.S. servicemen were killed during the refueling of one of the helicopters. The hostages were finally released on January 20, 1981, after 444 days of captivity. *Coincidentally,* this was just hours after Ronald Reagan's presidential inauguration.

So how did the hostages who had been held captive for 444 days finally get home? Was it military might? Political maneuvering? No, we simply bought them out. We gave the Iranians money and equipment, and they released the hostages. The Iranians did not trust or like Carter. It took the incoming Reagan team to make the deal. We promised we would not retaliate if all the hostages were released, and so it was arranged. We traded arms for them and we bought them their freedom.

No one within the Reagan administration would even talk about this for years. The Carter administration was livid, but they kept their mouths shut because the greater good was served—the hostages were released. Bottom line, we did not have the stomach for another failed rescue, so we decided to give in to the Iranian demands for money and gear, straight up. No one cared at the time. We had spent too long counting how many days the hostages had been in captivity. We had had enough, plain and simple.

This was wrong then, and in the light of 9/11 it is tragic beyond all measure. I mean, we had people working their butts off to free the hostages, and in the end it was politics that got in the way. The hostages were used as a political tool, and that is criminal. We appeased a terrorist nation and twenty years later we experienced the single largest loss of life on U.S. soil since the Civil War. This capitulation is just one example of the larger and constant capitulation to terrorists over a thirty-year period.

Of course, you would assume that we exacted a terrible price for what the Iranian government did to our citizens. You would assume incorrectly. Not a single, solitary act was ever perpetrated against Iran's government for what the Iranians did. To this day Iran remains an active member of the "Axis of Evil" and is officially recognized by the State Department as a state sponsor of terrorism, and to this day it remains free from punishment. The Iranians are free to plan their next attack, free to build and acquire nuclear weapons, free to support terrorism, and free to kill us.

Were the bad guys watching and studying how we handled these crises? You bet! And our government bet your families' lives and well-being when it bet that our reaction didn't matter.

During those 444 days we worried, sweated, looked scared, and let our president hide in his Rose Garden. We did try to rescue the hostages, but we looked inept and lost some very brave servicemen when the rescue went south. Then we gave up. We never tried again.

What happened? It was not that we didn't have dedicated military and intelligence professionals that were willing and able to risk all to rescue the hostages. We did. The problem was, our political leadership never had the backbone to risk another rescue. We backed off and rode the bench. You get wood chips in your butt when you ride the bench, and in this instance and almost every other instance involving terrorism, we were too busy picking wood chips out of our butts to do anything.

Why Didn't We Use These Guys?

In the late 1970s, the Army realized that it needed a new way to deal with terrorists and actually convinced our government to let them do it. The Army created a new unit, Special Forces Operational Detachment Delta, modeled after the British SAS, which had been around since World War II. The Navy, not to be outdone, correctly assumed that a SEAL unit would also be helpful in the fight against terrorists, so in the early '80s the Navy formed SEAL Team Six.

Here is the recipe to make a Delta Force warrior: You start with an already spectacular soldier who has a proven service record of, say, five years, usually as part of Special Forces or as a Ranger. He volunteers to go to the mountains of West Virginia, where he must run four kilometers an hour over mountains with over sixty pounds on his back plus his weapon. He must pass a series of mental and physical tests. Only one in fifty will make it through this process. Once you make it through this "selection," you then spend almost a year learning the "deadly arts" in a training program that is designed for masochists. And there you have it, a Delta Force warrior!

The SEAL Team Six formula for perfection is arguably more grueling. The recruit must first make it through a training course called BUDS—nine months of hell at the beach in Coronado, California. If you are one of the lucky 30 percent who graduate, you are then assigned to a SEAL Team, where you are evaluated for a year before you are awarded your "trident," or SEAL badge. After running around the world as a SEAL for five years, you volunteer for SEAL Team Six, where you are put through six months of "selection" training, which might be even more difficult than the first six years you have already spent being a SEAL badass.

These two superior organizations represent the very best the American military has to offer. The military had to convince the politicians that such forces were needed. Fortunately, even President Carter agreed that these organizations should be allowed to be formed, but this one bright shining moment cannot come close to making up for all the things that went wrong during his presidency—four years of malaise, no Olympics, Iran hostages, and a black cloud that followed him around the White House.

Here's the criminal part of all this: We created these guys to kill terrorists and then hardly ever used them, or when we did use them, we put so many restrictions on them that we made them almost ineffective.

On April 18, 1983, a pickup truck packed with over a thousand pounds of explosives rammed into the U.S. Embassy in Beirut, Lebanon, killing sixty-three people. Of the seventeen Americans killed, eight were employees of the CIA, including chief Middle East analyst Robert C. Ames and station chief Kenneth Haas.

At that time, our government was led by Ronald Reagan, one of the most popular presidents in modern memory. Reagan said that the attack was carried out by Hezbollah operatives. Hezbollah was receiving financial and logistical support from both Iran and Syria. This time, instead of doing nothing, we sent in our own operatives to gather information. *Then* we did nothing. The leadership looked at the information and decided, "No, not today." We decided that terrorists killing a few Americans and attacking a U.S. embassy was not enough reason to retaliate. Look, I am not saying our leaders didn't care; I'm sure they did. But they acted without honor and without courage. Politics was more important.

So again we did nothing. Again the terrorists watched and waited for our response. There was none, and the murdering sons of bitches hit us again, this time with even more deadly results. On October 23, 1983, almost six months to the day from the April embassy bombing, a suicide bomber detonated another truck in Beirut. This time the truck held over fifteen hundred pounds of explosives and the attack was on the Marine barracks located at Beirut International Airport. Two hundred and forty-one U.S. Marines were killed. More than a hundred others were wounded. They were part of a contingent of the 1,800 Marines that had been sent to Lebanon as part of a multinational force. Their mission was to try to keep opposing Lebanese factions from killing each other.

Secretary of Defense Caspar Weinberger said, "The U.S. lacked actual knowledge of who did the bombing." He said this in spite of the fact that the National Security Agency had an intercept from the foreign ministry of Iran ordering the murder of our Marines. We strongly suspected Hezbollah and we knew they were supported by Iran and Syria. Hezbollah, of course, denied its involvement. Can you believe this? We are attacked twice, our guys are killed, and we lacked "actual knowledge" or something. Yes, we lacked something: *gonads.* We knew who bombed us and we knew what countries supported them. Our soldiers, flag, and embassy had been attacked. That was an act of war. We had all the legal and moral authority we needed; instead we turned tail and ran.

This time was a little different; we did actually plan to retaliate. Our target was to be the Sheik Abdullah barracks that housed Iranian Revolutionary Guards who were believed to be training Hezbollah fighters. We had a plan, we had a target—and then Secretary Weinberger called it off, reportedly because of his concerns that retaliation would harm U.S. relations with other Arab nations. Can you imagine, we might harm our relations? Hey, Mr. Secretary, take a nap, and when you wake up you might want to notice that we had no relations with these countries. You might also notice these countries gave aid and support to those who were trying to kill us.

Instead of taking the fight to the enemy, President Reagan ordered the battleship USS *New Jersey,* stationed off the coast of Lebanon, to shoot shells into the hills near Beirut. Can you believe this? Evil men spill our soldiers' precious blood and we blow up some hilltops? As if that wasn't bad enough, four months later we finally did do something: we ran. Our government's reaction to the attack on the Marine barracks and the death of 241 of our Marines was to pull out of Lebanon, against Marine wishes. So the terrorists got yet another lesson in how our great nation intended to fight: we would run. Sadly, we would keep running away from this fight for another eighteen years.

Early one morning in 1988, a tough Marine named Lieutenant Colonel William Higgins, while assigned to the United Nations peacekeeping operation in Lebanon, was checking on his men, as any good leader does—seeing how they were doing in their jobs, checking on their welfare, making sure they were safe. He did this two or three times a day, but this time, as he was making his rounds in a UN-marked vehicle, he was ambushed by twenty Hezbollah terrorists. He was taken to the back alleys of Beirut, where he disappeared.

Lieutenant Colonel Higgins's family and his country waited more than eighteen months before knowing the fate of this brave man. He was beaten, tortured, and starved, and in the end, the terrorists put a three-quarter-inch hemp rope around this great guy's powerful neck, had him stand on a gas can, brought the rope up tight, and then kicked the can out from underneath him. He struggled for almost five minutes before life finally left him. They dumped his body on a street in Beirut. They showed this on television for all to see. He was one of a dozen or so Americans, including the head CIA guy in Lebanon, who were captured and murdered. We did nothing against Hezbollah. There is simply no excuse or explanation that can be offered to justify our inaction.

The pattern of devastation and inaction continued. On December 21, 1988, Libyan terrorists blew a plane out of the sky over Lockerbie, Scotland, killing 281 people. The Libyan government refused to turn over the suspects, so we imposed sanctions. Fifteen years later Libya coughed up $2.7 billion in compensation and the UN lifted the sanctions. Now Libya is almost a trading partner, for pity's sake. Back in 1988 we should have made a glass factory out of the place.

On June 26, 1996, a truck exploded at Khobar Towers, a U.S. military housing complex in Saudi Arabia. The explosion killed 19 Americans and wounded 372 people. Not only did the Saudis not protect us from these killers, they would not even allow the FBI to conduct an investigation into the activities of al Qaeda, the suspected assassins. Many members of our intelligence community believe that elements within the Saudi government worked closely with al Qaeda on this attack.

For this attack alone, we should have, at the very minimum, demanded free oil from the Saudis for a year, and that would have been just a down payment. The down payment would not, of course, have covered our killing all those involved, from paupers to kings.

On August 7, 1998, the U.S. embassies in Nairobi, Kenya, and Dar es Salaam, Tanzania, were bombed by terrorists. The bombings left 258 people dead and more than 5,000 injured. In response, the U.S. government launched cruise missiles that struck an abandoned terrorism training complex in Afghanistan and destroyed a pharmaceutical manufacturing facility in Khartoum, Sudan. The factory reportedly produced nerve gas. I say "reportedly" because it turned out to be an aspirin factory. Whoops! (Don't worry about the factory; the owner sued, and the United States paid to rebuild it.)

U.S. intelligence believed that Osama bin Laden was behind the embassy bombings, and both of these targets were chosen because he had reportedly financed them. This was the same man who had declared a jihad on the United States of America.

My, my, my—missiles? What a brave response. Let us evaluate this response for its effectiveness, shall we? We missed Osama bin Laden; he was not in either place. The Sudan mission turned out to be an aspirin factory. Then we gave up. Now, I have nothing against cruise missiles or missiles in general. They are accurate and deadly and can be fired from great distances. Missiles are really good at shooting down planes, blowing up buildings, and sinking ships. But when going after terrorists, we have to be willing to really commit ourselves. That means commitment of soldiers, sailors, and spies. We have to be willing to put them all in harm's way. That's their job. And by the way, they love it. In order to kill those who have proven time and time again their willingness to kill us, we have to be willing to use every weapon in our arsenal—the people we train to kill bad guys included.

On October 12, 2000, al Qaeda blew a 40-by-40-foot hole in a 505-foot destroyer, the USS *Cole*. Richard Clarke, the White House terrorism coordinator, said, "I don't agree we've had a failure of intelligence." I wonder what Mr. "It-Ain't-My-Fault" Clarke considers an intelligence failure. I mean, we had a U.S. Navy warship almost sunk. They killed seventeen and wounded thirty-nine U.S. sailors. Only those in the "cover your ass" business—and here I mean politicians—could possibly think that this was not an intelligence failure. These politicians are certifiable, self-medicating, fawning sycophants who care more about their "place in history" than the safety of our country and her citizens.

Once again al Qaeda watched our response. They watched as the Yemeni government denied the FBI access to important information and witnesses, and we took it. Hell, our agents were not even allowed to carry weapons. They were prohibited from doing so by our *own* government. Seems we did not want to upset our friends in Yemen. My God, we were investigating a terrorist attack and we were getting crap about the good guys carrying guns?

This is where I throw up. Have you still got your bucket handy? As our friends in Hollywood would say, "Are you feeling me?" "Are you getting it?" September 11 did not just happen. It was a culmination of errors—our errors. Could we have been more inept, more ineffectual, and more weak-kneed? Maybe. Maybe if we had done absolutely nothing; maybe that would have been worse—but not by much. This was next to nothing.

By 1998 we had developed the finest counterterrorism teams in the world with Delta Force and SEAL Team Six. So what about them? We trained two unique units to the point of perfection. These guys shoot 50,000 rounds of ammunition a year per man. They train attacking trains, planes, and automobiles. They train in tunnels, in sewers, on high wires, and even in trees. They actually run with 60 to 100 pounds on their backs. They jump from airplanes carrying more than 500 pounds. These supersoldiers can do amazing things . . . if you let them. And therein lies the rub.

We can only imagine where we would be today if we had allowed these Special Forces to sneak into Afghanistan and kill bin Laden in 1997. What if they had helped the Israelis take care of Arafat? Maybe somebody would be safer today. What if we had actually turned them loose in Bosnia early enough in the war to remove a Karadzic, a Mladic, or Milosevic? How do we explain the thousands of lives that could have been saved but weren't because politicians wouldn't allow these guys to do what they do? Moreover, wouldn't the bad guys have thought twice about hitting us if they had been looking over their shoulders worrying about when Delta or Six would hit them next? The truth is that no administration—neither Democrat nor Republican—had the guts to let loose these forces, and those decisions have cost us all.

We had these supersoldiers with guns primed and ready, but we sent cruise missiles into Lebanon and did nothing in Yemen. My God, we were, and still are, the most powerful nation on the planet and we sent missiles to do men's work. What a damn waste! What would it take for our government to get serious? Let them kill Americans by the thousands? No, it would never come to that—would it?

Blown Chances

On Friday, February 26, 1993, a massive explosion occurred in the parking garage of the World Trade Center in New York City. As a result of the explosion, six people died and more than a thousand were injured. Up until this point, we had always been protected by two myths. The first myth was believed by the terrorists. They thought we were omnipotent. Our intelligence services, especially the CIA, knew everything—period. The second myth was our own. It was that we were surrounded by two huge oceans that kept us safe. Both myths went away in 1993 when the World Trade Center was attacked.

Within a month of the blast, the four individuals responsible for the attack were apprehended. The suspects went on trial on September 13, 1993. On May 25, 1994, a judge sentenced each of the four defendants to 240 years in prison and a $250,000 fine. I can hear some of you saying, "Aha! We did do something here. We caught the bad guys and put them in jail." Yes, we did. And that's the problem.

Many things were wrong with the way we dealt with terrorists, but deciding to treat them as criminals may have been our worst mistake. They were much more than criminals. They were murdering, evil subhumans that came in the night and killed innocents. They were terrorists, and the only way to deal with terrorists is to kill them. In typical American fashion, we tried to impose our sense of justice on people who view the world in a completely different way.

The fact that we even managed to convict the guys responsible for the first World Trade Center bombing is something close to miraculous. The FBI was not getting full cooperation from the CIA on this one, but they still managed to crack the case. Only one small problem: putting four terrorists in jail for this crime did not stop or even delay others from continuing their murderous rampage. We simply chose the wrong path. We tried to deal with barbarians in a *legal* way. We spent millions chasing and prosecuting those responsible for the first World Trade Center attack and eleven years later we got ... 9/11. Not a very good deal.

The Clinton administration has pointed to two "victories" against terrorism to justify its policies: the discovery of the "Millennium Bomb" plot and the discovery of plots to blow up the Lincoln and the Holland tunnels. In the book *Against All Enemies,* Richard Clarke wrote that he and others coordinated a "massive" government effort to foil al Qaeda from blowing up Los Angeles International Airport on New Year's Eve 1999, and he has reiterated these claims during any number of TV appearances. Yeah, right. What really happened is a stupid SOB named Ahmed Ressam filled his trunk with explosives in Canada and tried to drive through a customs checkpoint in Washington State. A well-trained and very competent border guard spotted the nervous, sweaty Ressam and hauled his ass over to the side to inspect him and his vehicle. She found the trunk full of nastiness.

Clarke and others attempted to take credit for this find, which might have worked except that an alert press corps just asked a simple question of the brave and alert border guard: *So is it true that you found this terrorist because of the massive effort on the part of the U.S. government, sending out notices, alerting you to the possibility that this deadly terrorist might cross the border?*

"I don't recall any specific threats," answered Diana Dean. "I don't recall anybody saying watch for terrorists." Customs officials confirm that no alert had gone out to the field.

Bottom line: we got lucky. Neither Clarke nor anyone else in D.C. had diddly to do with catching Ressam. It was blind luck—good for us, but it was blind luck just the same.

Now, as far as the Clinton administration having anything to do with uncovering the plots to blow up the Lincoln and the Holland tunnels, uh, that would be a big no. The FBI and the NYPD got wind of this one through solid police work. Nice going, guys. I am very happy we caught them. But this had nothing to do with anything but great cops doing a great job. It was not the result of a coordinated antiterrorist campaign. We were so desperate for a success, we could not even give credit where it was due.

You have to understand something: not only was the Clinton administration not doing anything, it was taking credit away from underpaid, overworked, competent, and brave public safety officers who could not put their hand up and say, *"Bullshit."*

Well, I just did.

If doing nothing was all we did, that would be bad enough. But at times we actually worked against ourselves. We made decisions that weakened us and made the terrorists stronger. We actually had rules inside our government that prohibited the CIA from sharing information with the FBI. We had the FBI with computer technology that was more than ten years old. Technology is a key weapon in the terrorism fight and one that we must master *immediately.* The FBI is *still* behind in computer technology. It is trying to make advances but not at the speed of DSL—more like dial-up.

We treated and are still treating terrorism as if it were the Cold War. Hello, we are not fighting the Soviet Union in the Fulda Gap any longer. News flash! A guy named Reagan put the hex on the Russian Bear. So if we are not fighting the Soviet Union, shouldn't we change the way we gather intelligence and fight to suit the enemy we are fighting? The answer is, Yes, we should. But we didn't. Terrorists are killers. They live in closed societies. We will continue to fail to infiltrate them if we use Cold War tactics.

"We don't have the money. We don't have the money." That was the actual answer the FBI gave me in October 2001 as to why we could not visit with a former Special Forces general in the Pakistani army who had access to Afghanistan, the Taliban, and al Qaeda. The same answer was given when the Moroccan government offered to give us agents to infiltrate al Qaeda—"No money to pay for a visit to Morocco." You have got to be kidding me! We turned down real offers of help because of the price of plane tickets. What is wrong with this picture? I know. *Everything!*

In 1996 the CIA actually got it right. It had tracked bin Laden to a ranch in Afghanistan. It had him in its sights. The agency only needed permission from the Clinton White House to pull the trigger. So what did the passive-aggressive Clinton administration do? It would not give the order. A government official from the United Arab Emirates was present at the camp with bin Laden, so we chickened out. The reason this other guy was hanging with bin Laden couldn't have been good. Did we think they were forming a church group? Did we think they were planning to turn themselves in? No? Then we should have killed them both. We could have paid retribution for any real or perceived harm done to innocents. This was a camp out in the middle of nowhere. We could have turned it into a puddle. Bin Laden would have been dead, and maybe, just maybe, 9/11 wouldn't have happened. These guys let him go. The response should have been, "Nice job guys, now *you're fired!*" But it wasn't. It wasn't because we don't ever fire anybody for failures tied to terrorism, not even when almost three thousand Americans are killed. Hell, under Clinton, missing bin Laden probably meant a promotion.

Six months after we said no to blowing bin Laden into little pieces, our very brave and capable spies got another shot at, or at least a close-up of, the leader of al Qaeda. The CIA had someone inside al Qaeda next to bin Laden and was able to track him and set up an ambush. The plan was brilliant in its simplicity. We knew where he was going. We would set a trap on the back roads of Afghanistan with our Special Forces and CIA. We would take him and hide him in a cave until we could get him out of the country by air.

The CIA believed it could get this done with minimum loss of life. The plan was set. But then the answer from the Clinton White House was, yet again, "Nope, too risky. Someone could get hurt. A mistake might occur." The mission was canceled.

How could a real president turn down two chances to get the leader of the most deadly, most effective terrorist organization to come out of the depths of hell? No competent authority would do nothing twice, would he? All of this would make a great movie, except no one would believe it. Well, believe it. It happened. Unfortunately, it is still happening today in Iran, Syria, Saudi Arabia, and other places.

What was behind the Clinton administration's unwillingness to be aggressive when it came to terrorism? In 1993, while trying to keep the peace between warlords in Somalia, we lost eighteen of our soldiers. Two bodies were dragged through the streets. From that point on, Clinton was obsessed with not letting it happen again. It handcuffed every decision about aggressive action from that moment on. With Clinton it wasn't just with terrorism where our hands were tied; it was with all things military.

For example, one of the constant factors in the Bosnian war of the mid-1990s was the presence of mass graves. The Serbs created them by burying Muslim men, women, and children in open pits. In Srebrenica alone more than 7,500 bodies were found in eight graves. The United States and NATO had a chance to capture a Serbian bad guy named Mladic, who was responsible for the murder of *thousands* of innocent Muslims. Yay for the good guys! We were going to take action. We were going to arrest a war criminal. We might even kill him. We might have, but we didn't.

We had the U.S. Navy's SEAL Team Six—remember, the finest Special Operations warriors anywhere, anytime—on the ground in Bosnia, as well as a very talented group from the CIA. Together they came up with a brilliant plan to arrest and bring to justice the mass murderer Mladic. But the Clinton White House put restrictions on the mission, keeping these supersoldiers from doing their job. The administration actually ordered the SEAL assigned to approach Mladic to do so *unarmed.* Why, you might ask, did we do such a stupid thing? The answer from the White House—please, sit down— was, *If the SEAL had a gun, someone could get hurt.* Get hurt? *Get hurt?* Mladic was a *mass murderer* and we were going after him in the middle of Serbian territory, and the White House didn't want any-body to get hurt? You have got to be kidding me! How about if somebody worried about the Navy SEAL—you know, our guy—getting hurt?

You can't fight anyone this way. You certainly cannot fight ter-rorists this way. We had hundreds of chances. Every time an Ameri-can citizen was murdered by terrorists, we had another chance. Every time, we blew it. Each citizen has the right to expect that this great nation will protect him or her. Failing that, we have the right to expect that our leaders will at least *try* to bring those responsible to justice. In the twenty-nine years prior to 9/11, we have on fewer than three occasions put up even a half-assed effort. Our government's conduct has been criminal.

But surely by the year 2000 we would take some action besides preparing for the next press conference. After this many deaths, this many worldwide humiliations, this many examples of cowardice, surely we would fight back, attack, put sticks in terrorists' eyes, and punish those countries that supported the terrorists who had taken the lives of our sons, brothers, and fathers. Right? Now, very slowly, go to the front door, open it, and scream into the night. We *still* did nothing. *Ahhhhhhh!*

We not only guaranteed further attacks, we actually helped make them possible. Hell, if your child kept getting into the cookie jar, would you not stop the child or at least take the cookie jar away? Well, our leaders didn't take the cookies away; they actually put more cookies in the jar. *Unbelievable!*

So where did all this governmental inaction get us? Did the ter-rorists get tired of killing us? Did the terrorists give themselves up? Did the countries that sponsor terrorism suddenly stop? Did Osama bin Laden have a heart attack? Did the Saudis stop supporting al Qaeda? Were we now safer somehow? The answer, my friends, came one beautiful morning in September 2001.

Remember Your Anger

Son of a bitch! They did it. We watched the beautiful blue-skied morning of September 11, 2001, as not one but two planes flew into the World Trade Center. Another flew into the Pentagon and one fell into a field in Pennsylvania. Terrorism had once more come into our living rooms.

By the time the Boeing 767 flown by Mohammed Atta slammed into the ninety-seventh floor of Tower One, the plane weighed 500 tons because of the principle of momentum—you know, mass times velocity. The second plane flown by Atta's associate killer, Al-Shehhi, weighed slightly less, but to the tortured souls on board and those in the buildings, it really did not matter. The first plane hit at 8:46 A.M. What if the planes had flown into the twin towers thirty minutes later, when the entire workforce of more than fifty thousand people would have been inside?

We seem to have forgotten the horror of all of this. Right after 9/11, we put American flags on our lapels, our cars, and our barns. Now most of these are tattered or have been taken down. Apparently, in order to keep our anger, we need to see photos and film footage of American citizens jumping more than a hundred stories to their deaths. Some would call this exploitative. Fine! Exploit away. We need whatever it will take to get us back in the mind-set that we had following 9/11.

"Dad, I am scared," said my then-twelve-year-old son. My wife came home early. I went to Boston to be on *The O'Reilly Factor.* On the ride down from Maine, both sides of Interstate 95 were abandoned. It was not until ten miles outside of Boston that I saw any traffic, and then it was being escorted by the Massachusetts State Police. The terrorists had won the day. Our great nation was shut down for four days. Never in our history had the nation's air transportation system been closed—not through two world wars, Korea, or Vietnam. Ronald Reagan Airport in Washington, D.C., was closed for an additional month. We were scared, and rightfully so.

Al Qaeda had killed close to three thousand human beings. They had killed more than the Japanese killed at Pearl Harbor. The weapons used were simple box cutters and our own planes. All the walls were down; we were naked and vulnerable.

Now we would have to get serious. Now we had no choice. We would finally strike back: strike at them all; kill those who killed us; an eye for an eye—biblical justice. We would surely make all involved pay, which would of course include those countries that supported the murderers. We would leave no stone unturned. There would be no place to hide. No more politics; just do the right thing.

Right? Wrong.

We did finally attack al Qaeda and its host, the Taliban, in Afghanistan. Some very brave CIA and Special Forces guys jumped in the middle of the night, got on horses, spread some money around, and took this country in less than three weeks. Perfect. Nice going!

Then there were speeches. "No place to hide." "We will hunt the terrorists down, wherever they are." We heard this over and over. Except it didn't happen.

We not only did not hunt down bin Laden, we allowed him to hide in Pakistan, the country right next door to the one we had just invaded.

Pakistan is a troubled country. Two years before 9/11, a supposed friend of ours, a four-star general, had taken over the country in a coup. But during the War on Terror we have been denied entry into Pakistan for any, all, and no reason. Guess what? With friends like Pakistan, we won't need a lot more enemies. We can't chase bad guys into the mountains between Afghanistan and Pakistan. The Pakistanis don't want us to, and we have caved in to them. We are working against ourselves here, and if we keep it up, we will pay with more American lives.

Our elected officials told us that they would do whatever it took to get these guys and to make our country safe. Immediately after 9/11, a billionaire computer-business owner offered to give the U.S. government a million-dollar computer tracking program currently used in the banking industry. This program can track anything with numbers—money and phones in particular. He offered all the training and equipment necessary to implement the program and free follow-up. He wanted nothing in return: no contract, no acknowledgment. He was a former Marine and just wanted to help. I know all this because I was the guy carrying the message between the rich guy and the government. But you know what? He couldn't even get a serious callback on his offer.

This is not doing whatever it takes. This is doing nothing—again.

In the first three years after 9/11, our government repeatedly reminded us that we hadn't been attacked again. Trust me, those doing the reminding have their own agendas. Some have political reasons, some need to be elected or reelected, and some need to have legislation passed. Do we really think that the terrorists who waited and planned for five years to attack and kill us are finished with us? Do we really want to trust those who did not see 9/11 coming? Do we want to trust those who, for twenty-nine years, did nothing? I think not. Hell, these are the guys who got it wrong on the weapons of mass destruction in Iraq.

We must get our focus back. Taking Afghanistan from the Taliban was righteous. It was a long time coming. Glad we did it. But we missed the prize. Osama bin Laden became Osama bin Forgotten. That can't be! Go get him! Stop at nothing! Kill him now!

Taking Saddam down was fine. We can now have military bases in the Middle East to help us fight terrorism. That's a good thing. But for some reason, we are now putting up with Syria and Iran killing our soldiers. They do this by sending their agents, supplying money, and supplying training for the insurgents fighting us. And yet we didn't seal the damn borders. How can this be allowed? It can't. No, we must keep up the pressure. Syria and Iran have to be addressed in the most direct and unambiguous fashion possible. We have the proof. Hell, we have the dead and wounded soldiers that are a direct result of these terrorist states assisting the insurgents in Iraq. Time to pay up, boys. Time to pay up, now!

We can't let our government get distracted. Right now, it is distracted. America's future is at stake—my family, your children, and our way of life. No more distractions! Wake up! Snap to it! Stop the slide! The terrorists are right over there, go get them—now!

My concern is that we seem to have forgotten. Time has helped heal our wounds. Our successes have masked our pain. We have been distracted by our daily lives. We can all keep our heads buried in the sand. We can keep thinking that the fight is over there and not here. I suppose we could all visit Oz too, or we can get serious.

You needed to know this stuff. You needed to know this stuff so you could get angry. Actually you need to be more than angry; you need to be outraged. Your government let you down. Our record of inaction is staggering. There are enough excuses and bureaucratic mistakes to fill a supercomputer. We have been lied to and neglected. It seems that we are not important enough for our government to bother with the business of protecting us.

I will say it again. We lost more than 780 American lives to acts of terrorism over a twenty-nine-year period, and that's not counting 9/11. That's 612 more Americans than were killed in the Oklahoma City bombing. Do you remember watching as men, women, and children were pulled from the Murrah Federal Building? Do you remember how difficult it was to watch as rescue teams searched in vain for any life? Do you remember?

After Oklahoma City, we arrested the murderers. That was good. Did we do anything else? Do you recall a massive governmental antiterrorist reorganization? No? You don't remember anything else happening because we didn't do anything.

Oh, I'm sorry, that is not entirely true. The government *did* fund four studies on terrorism. That's right, we decided to *study* terrorism. *Study terrorism?* You don't stop terrorism with a study. You stop it by killing the terrorists.

The 9/11 terrorists took close to five years to plan and execute their attacks. It was a very complex operation, yet sadistically simple in its outcome. Those of us without our heads in the sand know that because of al Qaeda's success here and throughout the world, they will attempt to hit us again. Our incompetence makes it inevitable.

The government is still trying to figure out what to do and how to do it. This condition of ineptitude has been with us for a long time. We have been as limp as an old man in need of Viagra. Just how far down the ladder of incompetence have we fallen? With 9/11 as a gauge, I would say all the way to the bottom.

CHAPTER 3

Just Who the Hell Is Trying to Kill Us?

Now that you know a little bit of history, are you interested? Have the things I've told you so far pissed you off? No? Well maybe a look at the *who* and the *why* behind all of this will help. For twenty-nine years we looked the other way and we paid an enormous price for it. So do you care that governments, through their support of terrorism, are killing us? The A-Team of terrorist sponsors is made up of Iran, North Korea, Syria, Yemen, and of course my personal favorite, Saudi Arabia. The Saudis have the best of both worlds: they've figured out a way to be both enemy and friend.

During the Cold War we stationed troops in Saudi Arabia to protect the Saudis from the Russians. Then we stayed, because of the aggressive nature of Iran and Iraq. For them it's been about protection; for us, it's always been about oil. The bottom line is, we need the oil that's under the Saudi sand. Until we come up with an alternative energy source, that's the way it will be. The Saudis hate us because of their dependence on us for protection, because we are Westerners, and because we are willing to take Saudi money. We take money in the form of political donations funneled through middlemen; we take money in the form of consulting jobs for former influential government officials getting hundreds of thousand of dollars a year; we take money when the Saudi government buys our weapons (which the Saudis don't even know how to use); we take money from our trade with the Saudis; and we even take money in the form of bribes. We take Saudi money all the time.

Robert Baer, a very brave and competent former CIA spy, wrote a great book called *See No Evil.* In this book he says that the government of Saudi Arabia has given al Qaeda more than $500 million— that's *half a billion dollars*—as a bribe so Osama bin Laden's terrorists would focus on killing Americans, not Saudis. So let's see: we protect the Saudis from their enemies, including al Qaeda—Osama ain't too fond of the Saudi ruling family either—and they give money to the terrorists that kill us. Let me be crystal-clear: the money the Saudis gave to al Qaeda was used to kill almost three thousand Americans. Al Qaeda used this money to build and run terrorist training camps, to buy plane tickets for the 9/11 attacks, and to provide support for the murderers who used our own airplanes as missiles.

So we are in bed with our own killers. What is that? I'll tell you what that is, it is governmental suicide. Well, if our government wants to kill itself, that's fine. Just leave my family out of it.

The Saudi government has denied supporting al Qaeda. What a surprise! They probably always tell the truth. These are the same people whose state-sponsored religion is Wahhabism, a religion that has two main principles: the elimination of Israel and the death of all "infidels" (non-Muslims). Nice guys, huh? We don't have a reason to suspect that they would lie to us, do we?

So what does our government say? Tellingly, it didn't refute Baer's well-documented claim, even though it counts Saudi Arabia among America's "friends" and consequently has a vested interest in proving that the Saudis are not supporting the world's most lethal terrorists. In the summer of 2004, Saudi apologists seized on the 9/11 Commission's final report, which stated, "Saudi Arabia has long been considered the primary source of al Qaeda funding, but we found no evidence that the Saudi government as an institution or senior Saudi officials individually funded the organization." But these defenders of Saudi Arabia often neglected to mention the next two sentences from the report. The first was offered as a parenthetical: "This conclusion does not exclude the likelihood that charities with significant Saudi government sponsorship diverted funds to al Qaeda." The second noted that al Qaeda still "found fertile fundraising ground in Saudi Arabia, where extreme religious views are common and charitable giving was both essential to the culture and subject to very limited oversight." Not exactly letting the Saudis off the hook. Consider that in June of 2002, the Saudis held a nationwide telethon whose sole purpose was to collect money to aid the families of *suicide bombers*. The telethon collected millions of dollars. Can you imagine this? (By the way, those suicide bombers were killing the citizens of Israel—an ally of the United States.)

And remember that before the 9/11 Commission issued its final report, a joint congressional committee had investigated the Saudi connections to al Qaeda. The joint committee's final report remained classified, but the *New York Times* reported that by most accounts the study concluded that the Saudi government and Saudi government officials were financing al Qaeda. At the time, the Democratic co-chairman of the committee, Senator Bob Graham of Florida, refused to publicly call out the Saudi government, but he did say, "In my judgment there is compelling evidence that a foreign government provided direct support through officials and agents of that government to some of the September 11 hijackers." Moreover, according to the *New York Times,* "People who had read the report said it described senior Saudi officials as having funneled hundreds of millions of dollars to charitable groups and operatives who may have helped finance the attacks." Even when the joint committee's classified report was made public in July 2003, the section of the report addressing Saudi Arabia's role in 9/11 was deleted.

So let's review:

- Fifteen of the nineteen terrorists involved in 9/11 came from Saudi Arabia.
- The Saudis have given millions to al Qaeda.
- The Saudis have never cooperated with the investigation into the Khobar Towers bombings, in which nineteen Americans were killed and hundreds were injured. Those responsible for killing our citizens are still at large as a direct result of this. And to add insult to injury, these friends of ours, these partners in peace, have the temerity to hold a telethon that will reward the families of people who blow up our allies (and themselves).

Just in case anybody had doubts about Saudi Arabia, in June 2004 we witnessed the barbaric beheading of yet another American, Paul Johnson. Al Qaeda terrorists based in Saudi Arabia kidnapped him, cut his head off with a sword, and then distributed pictures and a video of this for the whole world to see. They somehow had access to Saudi police uniforms, IDs, vehicles, and weapons—that is, official property of the Saudi government. Has to make you a little suspicious, doesn't it?

Of course, immediately after Johnson was murdered, Saudi security forces killed four of the terrorists responsible for the beheading. But that timing has raised a lot of eyebrows. Just as Johnson's body is being dumped, the Saudis show up? When a police agency or government is right there, and I mean *right* there, when the crime is committed, it means the police and/or the government was watching the whole time. And it would make sense that the Saudi government would want these terrorists, what with the Saudi government identification and uniforms providing evidence that might implicate Saudi officials.

The attack on the terrorists responsible for Paul Johnson's beheading was part of a larger Saudi effort to show the government's renewed commitment to fighting terrorists. Responding to a series of kidnappings of foreign workers, the Saudi government took supposedly aggressive action: it offered the terrorists one month to turn themselves in, and to sweeten the deal, it also offered amnesty to any terrorist who was a terrorist for *religious* reasons. In other words, in a country that holds public executions for far lesser crimes than murder (such as drug dealing and sorcery), terrorists are receiving amnesty because they have done their deeds in the name of Allah. Sure glad our so-called friends the Saudis are taking such an "aggressive" stance against terrorism. We can't afford much more "support" like this in the War on Terror.

Tell you what, how about we decide that we don't like the House of Saud, the family that rules Saudi Arabia? How about we decide that protecting this kingdom is no longer in our national interest? How about we do *something*? How about we do anything but deny that the Saudi ruling family is up to its armpits in American blood? I for one would be in favor of a little biblical justice when it comes to the Saudis.

Russian Gangsters

Okay, if that news flash about Saudi Arabia does not incite you to action, or at least give you a mild jolt, then let's pile it on. Let's talk about Russia. Let's talk about the *new* Russia. It is a country rife with corruption. The Russian mafia is not just a worldwide, slave-trading, gunrunning, drug-peddling criminal organization; it is part of the Russian government. A government intelligence source told me that the Russian government, in exchange for cash, gives intelligence, weapons, sanctuary, and full support to the Russian mafia. The Russian mafia then proceeds to sell terrorists nuclear weapons and anything else it can get its hands on. Sources reveal that the intelligence community has clear documentation on this subject. And acclaimed national security reporter Bill Gertz confirmed the reports of the Russian mafia's arms deal with terrorist groups like al Qaeda in his 2004 best-seller *Treachery: How America's Friends and Foes Are Secretly Arming Our Enemies.*

Both the FBI and the CIA have learned that as recently as 2002, Ivan Patanski, a Moscow businessman, also a bad guy, was attempting to sell nuclear bombs to both North Korea and al Qaeda. He reportedly tried to set up a multimillion-dollar deal. The reason the deal didn't go down—this time—is that the Russians were selling fake weapons materials. Imagine, can't even trust the bad guys anymore. Get this and get this now! The Russian mafia, for the past ten years, has provided the Iraqi military as well as al Qaeda with training, intelligence, and antitank missiles. The Russians did this in Iraq as recently as March of 2003, according to the U.S. intelligence community. And the bad guys have used this stuff to kill our soldiers. That's exactly what the U.S. Army concluded in an after-action report on how our tanks got destroyed; we were getting hit with both Russian and French antitank missiles.

Oh yeah, these guys are our friends all right!

For the terrorists, all of this is a great thing. The terrorists get weapons, training, and intelligence, all through groups connected to the Russian government. Russia is a member of NATO and the G8, the international organizations invested with the power to set the international agenda. We know this. We allow this. Why didn't the president invite Vladimir Putin to Texas for another steak dinner? Maybe, just maybe, he could have brought up the subject with the Russian president over dessert.

The Russians are up to their eyeballs in blood, and yet our government claims they are friends. Why does this sound familiar? It sounds familiar because once again countries we do business with, countries that need us, and countries whose leaders are photographed smiling in the White House Rose Garden are openly supporting the guys trying to kill us. It's true. You can't make this crap up. Don't put that bucket away just yet; if you aren't sick yet, just wait.

Thanks for the Help, Pakistan

How about our buddies in the Pakistani government? This country is another one of our friends. But as we discussed earlier, Pakistan refused to allow U.S. forces to pursue Osama bin Laden into the mountains along the Pakistan-Afghanistan border. In other words, the Pakistanis were providing sanctuary to the people who brought us 9/11, and yet our government gave this sanctuary tacit approval. If we were serious about finding bin Laden and fighting terrorism, we would have told the Pakistanis to pound sand. We would have gone in anyway.

I can remember President George W. Bush saying things like "no place to hide," "hunt them down," "bring them to justice." Well, we knew where they were. They were in those mountains. We could have walked over there and touched them. We should have walked over there and killed them. But we stopped at the border and looked mad and honored the wishes of the Pakistani government. Give me a break!

The Pakistani government, along with the governments of Saudi Arabia and other nations, fund the fanatical religious schools known as madrasses that have produced many of the world's most infamous terrorists. Madrasses have only one purpose: they create Islamofascists. That is, they make terrorists and disguise them as religious nut jobs.

Our friends within the Pakistani government refuse to close down the madrasses. How about we make a deal? Pakistan closes the damn schools or we will support India. This country has been the sworn enemy of Pakistan since 1947, when the Brits left the area and did not settle disputes on the borders of both countries. Both countries also have nuclear bomb capability. Look, these are our lives here. Can we stop pussyfooting around? The longer we delay, the closer we come to a disaster of 9/11 proportions or worse.

There are those in the government who dismiss my solution. They say straight-faced that this is too simple an approach and that I don't understand the nuances involved. Hey! Jerkoff! Nuance this! You are allowing murderers to remain free. Shut up and do your job.

So Pakistan is hiding bin Laden and his followers, supporting schools that make more bin Ladens, and we put up with it. Surely we wouldn't put up with any more. Right? Wrong.

Abdul Qadeer Khan, the father of the Pakistani nuclear industry, with the approval and logistical support of his government, sold nuclear weapons technology to at least nine other countries, including rogue states like North Korea, Libya, and Iran. He sold *nuclear weapons*—the most dangerous weapons in the world. And he did this for more than ten years before we even noticed. Why we didn't notice, I don't know, because Dr. Khan and the Pakistani government were so blatant that they had marketing brochures with color pictures.

You would assume that Dr. Khan is now in a dark hole somewhere rotting away. You of course would be mistaken. He has been completely pardoned by—yes, you got it—our *friend* the Pakistani government. Pardoned, by the way, with hardly a complaint from the United States of America.

Syria: State Sponsor of Terrorism

Are you angry yet? No? How about just a little pissed off? Well okay, then, let's talk about Syria.

In downtown Damascus, the capital of Syria, a little piss-ant country northwest of Iraq, street signs direct pedestrians to Hamas and Hezbollah headquarters. These are two of the world's leading terrorist organizations and the Syrians have signs pointing to them as if they were Disneyland.

Let us be clear: Syria is a partner in the planned destruction of Israel. It is one of the major forces in this murderous movement. The Syrian government provides safe haven and support to the scum of the universe, the killers of Israeli children.

In the 1970s Syria gained power and prominence with the backing of the Soviet Union, which was trying to build its presence in the Middle East. Syria is on the world stage for only one reason: it is a state sponsor of terrorism. When civil war broke out in Lebanon, Syria moved in to act as a stabilizing power—by siding with Hezbollah and decimating Lebanon for more than twenty years. We lost 241 Marines in Lebanon to suicide bombers. Care to guess who, along with Iran, was backing the terrorists responsible for that? You guessed it, Syria. Our government's reaction? You already know—none at all.

So why do we put up with the Syrians? We put up with them for no other reason than "Middle East peace." Uh, excuse me, what Middle East peace? This phony excuse cannot stand any longer. We need to have a sit-down with President Bashar al-Assad of Syria. We could show him a nice movie titled "Shock and Awe." We could have an F-16 fly over the meeting with this young president. That would make the point: "You don't want us to come back and produce a 'reality show' using the weapons you've just seen." Oh, but in order for this to work, we actually have to mean it.

The North Korean Threat

Ready for more? North Korea is part of the infamous Axis of Evil. Seven years after World War II we went to war against this Communist regime. We have had thousands of soldiers stationed at North Korea's border with South Korea for more than fifty years just in case it gets frisky again. North Korea is the wild card of states that support terrorism. It has at least three nuclear bombs, and the number could be as many as six to eight; the intelligence community loves to argue about the total. It has more artillery than the rest of the world combined—over 500,000 pieces. It has a million-man army. But North Korea also is in a state of perpetual starvation. And it is a dark, dangerous, and predatory nation that we really know

squat about. The U.S. intelligence community has never successfully penetrated North Korea; we have only gotten some satellite
shots and listened to a few telephone conversations involving officials
who knew we were listening. We are blind when it comes to North
Korea.

Deadly Iran

Okay, what about Iran? Iran is the leading member of the Axis of
Evil. It is the principal supporter of one of the world's deadliest terrorist organizations, Hezbollah. Hezbollah, besides killing innocent
Jewish children in Israel, has been a major reason that Lebanon has
gone from the Riviera of the Mediterranean to a war zone. Iran gives
Hezbollah support in the form of military training, weapons, money,
intelligence, and safe haven.

If that's not enough, the Muslim clerics who run this place now
have or are a hair's breadth away from having the Bomb—that's
right, nuclear weapons. In the summer of 2004, in fact, the Iranian
government publicly declared that it would resume building centri-
fuges for its nuclear program. It caused an outrage, but the Iranians
don't seem to care. All this puts Iran on the "Ready for Prime-Time
Shock-and-Awe Show."

And that's just what we *know*. What is Iran doing that we don't
know about? It could be a lot. Frighteningly, we are flying as blind
with intelligence in Iran as we are in North Korea and as we were in
Iraq before the war. In the Iraq situation, we've learned that we did
not have a single dependable intelligence source there after 1998. In
Iran, we haven't had one since *1985,* according to my national intelligence sources.

Anybody worried yet?

We really need to understand the U.S. position on Iran, Syria,
Saudi Arabia, Pakistan, North Korea, and of course Russia. To some
we give money; to some we give military aid; some we save from

starvation; some we even call partners in the War on Terror. But guess what they all call us? The enemy. Pakistan for example, votes against us 75 percent of the time at the United Nations. Saudi Arabia provided more than 75 percent of the 9/11 murderers from among its own citizens, and has given millions of dollars to al Qaeda. Syria supports any number of terrorist organizations and is clearly no friend of ours. The Russians have their friendly mafia arming terrorists and tyrants.

The point here is that none of them will truly help us—or at least stop hurting us—unless there is something in it for them. We could easily provide them with the reason; how about survival! In the words of the immortal Bard, "They all suck." (Okay, so maybe he didn't say it, or if he did, he said it in iambic pentameter, but you get my point.)

Al Qaeda's Deadly Ambitions

Born of these countries—with their corrupt governments, extreme religious views, and disenfranchised citizens—are terrorist groups. These groups have a membership of ruthless murderers who are well organized and dedicated to our destruction. Terrorist groups like Black September, Hamas, Hezbollah, and the Muslim Brotherhood are all well organized and have a clear direction. They all have excellent funding, logistics, intelligence, and state sponsorship. But none have displayed the deadly flair, the organizational skills, the deadly consistency, and the tragic success of al Qaeda.

Al Qaeda has a presence in over eighty countries and has recruited more than twenty thousand killers. During his testimony before the 9/11 Commission, former acting FBI director Thomas Pickard said, "The camps in Afghanistan and elsewhere were graduating thousands like them who are educated, committed, and even computer savvy. Al Qaeda was turning out five times more graduates from their camps than the CIA and the FBI were graduating from their training schools." Obviously our leaders and the national intelligence community had known about al Qaeda for some time. They just didn't bother to tell us.

On September 11, 2001, most Americans had never heard of Osama bin Laden or al Qaeda. All we knew was that we had been attacked by Muslim extremists. We knew they had killed thousands of Americans. We knew we were at war.

So who is Osama bin Laden? Who is this devil, this murderer of innocents, this cave dweller, this bogeyman that the world can't seem to find? Well, unless you have been living under a rock for the past few years, you probably already know something about him. He's a bad guy who learned the art of guerrilla warfare when he went to Afghanistan to help fight the Soviets. At that time he had the backing, support, and approval of Saudi Arabia, Pakistan, and the United States of America. Yes, you heard me, at one point we backed Osama bin Laden. Bin Laden's guys were all using U.S. Stinger missiles and were trained in our communications. Hell, at one point he even received some very specialized training from none other than our own CIA. Oh, in case you were wondering, the CIA is not happy that we know this, and the agency—surprise, surprise—denies it. But we have plenty of sources: the Afghans have told us, the Russians have told us, the guy who *ran the training* told me.

Ayman al-Zawahiri, bin Laden's second in command, is the diabolical genius behind al Qaeda's operations. Al-Zawahiri is an Egyptian surgeon from an upper-class family. He joined Egypt's Islamist movement in the late 1970s. After serving three years in prison on charges connected with the assassination of Anwar Sadat, he traveled to Afghanistan, where he met bin Laden.

Al-Zawahiri is suspected of helping organize the 1997 massacre of sixty-seven foreign tourists in Egypt. He was indicted in connection with the bombing of U.S. embassies in Tanzania and Kenya. In 1998, he was one of five Islamic leaders to sign on to bin Laden's declaration calling for attacks against U.S. citizens. He is wanted by the FBI and has been sentenced to death in absentia by Egypt. In March 2004, the Pakistani military began an assault on al Qaeda's troops along the Pakistan-Afghanistan border. These troops were believed to be defending al-Zawahiri, who managed to escape.

These are bad guys. They are murderers who run one hell of an effective terrorist organization. Al Qaeda's leadership oversees a loosely organized network of cells. It recruits members from thousands of Arabs who are veterans of the Afghan war, as well as radicals from around the world. Its infrastructure is small, mobile, and decentralized. Each cell operates independently and its membership reports directly to the cell leader. The cell's members operate without knowing the identity of other cells. Local operatives rarely know anyone higher up in the organization's hierarchy. They are well prepared, well trained, and disciplined—all the elements necessary to have a successful organization.

Videos of their training camps have been aired on television. These guys train like . . . well, like the good guys, like us. They train on how to use all types of weapons, from small handguns to rocket-propelled grenades (RPGs) to antiaircraft missiles like the SA7. They do extensive live fire training while entering confined spaces—the technique used in order to take hostages, rob banks, or just kill everyone in a room.

Now when we—the good guys—train, we do so with an eye to preventing friendly fire. We worry about, and try to minimize, hurting or killing civilians. We worry about getting ourselves wounded or killed. These terrorists don't concern themselves with any of this. That makes them extremely dangerous. They train very hard in very realistic ways using live bullets. They are impressive indeed. We don't have to admire these jerks, but we do have to acknowledge their efforts. We can never again take them for granted, or worse, ignore them.

When U.S. forces launched their military campaign in Afghanistan in the fall of 2001, they turned up videos and other al Qaeda training plans. Writing in National Review Online, journalist Bryan Preston described the sorts of follow-up attacks against the United States that al Qaeda apparently was planning—all of which would occur on the same day, "at roughly the same time":

On a sunny day in rural Ohio, a routine traffic stop becomes a nightmare. As a sheriff's deputy approaches an apparently disabled pickup truck, armed men leap from its bed, spray him with gunfire and toss a homemade bomb into his squad car before escaping.

In Los Angeles, masked men capture a small office building, killing its security guards before taking more than a dozen hostages. As the day unfolds, the masked men demand time on local television, and use it to rail against American "decadence." Sometime near midnight, the terrorists kill all of their hostages in front of live cameras before setting off a bomb that destroys the building, kills themselves and leaves an indelible impression on the horrified audience.

In suburban Washington, D.C., a band of terrorists attack and kill a senator out for a round of golf. In Dallas, an unknown attacker gains entry into the house of a wealthy local businessman, and kills him by pumping 15 rounds from a .45 into his body. The assailant escapes into the night.

It is a scary picture. As Preston said, these sorts of attacks could happen. They will happen if we don't stop the terrorists.

If you doubt al Qaeda's ambitions and capabilities, you need only recall the string of deadly successes the al Qaeda band of murderers has already executed in little more than a decade (as well as the terrorists' thwarted plans):

1993 — Terrorists bomb New York City's World Trade Center, claiming six lives.
    — In Somalia, al Qaeda operatives launch attacks against U.S. soldiers.

1994 — U.S. officials investigating the World Trade Center

bombing discover that the terrorists had seen the
New York City skyscraper as only one target in a
much broader plan; plans also called for hijacking a
plane to fly into CIA headquarters.

1996 —A bomb explodes outside an American military
complex at Khobar Towers in Saudi Arabia, killing
nineteen Americans and injuring hundreds of others.

1998 —The bombing of the U.S. embassies in Tanzania
and Kenya claim 224 lives, including 12 American
lives.

1999 —Customs agents in Washington State foil the
"Millennium Bomb" plot when they discover
explosives in Ahmed Ressam's car.
—Police in Jordan arrest terrorists who have been
planning attacks against vacationing Westerners.

2000 —The USS *Cole* is bombed while in port at Yemen;
seventeen sailors are killed.

2001 —Nearly three thousand people are killed when
al Qaeda attacks the World Trade Center (again) and
the Pentagon, and crash another hijacked plane in a
Pennsylvania field.

2002 —A bomb explodes in a Tunisian synagogue, killing
seventeen.
—A car bomb goes off outside a hotel in Karachi,
Pakistan, and kills fourteen.
—A car bomb kills twelve outside of the American
consulate in Karachi.
—In Bali, Indonesia, 202 people are killed in nightclub
bombings.
—A suicide bomber in Mombasa, Kenya, kills sixteen.

2003 —Suicide bombers attack a housing compound for
Westerners in Riyadh, Saudi Arabia, killing thirty-four
people.
—A series of bombs goes off in Casablanca, Morocco,
killing thirty-three.
—A car bomb in Jakarta, Indonesia, claims twelve
lives.
—Seventeen people are killed in another bombing of a
housing compound in Riyadh, Saudi Arabia.
—Suicide bombers attack two synagogues in Istanbul,
Turkey, killing twenty-five.
—A British bank is bombed in Istanbul.

2004 —An al Qaeda affiliate launches a series of rush-hour
bombings in Madrid, killing 191 people and injuring
some 1,800.
—Twenty-two are killed in Khobar, Saudi Arabia,
when an oil company is attacked.
—American Paul Johnson is beheaded in Saudi
Arabia.

This list is hardly complete, but it is both a testimony to al
Qaeda's deadly skills and a sad commentary on the world's inability
to stop it. We cannot allow this list to get any longer. We must pull
out all the stops. We must do whatever it takes, and I mean *whatever*!
We must squash these killers now. Not tomorrow, not after we have
negotiated. Now! For those who do not have the stomach for this,
please, get the hell out of the way.

Do you think that there is a better way? Do you think it will all
get better if we try sanctions and diplomacy for a little bit longer? I
don't believe you would feel the same way if you took a good look at
the al Qaeda training manual. Reading it would convince you that in
the face of this evil we can no longer afford nice. We can only afford
success—and success in this business occurs only when the terrorist
is dead.

The manual I'm describing is 180 pages long. The British SAS discovered it in Afghanistan and turned it over to British intelligence, who shared it with the CIA. The manual's sole purpose is to teach killers how to kill better—to serve the ultimate goal of bringing down the United States of America. It contains chapters on kidnapping, assassinations, explosives, knives and guns, and torture, among other things. But the manual also makes clear that the terrorists consider *all* ways to kill us, and think deeply on how to perfect their methods. I'm going to give you a firsthand view of this manual (portions of which are reproduced in Appendix A, at the back of the book). How about these instructions from the chapter on "Assassinations Using Poisons and Cold Steel"? And trust me, this is only the beginning:

> *Assassinations with Poison:* We will limit [the discussion] to poisons that the holy warrior can prepare and use without endangering his health.
>
> *First—Herbal Poisons*
>
> *A—Castor Beans*
> The substance Ricin, an extract from Castor Beans, is considered one of the most deadly poisons. .035 milligrams is enough to kill someone by inhaling or by injecting in a vein. . . . It is a simple operation to extract Ricin, and Castor Beans themselves can be obtained from nurseries throughout the country. . . .
>
> *B—Precatory Beans*
> The herbal poison Abrin, extracted from Precatory Beans, is very similar to Ricin. The seeds of this plant are red and black and are used in prayer beads. Prepare a very dark ink or refine some normal ink to be as fine as possible while keeping it strong enough to penetrate the shell of Precatory Beans. Put on a pair of leather gloves and very carefully

bore about twelve holes in each of the prayer beads. After completing that, spray the prayer beads with DMSO [Dimethyl Sulfoxide]. The Abrin will kill your victim slowly, but relentlessly. . . .

C—The Water Hemlock Plant

A lethal dose is 3.2 grams. It has a palatable taste, and is very similar to another plant, parsnip.

Symptoms: Nervous spasms within 15 to 60 minutes, including severe locking and clenching of the jaw to the extent that the tongue could be cut off. . . .

Poisoning from Eating Spoiled Food

Since .000028 grams will kill a person, this poison is absolutely lethal. After consumption, the symptoms appear in 12 to 36 hours. They include dizziness, headaches, constipation, difficulty swallowing and speaking, fluids coming from the nose and mouth, and lack of muscle coordination. It results in death from respiratory failure. If it is received in the blood stream, death is very swift and almost without symptoms.

How to Prepare Spoiled Food

Fill a pot with corn and green beans. Put in a small piece of meat and about two spoonfuls of fresh excrement. Pour the water into the pot until there is surface tension at the lip of the pot. Cover the pot tightly. If you do that correctly, there will be no air trapped in the pot. Leave the pot in a dark, moderately warm room for 15 days. At the end of that period, you will notice a substance on the edge of the pot and a small amount of rottenness. These are known as bacteria colonies, which secrete their external poison as a result of the process of bacterial digestion. You can make three or four pots at the same time.

> During the time of the destroyer, Jamal Abdul Nasser,
> someone who was being severely tortured in prison (he had
> no connection with Islam), ate some feces after losing san-
> ity from the severity of the torture. A few hours after he ate
> the feces, he was found dead.

Interesting reading. There is a tendency for us to think that these guys are stupid. Clearly the instructions above, not to mention al Qaeda's string of successes, demonstrate that this is certainly not the case, at least when it comes to things like killing. We need to focus on the fact that they are sophisticated assassins. And they are coming for us.

A Religious War

Why? Why are they coming for us? Why do they want to kill *us*? What is this interest in killing Americans, flying planes into buildings, causing terror and mayhem all about? Why, indeed.

The U.S. government—meaning politicians who don't want to offend anyone—say that the War on Terror is against a few radicals. They say that most of the people in the Middle East are friends of America—whatever that means. Funny, politicians know how to read a poll here at home, but they can't seem to wrap their minds around the fact that pretty much every poll taken in the Middle East says most of the people there hate us. (For example, in June 2004 Zogby International produced a detailed survey of "How Arabs View America," which showed that the overwhelming majority of Arabs in Morocco, Saudi Arabia, Jordan, Lebanon, the United Arab Emirates, and Egypt have an unfavorable impression of the United States. In Egypt, a whopping 98 percent had an unfavorable impression, and 94 percent of our "friends" the Saudis felt the same way.)

We all seem to be avoiding an essential fact about those who are trying to kill us: 99.9 percent of the bastards are devout Muslims. Care to guess at the number of Muslim religious leaders that condemned terrorism in the three years after the 9/11 attacks? Give up? It's two. Extensive research into the clerics' statements reveals that *two* Muslim religious leaders have said publicly that terrorism is a bad thing. Gee, thanks.

One of the issues is simply that Islamofascists see the United States as preventing the "great nations of the Middle East" from regaining what they view as their rightful place at the table of world leaders. But there is an even bigger issue, one you must comprehend. Jihad, or "holy war," is a tenet of the Muslim tradition. True, mainstream Islam has moved away from more militant interpretations of jihad; some radical sects believe all Muslims are obligated to wage war against those who commit crimes against Muslims and/or occupy Muslim land. In many Muslims' eyes, we are supporting the oppression of Muslims in India, the Philippines, Russia, Uzbekistan, and of course Palestine and Israel.

That last one is most significant. Since the United States of America supports the right of a Jewish state to exist in the middle of what the Arab world views as Muslim territory, in the minds of most Muslims we are committing crimes that require Muslims to wage war against us. After all, the United States is the principal supporter of Israel, providing billions of dollars' worth of aid every year. Less noticed, but nonetheless important, are the billions that American citizens give to Israel. Since Israel became an independent Jewish state, Muslim extremists have been trying to destroy it, and they see the United States as the only reason Israel has survived for as long as it has. (This is not true, of course. As early as 1948, Israel clobbered Syria, Egypt, and Jordan simultaneously, simply outgunning and outclassing the poorly trained, poorly equipped, and even more poorly led Arab forces. The United States had little to do with it.)

Now, in fairness, not all Muslims are calling for the annihilation of Israel and the United States. But even those who aren't have a hard time reconciling their religious obligations with our foreign policy. That said, I am not suggesting that we should do a damn thing different in regard to Israel, unless maybe we should do even more for Israel. But in this War on Terror we must understand that we are an enemy of those who practice the Muslim religion because we are friends of the Jews.

Simply put, we are fighting a religious war, and knowing it is the first step in winning it. Our refusal to acknowledge this—and we don't because it might offend our Muslim and Arab friends, or because a politician might lose the Muslim voter here at home—does not make it untrue. We can't duck this. I do not want our government to change because the Muslims hate us, but I do want our government and you the reader to understand what we are up against. (To understand more of this mind-set and where it comes from, read *Imperial Hubris*, by Anonymous. He doesn't get it all right, but he makes an interesting argument, one definitely worth reading.)

By this point we've looked at the major players—the countries that support terrorism out in the open. (And this doesn't even include the governments that publicly condemn terrorism but make deals with the radicals who run the madrasses and incite violence and jihad against the West, including Egypt, Yemen, Jordan, and the United Arab Emirates.) We've looked at al Qaeda. Now it's time to look at ourselves.

Let's talk about the old Uncle, the United States of America, shall we? We are more than a bit bloody in all of this. Does anyone really believe that the Israeli government could not defeat its internal enemies if it really wanted to? It could. But it doesn't, because the United States government does not allow it. Sorry if this insults your American sensibilities and pride.

The United States doesn't want Israel to defeat its enemies. The reason for this is bizarre but true. There is a small but powerful Palestinian lobby inside the State Department who reason that Israel is part of the Middle East problem. This crowd says the Palestinians are simply defending themselves, that the Palestinians need representation. These are bleeding hearts, misguided government workers—some might even call them liberals. Whatever we call them, they are wrong.

They managed to convince five American administrations that it was not in our interests to kill Yasser "the Rat Man" Arafat. Well, it was surely in Israel's interests. How can ending the daily slaughter of innocents not be in our best interests? I wish that this were conspiratorial. It is merely bureaucratic. It would be easier to accept this mentality if it were a plot devised by evil men, but it is not. It is merely the ignorance of government employees and the laziness of elected officials. Now that the terrorist Arafat has finally died, that one obstacle to peace has been lifted.

We have tried for almost *thirty years* to broker a peace between Israel and the Palestinians and it hasn't worked. In the last three years alone, hundreds of Israeli men, women, and children have been murdered by suicide bombers—by men and women, young boys and girls, who strapped bombs to their chests.

Concepts of common decency and world opinion will not stop this. They haven't so far. It is time for us to get out of the way. It is time to let the Israelis take care of it. We helped the Israeli government build the most powerful military in the Middle East. Let's let them use it. The Israelis already had the most effective intelligence service in the world. This is their backyard. They can solve this problem, even if it gets ugly.

Know Your Enemy

For all the reasons we've talked about, Muslim extremists want to kill us. They want to kill us because in their twisted minds, we are decadent, we are solely responsible for any disrespect shown toward Arabs and Muslims, and we support Israel. They use their God to justify our annihilation.

These guys don't think like us. To understand the nature of our enemy, you have to understand what they believe. And to do that, you need to look at their guiding principles. The al Qaeda training manual makes it crystal-clear what they are fighting for, and who they are fighting for. Look at this passage taken from the opening pages of the manual of death:

> In the name of Allah, the merciful and compassionate
>
> To those champions who avowed the truth day and night . . .
> And wrote with their blood and sufferings these phrases . . .
>
> The confrontation that we are calling for with the apostate regimes does not know Socratic debates . . . Platonic ideals . . . nor Aristotelian diplomacy. But it knows the dialogue of bullets, the ideals of assassination, bombing, and destruction, and the diplomacy of the cannon and machine-gun.
>
> Islamic governments have never and will never be established through peaceful solutions and cooperative councils. They are established as they [always] have been by pen and gun by word and bullet by tongue and teeth.

Had enough yet? No? Then try this one:

Pledge, O Sister

> Covenant, O Sister . . . to make their women widows and their children orphans.
> Covenant, O Sister . . . to make them desire death and hate appointments and prestige.
> Covenant, O Sister . . . to slaughter them like lambs and let the Nile, al-Asi, and Euphrates rivers flow with their blood.
> Covenant, O Sister . . . to be a pick of destruction for every godless and apostate regime.
> Covenant, O Sister . . . to retaliate for you against every dog who touch you even with a bad word.

These are not reasoned men. These are killers of children. These are killers who use theology and deception to justify their actions.

They live in caves, plotting and scheming, blaming everyone else for what they have done. There is no reasoning with them. Once you understand what they are about, you understand that there is only one way to deal with them: kill them all.

Too strong for you? Just think, they're trying to kill *us* all. Let's dig back into the instructions in the al Qaeda training manual. Remember when I said the section on poisoning was just the beginning of it? Well, now you'll see how prepared and how very deadly they truly are:

> **A—*Assassinating with a Knife:*** When undertaking any assassination using a knife, the enemy must be struck in one of these lethal spots:
>
> *From the front:*
> 1.   Anywhere in the rib cage.
> 2.   Both or one eye.
> 3.   The pelvis (under target's navel).
> 4.   The area directly above the genitals.
>
> *From behind:*
> 1.   The axon (back of the head).
> 2.   The end of the spinal column directly above the person's buttocks.
>
> **B—*Assassination with a Blunt Object:*** A blow with a club must be in lethal areas.
>
> *From the front:*
> 1.   The two eyes.
> 2.   Where the veins and arteries converge in the neck.
> 3.   Top of the stomach, with the end of the stick.
> 4.   Above the genitals, with the end of the club.
> 5.   The area of the tongue.
> 6.   Choke the neck with the stick, like in a hanging.

From the rear:

1.   The area of the left ear.
2.   The back of the head (axon). . . .

C—Assassination with a Rope:

1.   Choking (Neck area). There is no other area besides the neck.

D—Assassination Using Hands:

1.   Choking.
2.   Poking the fingers into one or both eyes and gouging them.

Check out the detail here—where to stab, where to choke, how to strike. This is just one page of more than 180 pages of how to kill, maim, and destroy. Maybe TV and movies have made some of us jaded. Is it possible that you are not getting this? Here is another page from the terrorist manual to give you one more slap.

Booby Traps

These consist of creative, innovative methods aimed at planting anti-personnel and anti-vehicle explosive charges, and the enemy is blown up as a result of normal movement without paying attention to what is around him. Booby traps are considered one of the best ways to execute an assassination operation against enemy personnel because we have gotten a long distance away from the site of the incident without leaving any evidence or trace enabling the enemy to know who were the perpetrators.

However, a brother should not be allowed the opportunity to work with setting booby traps until after he has mastered the use of explosives and has successfully worked in

the electrical and mechanical fields, because the first mistake a brother makes could be his last mistake.

One of the most important considerations in placing a
booby trap is to make the right choice of the appropriate
switch that the enemy would not notice [and avoid his de-
tecting] and removal of the charge.

Any sign of our work or presence in the area where the
booby trap was placed must be removed, because any tools,
pieces of electrical wire, tape, etc., would put the enemy on
the alert, and the plan and operation would fail.

These booby traps should sound very familiar to all of us. We
have heard about them almost daily in news broadcasts. They are the
very same devices that have killed so many of our loved ones in Iraq
and Afghanistan.

Al Qaeda looks at itself as a paramilitary organization. It is waging war, even if we refuse to participate. The manual says its mission
includes the following:

1. Gathering information about the enemy, the land, the in-
    stallations, and the neighbors.
2. Kidnapping enemy personnel, documents, secrets, and
    arms.
3. Assassinating enemy personnel as well as foreign
    tourists.
4. Freeing the brothers who are captured by the enemy.
5. Spreading rumors and writing statements that instigate
    people against the enemy.
6. Blasting and destroying the places of amusement, im-
    morality, and sin; not a vital target.
7. Blasting and destroying the embassies and attacking
    vital economic centers.
8. Blasting and destroying bridges leading into and out of
    the cities.

Look at this list. Consider what it says: blast, kidnapping, assassination. Can the terrorists be any clearer? There is no doubt what is going on—and there should be no doubt what we have to do in return.

None of what I've said in this chapter is *politically correct,* but all of this is too damn important to pussyfoot around. Hey, this is me tapping an annoying knuckle on your forehead. Al Qaeda is the most dangerous threat this nation has faced since the fall of the Soviet Union. So yeah, you really did need to see in black and white, in the killers' own words, what they intend to keep on doing. An ancient Chinese proverb sums it up completely: "Know your enemy as you know yourself and you can fight a hundred battles with no danger of defeat."

CHAPTER 4

The Intelligence Disaster—and How to Fix It

So far we have talked about how we got into this mess and who is killing us. Now it's time to start looking at how we fix it. So first and foremost, we must look at intelligence. Without it we are going nowhere and looking decidedly incompetent doing it. We can't even point in the general direction of the terrorists without it. It is the single most important aspect of the War on Terror.

Intelligence is, simply put, all the information and news from entities that don't want us to have that information. Intelligence can be gathered in many different forms. It is collected through satellites, by listening to phone conversations, by reading computer hard drives, by tapping fiber optic cable, and much more. That's the technical side. But when it comes down to it, any intelligence service needs to rely on human means—spies. And unfortunately, human intelligence is our Achilles' heel.

The fact is, the War on Terror cannot be won if the United States does not possess the world's best intelligence service. Unfortunately, we're not there yet. We're not even close.

As we all know now, 9/11 was a massive intelligence failure. (Hell, even Richard Clarke, who didn't think a hole being blown in the USS *Cole* was an intelligence failure, admits 9/11 was one.) We didn't see 9/11 coming. We weren't prepared.

The trouble is, for all the time we've spent agonizing about what the U.S. intelligence community knew or should have known before 9/11—for all the bickering, all the finger pointing—we've done almost nothing to solve the problems that *still* plague our ability to spy on our enemies and to detect the many threats to our safety. In late 2004, we passed a rather toothless intelligence bill. The bill did some good things, but, as we will see, it hasn't addressed some of the biggest problems.

Everyone, and I do mean everyone, will tell you that in order to win this fight we have to lead with intelligence. We need intelligence—and lots of it—because we have to know the *who,* the *what,* the *where,* the *when,* and sometimes the *why* of the terrorist before we can get close enough to kill him. When you decide to kill someone, particularly one as well protected and operationally savvy as Osama bin Laden, you want to know where he eats, sleeps, and craps. You want to know how much gas is in his car. You want to know who his friends and enemies are. You want to know every damn detail you can because you just don't know what kernel of information will be the one you need to get him. Getting this information is the business of spying, and it is dangerous and dirty work. We're not equipped to do that work.

Thanks, President Carter

Once upon a time, the United States had a very aggressive, very successful national intelligence community. So what happened?

Jimmy Carter happened.

Gutted like a fish—that's what President "I-Should-Have-Stayed-a-Peanut-Farmer" Carter did to the CIA, the governmental agency charged with the necessary dirty work of spying. Carter got away with it because the American people, still reeling from Vietnam, didn't want to deal with any more scandals or crises. And after all, the famous Church Committee hearings of the 1970s had portrayed the CIA as an organization out of control, as a secretive agency intent on covert operations to circumvent the normal checks and procedures of government. So Carter began the crippling of the CIA. We lost 50 percent of our human intelligence-gathering capability. We lost our spies. Nice going, guys!

President Carter didn't think we needed those pesky spies hanging around because we had all this new technology. By then we had begun to develop satellites that could see the hair on a gnat's ass. We had listening devices that could hear every phone call anywhere in the world. By using these tools, our intelligence community became extremely adept at telling you what happened yesterday and what was going on today. There was only one problem: after gutting the CIA, we were completely blind about tomorrow.

You can't know about and prevent tomorrow without the best human intelligence assets on the planet—spies. Tomorrow always belongs to spies. Spying is humans talking to humans and getting people to betray their causes. It is watching someone sweat when you talk to him. These are the things technology could never do. Without knowing about tomorrow, we can't protect ourselves. We are an open society that leaves too many doors ajar, too many ways to get at us. We have too many trains, planes, and automobiles, too many borders.

So we were blind about September 11. Believing that technology would solve everything, we sat by as a bunch of terrorists armed only with box cutters brought this nation to its knees.

We're still blind.

Years have passed since the 9/11 terrorist attacks, and we still haven't dealt with the mastermind of those attacks. Every day we don't find Osama bin Laden we have failed, have been kicked in the teeth. Every day he is still out there, we get an F in intelligence.

If failure to find bin Laden weren't enough, what about Iraq and the weapons of mass destruction? When the secretary of state of the United States of America is forced to acknowledge publicly that our government's concern over WMDs in Iraq was *probably* a mistake, he is issuing an indictment of U.S. intelligence. (And that's putting it politely. It's really a full-blown disaster!)

Oh yeah, and what about all the intelligence predicting what kind of war we would face once we went into Iraq? Before we began the military campaign, our intelligence experts estimated that when our armed forces took out Saddam's army, we would be fighting only between two thousand and seven thousand insurgents and that the rest of Iraq would greet us with cheers and flowers. But more than a year and a half into the fighting, we were dealing with an insurgency that numbered almost twenty thousand, and many of the people who were supposed to be cheering us were insurgent sympathizers. How could this be? Once again, our intelligence failed us. We didn't have credible intelligence sources in Iraq after 1998, so someone lied or was stupid, or both. Off with their heads.

Getting Our Friends in Line

Part of our intelligence failure can be placed squarely on the shoulders of our supposed friends in the Middle East. The Saudis come to mind here. We have not done what is necessary to get nations like Saudi Arabia to share vital information with us. The Saudis need to *really* help; they need to give us access to the *real* intelligence, the *real* prisoners, and the stuff that really matters to us in this fight. There are two basic tools we can use to force the Saudis to cooperate— *money and power.*

When I say we have to use money as a tool, I mean *taking* their money. In the Middle East, oil is money. So what do we do to take the Saudis' money? We deny them the money we're throwing at them for their oil. We can take more oil from our own country—

stop all the dickering about Arctic National Wildlife Refuge in Alaska; just drill! (Despite all the hand wringing about the environmental effects, the truth is that we're talking about exploring for oil in just a tiny part of the massive area—and most of the time, this tiny, remote, barren part of the "wildlife refuge" isn't even inhabited by wildlife!) And in addition to taking advantage of our own oil resources, we can make a deal with Canada, which has huge oil assets. We could even go after alternative fuels. For years we've been researching and experimenting with alternative fuels. Now we need to apply all we've learned in this endeavor to free us from the bonds of oil dependency. Let's get all the bugs worked out so countries like Saudi Arabia can no longer hold energy hostage. Until that happens we can make them *pay*. We can demand higher prices for the services we provide the Saudis. Let's jack up the fees for training their military and selling them things like tanks and planes. The House of Saud has very deep pockets; we need to get much farther in them.

Just as we can take away some of their money, we can also take away *power* from the Saudi government; the Saudi ruling dictatorship—excuse me, "royal family"—will cooperate if they know we're not going to keep propping them up. We give the Saudis intelligence support. We have a defense agreement with them that says any country that attacks Saudi Arabia gets attacked by the United States. We give them access to presidents. We sell them our military gear and give them training. Without our support, the House of Saud would fall.

If we use these two things, if we affect their money and their hold on power, then we have got them by the short hairs. Odds are they will pony up.

What is the end result of our unwillingness to put *real* pressure on Saudi Arabia? A peaceful, hardworking American citizen, Paul Johnson, is captured. We are helpless to save him. He is beheaded by terrorists.

Other nations in the Middle East, who have every reason to be the enemy of bin Laden, help us even less than the Saudis do. They have failed to offer us the information necessary to find and deal with bin Laden. We lack this cooperation from others for many reasons, but we can do things to improve our chance of having a clue as to what is going on. Money and power are languages all countries speak. We need to start yelling in those languages, now.

But there is only so much blame we can place on other nations. We haven't fixed the problems here at home. For example, we have very few agents in the Middle East who even speak the language of the country in which they are stationed, let alone have access to tight-knit family-based cells that make up al Qaeda. This must change.

So Here's What We Do

In the summer of 2004, the 9/11 Commission released its report, complete with suggestions as to how we keep 9/11 from happening again. The commission's plan called for a complete overhaul of our intelligence community. Sounds like a radical step, right? Well, the fact is, *nothing the 9/11 Commission recommended in its report is new.* It shouldn't have taken 9/11 to make the government realize that the intelligence community needed to be remade entirely. I and other terrorism experts have been saying that *for years*.

That being said, and late being better than never, we are now going to look at how we can protect ourselves. Keep in mind, you can't do just *some* of these things. In order to effect real change, in order to make it so these guys can't get to us again, we have to make sweeping changes in every area of our intelligence community.

WARNING! You will find a few things in my plan you *won't* find in the 9/11 Commission's plan. This is because either the 9/11 Commission did not consider them or it did but the membership chickened out. Either way it is a big mistake. My plan is not for the politicians or the weak of heart, but it will get at it. Hang on to your hats, here we go.

When we talk about intelligence failures, we have a tendency to think of and blame the CIA. This is not quite accurate or fair. We have *fifteen* separate, large, cumbersome, very territorial, never-cooperating-with-the-others intelligence agencies in our government. They report to seven separate cabinet officers, who answer to fifty-seven separate congressional committees. So as you can see, all the blame can't possibly belong with the CIA. An inordinate number of bureaucrats and politicians deserve their fair share of the blame.

In theory, the director of Central Intelligence (DCI) is not only the boss of the CIA; he is also the boss of the entire intelligence community. He is *supposed* to control all the other national intelligence agencies. He is also *supposed* to put together the National Foreign Intelligence Program, which includes the budgets and priorities for all the nation's intelligence agencies. Upon completion, the program is sent to the president and Congress for approval.

Hey! This sounds good—one guy in charge of everything. It sounds streamlined and efficient. Except the government is involved, so of course it is screwed up. Our government put one guy in charge of all things related to intelligence but gave the DCI no way to hold any of the other agencies accountable. He can't direct how much money is spent by the other agencies. He doesn't have the tools to make other intelligence agencies coordinate with him. To be fair, the new intelligence bill provides some help. But not enough.

In business, in life, but particularly in government, the bottom line is, if you can't tell people what to do and you can't control their money, you are not in charge. Hell, the DCI is barely in charge of the CIA. He has more than ten thousand employees and spends more time testifying before Congress than running his agency. He and all surrounding him are political appointees with other masters and agendas—none of which have anything to do with our safety.

Again, we have more than fifty separate committees in both branches of Congress demanding to talk to seven separate cabinet-level secretaries, who run fifteen competing intelligence agencies; all of these congressional committees can demand information or testimony from the fifteen intelligence agencies! I will say this over and over in this chapter, because the sheer magnitude of it is mind-blowing. It is the perfect example of how screwed-up things truly are.

If you find all these layers of bosses and committees confusing, imagine how those who are actually trying to get things done, the guys within the intelligence community, feel about the structure. Here is the really bad thing: When the DCI is called to testify before Congress, all other things stop while he prepares. Position papers are written, e-mails fly all over the airways, and PowerPoint presentations are cranked out. Then he hauls his ass up to the Capitol and sits in front of a bunch of mostly white men who ask him stupid questions. While this is going on, nothing else is being done. This process is outrageous. In the middle of a war, our leaders are holding hearings, trying to figure out how to cover their asses if it all goes bad, instead of focusing on getting this fight right.

Even when the DCI isn't testifying, the only thing going on in these fifteen agencies is bad politics. Bad politics means nothing is getting done. Nothing getting done means more good guys die and we lose the War on Terror. That is how important intelligence is and why we must fix it now. One of the problems with the new intel bill is that it adds another layer of BS without flushing any agencies or bureaucracies.

We are going to have to drag the intelligence community into this fight. There is so much wrong with our national intelligence community that it is almost better to blow it up and start again. This is going to be very difficult and dangerous to do while we are at war, but that's the price you pay when you do nothing for thirty years and don't heed the warnings that have been sounded. You can't pretend that the bogeyman will just up and go away. For decades we accepted, without protest, the deaths of hundreds of our citizens. This inaction led us to the one day when thousands of our citizens died. You guys would not fix this, people died. It's our turn.

Here is a start. Put one person in charge—*really* in charge. Give him control over the money. Give him control over the hiring and the firing. Give him control over the whole deal. Every commission, every study done before 9/11 and since says that the national intelligence community needs *one* boss.

The 9/11 Commission also recommended the creation of a cabinet-level position for Intelligence. The commission wanted to call it the national director of intelligence, or NDI. So the intel bill did this, but it didn't give the position the necessary authority. Whatever you call this person, he/she must have the real ability to tell the other remaining agencies what to do. Sitting as a cabinet guy or gal in many instances is almost ceremonial; look, we even had a drug czar, who gave a lot of speeches but had no real power. If the NDI doesn't have any real power, then it is just another layer of crap to wade through and we will remain in a state of chaos.

Hey, zipperheads! Make the NDI the boss for real. Mr. President! Hey, Congress! Pay close attention. Make a damn order or law that gives the NDI what you hate to give anyone. It's called "tasking authority," and it's the ability to tell other governmental agencies what to do while having absolute control over budgets and those who work for you. The new bill did not. What a surprise.

This seems simple, but just watch. Every pencilneck in the Department of Defense, the National Security Agency, the FBI, the State Department, the Defense Intelligence Agency, and of course Congress will scream like a stuck pig. Too damn bad! If the 9/11 Commission is to be believed, if the Senate Intelligence Committee's report on 9/11 is to be believed, no one in the U.S. intelligence community was talking to any of the others; the fifteen different agencies wouldn't share information with one another; no one was in charge, and that got us killed.

In August 2004, President George W. Bush came out and endorsed the creation of the NDI. But he stipulated that he did not want it to be a cabinet-level position. He also said that the NDI would not have the power to control budgets or to hire and fire the people who work for him. Sorry, but our president got it *dead wrong*. We shouldn't bother to create the position if we're not going to make it what it has to be. As one member of the 9/11 Commission said,

"This is not a Chinese menu that you can pick and choose. It's a fundamental systematic change, a complete change of the way this nation does its intelligence. So it's pretty hard to say, 'Well, we'll do that one, that's easy; this one's a little tougher, we'll put that aside.'" We need broad, sweeping, meaningful changes. So the NDI needs real power. Let one bureau-rat get in the way and he's fired. Let one administrator say no to the DCI's request for a spy and that administrator is relieved. In order for this position to mean anything, this is how it must work.

The NDI must have full power, full budget authority, full hiring and firing authority, tasking authority, and insulation from being fired on political whim. In fact, let's take the politics out of this appointment right here and now. The person must be appointed from the pool of all qualified eligible men and women for a ten-year term. He or she should be protected from being fired unless malfeasance can be proven, not just alleged. He or she will serve no political master; the NDI will serve the American public. This seems only right, since that is whom the official is charged with protecting.

We came right to the edge of fixing the intelligence mess, but then backed away. So why the hell was this intel bill lauded by Republicans and Democrats alike as an amazing piece of legislation? Well, the fact that every politician this side of the moon likes it should tell you that it's not all it's cracked up to be. The fact that politicians wrote it should tell you that there are holes in the language big enough to drive a truck through. The intel bill became more about saving face than about saving the country.

Hey, has anyone actually *read* the new intelligence bill? I read it, and while it is nice and lofty in goal and intent, what we actually do with it, how it actually plays out, remains to be seen.

Seems the NDI has to get everyone, including his brother, father, and uncle, to concur with his hiring and firing decisions.

Seems that the NDI doesn't have any real control over the Pentagon or its budget—so you know there'll be some kind of contest between the National Intelligence Agency and the Pentagon, and it won't end until someone pulls out a ruler and calls it.

Seems that while the NDI has access to the president, it's up to the president to determine how much access.

Seems that we've created yet another important job—the director of the National Counterterrorism Center—and yet another agency, the National Counterterrorism Center, which in theory are good things, but if not executed correctly, they will add more layers within an already overwhelming bureaucracy.

I can't make out exactly what role the NDI has over the CIA, but it seems as though the bill gives the NDI some control and input while making sure the powers that be at the CIA have grounds to say no to him anytime they feel like it.

This piece of legislation is being touted as the solution to our terrorism problems. Maybe it is, but only if everyone really means that they are done playing politics with our safety. Only if everyone is really committed to making this work.

The politicians could have gone all the way with this. They could have given the guy in charge, the NDI, the power he or she needed to do the job, but they didn't. They didn't because when you give someone power, you almost always lose some of your own, and politicians, like homie, don't play that.

In June 2004, at least one good thing happened: George "I-Was-Not-Paying-Attention" Tenet resigned from the position of DCI—for "personal reasons." Those "personal reasons" might have included a big hole in New York City and nearly three thousand murdered Americans. Those failures happened on his watch. Sure, as we've seen, the DCI doesn't have the authority he's supposed to have, and Tenet was hamstrung by the way the system was set up. But he never made a convincing case that he *should* be in charge. His job was to manage our spooks all over the world, who spy to protect us. He did not do his job. So it's a good thing that Tenet went to "spend more time with his family." If we're ever going to make changes to the intelligence system, we have to demand accountability. He is now making more than $500,000 on the speaking tour and working on a book that will earn him millions.

That was a start. Then President Bush had to find a replacement for the DCI. He chose Congressman Porter Goss of Florida as his man. Nope. Sorry. Wrong guy! He is way too political. He is not a killer. He left the spy business to become a politician. Wrong, wrong, wrong on so many levels. He has decided to be a partisan politician and we do not need more of them. And as soon as Goss got to Langley, the CIA went into turmoil. At this writing it was unclear whether Goss would end up in the new NDI position, but it *was* clear that Goss was not the man for the job. The NDI has got to be nonpartisan, nonpolitical, and a killer—an ethical killer, but a killer all the same. Have we learned nothing from 9/11? We aren't changing anything. We aren't fixing anything. We are moving things around, using smoke and mirrors, and we are screwing it up even more than it was before.

The next thing we have to do, if we are serious about fixing what is wrong within the intelligence community, is stop the overlapping of efforts. There are basically three types of intelligence: military, domestic, and foreign. We need to decide who does what. Give over these responsibilities to the appropriate agencies and let them do their jobs.

Right now, the Department of Defense, the CIA, the FBI, the Defense Intelligence Agency, and the National Security Agency, to name just five, are all vying for the same information on the same targets. You can get five agencies looking for the same bad guy, buying up the same sources, and tripping over one another in the back alleys of Damascus and Kabul. Look, do you care how silly and ineffective it is to have a bunch of white guys tripping all over themselves in Kabul? Do you care that when the intelligence community acts this way, good guys instead of bad guys die? Well, you should.

Eighty percent of our intelligence budget is tied up in the Pentagon, but the Pentagon is hardly ever questioned about its failures on 9/11 or before. The Pentagon and the CIA are engaged in an ongoing turf war, and that war is killing the good guys; it needs to stop now. The budget issue—meaning who should spend money on what operation, who gets credit for what success, and of course who gets the blame for the failures (the last one getting the most attention)—is all a big part of it. Right now the CIA and the Defense Department are fighting over who should pay for operations, such as the Special Forces being deployed to our embassies in Africa. The campaigns in Iraq and Afghanistan have brought such a fierce territorial battle between Defense and the CIA that the two sides are barely speaking. Some blame Defense, others the intelligence community. Who cares? We can't have this going on during a war. All these guys are fighting for the same money, the same duties, the same territories, and it leads to sloppy, dangerous efforts. No one knows who the good guys are without a scorecard. The truth of the matter is that we have far too many intelligence agencies. The new bill did not stop this bickering; it just put someone in charge of it . . . sort of.

If the agencies won't stop working against one another, then the NDI, the guy we have invested with tasking authority, the Boss of all Bosses of Intel, will cut their budgets, or better yet, just close down the agencies that overlap. We can start by closing the Defense Intelligence Agency. Great people work at the DIA, but they develop very few things on their own. They basically collate information from the other agencies. While we are at it, the intelligence agencies for the State Department, the Department of Energy, and the Immigration and Naturalization Service (now called the U.S. Citizenship and Immigration Services) can go away too. They overlap, redo, interpret, misuse, tie up assets, spend money, and use a limited talent pool. It's a "too many pigs at the trough" kind of thing. When you have fifteen agencies repeating the same data, you have fourteen agencies too many, which can and does lead to lost information and the leaking of secrets.

We must also trim the fat off the CIA. First, we consolidate. The CIA has a ton of what are called "stations," or headquarters, all over the world. Most of these are inside established U.S. embassies. We can cut half of those. After that, we cut half of the headquarters' staff. See, without staffs, you can't have reports. If there are no reports, no one has to waste time reading them, or responding to them.

At the same time, we increase the number of spies and those people that directly support them—give the spies the things they need. This does not mean *staff*. This means people who live in caves and provide real help.

We don't have the time or money to do things three times or even twice. We don't have the time or money for reports and staff. We must have the ability to focus, with laser-beam precision, everything we have on the problem—every resource, every tool, and every weapon. The bottom line is that even after 9/11, even after we know what an intelligence failure looks like and what the cost is in human life, we are still not doing this. We keep getting in our own way.

Congress is in the way big-time. Our "do-nothing" Congress has actually done something when it comes to intelligence. It has managed to get in the way of almost every intel initiative brought before it for twenty-five years. It has been especially destructive over the past decade. There were at least six serious attempts to fix parts of the intelligence community; Congress blocked all of these efforts. Why? Because changing the way the intel community is structured and to whom it answers would also change who has the power. No member of Congress has ever willingly given up power or a choice committee assignment. Even when Congress passed an intelligence reform bill, it did cut its power to interfere with or mismanage the national intelligence community. So we get a boss without real reform underneath him. Nice going, guys. Well, now is the time for the congressmen to get out of the way. This is nonnegotiable. There is no give. There is no wiggle room. The United States of America is being hurt every day by the very national intelligence community and Congress that are charged with protecting her, even with this new bill.

Cutting Through the Red Tape

After we attack and fix the structural and design problems of the intelligence community, we need to turn to those things that are a result of too much bureaucracy. All intelligence professionals I talk to cite the same problems. There are too many meetings. No one trusts them to do independent operations. Their guys have no language skills; we are sending spies to do dangerous work in faraway places who do not know the language of the country or the target group on which they are spying. They can't coordinate with other agencies. The CIA operatives all hate their headquarters at Langley. They see it as overly concerned with politics and not sufficiently concerned with operational matters. They don't get support from Langley in the field. No one cares. Bottom line, they are not allowed to do their jobs.

"Black projects" and "black operations," euphemisms the press and the "unwashed" use to describe offensive intelligence operations, are aggressive actions. These are operations to get things our country needs, like information and access to people that other countries and organizations don't want us to have. The administrative vehicle to gear up one of these operations is called special access programs (SAPs). In the intelligence community, almost everything else takes a backseat to SAPs. This is where covert activity lives. These are the things James Bond would do if he were real. This is where we get the real information.

I was involved in a boatload of SAPs in my career. It took over 179 separate tasks, meetings, and/or approvals to get just one SAP going. That was before 9/11. Now we are at war. Naturally, you would think we would have streamlined this process. We have. The process now only takes about 100 steps. How the hell can we expect to beat these killers when it takes 100 or more steps to get permission for our good guys to go and get them?

SAPs, by their nature, are our nation's biggest secrets. They are aggressive operations, because they involve listening in on or taking secrets from other countries. Sometimes SAPs demand planting false information to influence other countries; sometimes they involve catching or killing bad people, or stealing secrets or faking out the other guy.

Spying on others is also dangerous business. If you are caught performing these activities, you are usually arrested, shot, hanged, or all three. All who are involved with SAPs are among our very best spies and military personnel. Not only do our military Special Operations soldiers and our spies display great courage when they embark on SAPS, but so do their political masters who give the orders. They know this perilous work is critical to the protection of our country.

When they get it right, no one knows about the SAPs. But when they get it wrong, our country is usually embarrassed. And these black projects are so difficult and dangerous that they go bad more times than not. The reason we're embarrassed when the operations go wrong is that SAPs require orders signed by the president; there is a direct line back to the White House, and presidents don't like the political fallout that results from that. Actually, though, political embarrassment is the least of the consequences; some people lose their jobs, which is bad enough, but when SAPs are discovered by the enemy, often some brave American pays with his life. This is serious business.

An infamous example of an SAP that became all too public came in 1993, during the Clinton administration. We had decided to go to the "dark side of the moon," a place called Somalia, to help a country in trouble. The place was being run by warlords who were stealing, raping, and otherwise hurting the population. The most powerful warlord was a guy named Mohamed Farah Aideed. We targeted him. (Oh, and by the way, for those of you keeping score, Osama bin Laden and his al Qaeda murdering goons were associated with and helping these warlords, including Aideed.)

To try to capture Aideed, we sent in the Joint Special Operations Command with Special Forces Operational Detachment Delta and Task Force 160—the Night Stalkers and the First Ranger Battalion. The major portion of the operation was an SAP. But when Delta Force and the Rangers went in, things went terribly wrong. Simply put, our leaders got arrogant and thought that we could do a daylight operation against guerrillas without an adequate backup plan; the greatest military in the world blew it. Delta Force and the Rangers got caught in a deadly gun battle with Aideed's forces—a disaster that has been the focus of a best-selling book and a major motion picture, *Black Hawk Down*. These great soldiers paid the price despite heroic efforts; their bosses screwed this one up. We lost very brave men in a very public way.

The political fallout from this humiliation changed the way the Clinton administration approved SAPs for the next six years. Translation: The Clinton White House put the equivalent of permission slips in the system. Suddenly the government required an endless series of phone calls, e-mails, written orders, and other reporting procedures before any SAP could be approved. It was all designed to slow down—not speed up—the process. It was all designed to give the Clinton administration cover, the ability to say, "It's not my fault." Whatever the reasons, the result was that operators no longer had the ability or authority to do their jobs.

This need to keep blame from being laid at the door of the White House infiltrated all things dealing with intelligence and the military. When I served in Bosnia in the mid-1990s as part of the NATO peacekeeping force, we were actually told that we were not allowed to go hunting war criminals. If they happened to come up to one of our roadblocks, we could detain them, not kill them. That is, we could not kill on sight one of the men who had ordered the massacre of more than *seven thousand* men and boys in a town named Srebrenica. Nope, just detain him. *That is much better.* Oh yeah.

Changing the Cold War Mind-Set

The Clinton administration's "no-one-gets-hurt" mentality played a big role in getting us in the mess we're in today, but something else has factored heavily into the problem: our national intelligence community was trying to fight terrorists the way they had fought the Soviets during the Cold War.

During the Cold War, spying was mainly a manner of listening to, watching, and stealing anything we could off, about, or from the Russians. That's not what it's about anymore. Now we have to infiltrate religious organizations and terrorist cells that are run by people who are related or who grew up together. These clowns live in caves and back alleys, not in Moscow or Kiev. Nevertheless, the CIA has been very reluctant to change. The agency has been very slow to come around to the new way of doing things that this new type of war requires.

Back in the 1980s two very special men, Arthur "Mick" Donahue and Duane "Dewey" Clarridge, attempted to convince the bureaucracy within the CIA to start looking at terrorism. These were field guys—action guys—who did not suffer fools or bureaucracies lightly. They spent all their time chasing Russians and began to notice the frequency with which they crossed paths with or were influenced by terrorists. They saw how unprepared we were for this eventuality. They knew how totally focused we were on the Russians to the exclusion of all other threats, especially the threat of terrorism. Clarridge and Donahue were not the first to realize that those who analyzed intelligence and those who used and supplied those analysts were often not on the same page, but they were the first to push for and win a new office in which all assets within the CIA would actually work for one person, on one issue—terrorism. Thanks to the heroic efforts of these two men, the CIA's Counter Terrorism Center was formed. But these guys encountered massive interference from bureaucrats, especially from the spies. As Clarridge recounted in his memoir, the Directorate of Operations (the spy guys) tried every trick in the book to block the creation of the Counter Terrorism Center.

And to this day, even after 9/11, the CIA has not fully embraced the fight on terrorism. Many in its ranks miss the Cold War way of doing things.

So to these bureaucrats I'll say this: Look, you Ivy League–educated, round-bottomed, coffee-slurping "stupid white guys," get over it! How much more evidence do you need? We got clobbered. We got killed. We need to change now. And if you are still fighting this, then you are not helping. And if you are not helping us, you are hurting us. You need to go away.

Things have gotten so bad at the CIA that some long-serving officers have felt compelled to speak out. Remember, these guys spend their whole careers learning how to keep secrets, how to disappear, how to use discretion. These guys don't blab. So when they do, something *really* bad must be going down. In late 2004, one senior counterterrorism official, a twenty-two-year CIA veteran, defied orders to stop criticizing the U.S. government's failure to deal with the al Qaeda threat. Michael Scheuer, who had already anonymously written the best-selling book *Imperial Hubris: Why the West Is Losing the War on Terror,* kept talking even after the CIA told him to stop and despite the fact that he knew it could cost him his job; he even kept talking long after he lost whatever protection his anonymity had afforded him. And his charges were highly specific. Get this: In a letter to Congress he gave *ten different examples* of how the CIA had failed to go after Osama bin Laden aggressively or to at least slow up al Qaeda when it had the chance. Think this is how things should work?

Here is an example of our government's refusal to change: Before 9/11 we were spying against people who looked like us. The bad guys talked on phones, ate at McDonald's, went to movies, and basically did things like us. That made spying on them easy; all we had to do was send in someone who knew the language. It also made hiring people to spy on them easy.

Things have changed. The bad guys changed. Hell, the world has changed. Only the national intelligence community hasn't changed.

Listen, tall white guys with American accents stick out in the Middle East. We have to completely change the way we look to get at the men who are trying to kill us. Here is a flash: John Walker Lindh—"Jihad Johnny," the young American that our forces captured with the Taliban when we invaded Afghanistan—got all the way to meet bin Laden. He was twenty years old. So we need to re-cruit young men who look even younger to be our spies. Hell, we need gay men, old women, large basketball players, and left-handed pygmies from Botswana. Whatever and whomever it takes! We need to get anyone and everyone who can get access to the terrorist organi-zations, and we need to get them now.

We must use every trick we can think of and some we have not. We will have to get in bed, maybe literally, with one bad guy to get to another. During the late '90s the CIA and the FBI actually had a for-mal policy that prohibited their agents from associating with indi-viduals who had criminal pasts. News flash: Bad guys hang around with bad guys. If you can't associate with the bad guys, it's going to be hard to figure out what the hell they're up to. Is it any wonder we had trouble, any wonder why we were flying blind?

Many have argued that intelligence oversight is necessary be-cause the CIA will overreach if no one is controlling it. After all, didn't the Church Committee hearings in the 1970s show that the agency was out of control because there were no checks on its author-ity? And didn't the Iran-Contra affair show what happens when the CIA overextends its assignment? In the 1980s, the agency sold arms to Iran in exchange for the release of hostages, and the United States diverted the money from the arms sales to help the Contra rebels fighting to overthrow the Sandinistas in Nicaragua. Because of this, Congress got pissed and decided to cut the CIA's hamstrings, hob-bling the agency even more.

I am not advocating free rein for the CIA. Rogue agents make good movies but bad policy. I am advocating letting these guys do their jobs and instituting serious changes to allow the intelligence community to make us safe. Hell, mistakes will be made. Innocents will be killed, and that is terrible. When things go wrong, those who are responsible must be held accountable. I am not suggesting a rewrite of the Constitution here.

What I am suggesting—no, *demanding*—is the removal of layers upon layers of bosses and committees. I want, and we need, a much more streamlined system that takes minutes to get an operation approved, instead of weeks and months. I want a responsible and accountable chain of command made up of people who understand that their job is to support operations, not get in the damn way. But again, this doesn't mean that no one answers for mistakes. For it all to work right, they have to.

A Plan of Action

Here is how we make the rest of it work: We need more of almost everything, but we especially need more good people. A CIA case officer, taking risks every day for thirty years, will not make more than $125,000 a year. This may seem like a lot of money, until you take into consideration just how dangerous his/her job is. We need to pay more in order to attract more qualified people. While we're at it, we should be paying extra to all who are directly involved in the War on Terror. Those in the most danger get the most pay, period.

We should pull the FBI back from the terrorism fight. The FBI is still the best federal police force in the world—but they are cops, not spies. We need intelligence officers, spies, and a force that goes and kills the bad guys. That is not the mandate of the FBI. We need the FBI to enforce the laws, go after white-collar criminals, the Mafia, and drug cartels.

These are drastic times, and being so, they call for drastic measures. We are going to have to form an internal intelligence service like Britain's MI5. MI5 was formed to combat such lovable organizations as the Irish Republican Army and the Irish Brotherhood. It was created to combat terrorism. Well, we are now in the same position of having to defend ourselves against terrorists here at home. This new organization would do what the FBI and CIA cannot do: spy inside the United States. The FBI—cops, remember—are not equipped to fight terrorists, and the CIA is forbidden by about three billion laws from conducting operations domestically. Whether you agree with this or not, we would have to change too many laws to allow the CIA to operate here. Creating an internal intelligence service circumvents this problem and leaves the CIA free to do all overseas stuff.

We can call our new agency the Internal Intelligence Agency, or IIA. When we create it, we need to do so with an eye toward the enemy we are fighting. We will need laws that allow us to get into bank accounts and tap multiple phones to provide us with the means to fight these guys. We should not create it with the civil liberties violations contained in the Patriot Act. We will talk about the Patriot Act and civil liberties later on, but suffice it to say for now that the Patriot Act contains some good elements but needs to be tweaked. You cannot give this much power to the state. You cannot allow the attorney general to arrest U.S. citizens without cause or deny them access to representation. We cannot win this or any other war by taking away what makes us Americans—our Bill of Rights, our Constitution. If we take away our citizens' civil rights to win the war, we have then lost the war and we become our worst nightmare—*we become the French*. Stripping away the rights of our citizens doesn't make us safer; it puts us in a different kind of danger. Specifically regarding the creation of the IIA, we must make the laws specific to intelligence gathering and not criminal prosecution. Those laws governing operations will be temporary and require Congress to review them every two years.

So we close the agencies that are redundant; we create a cabinet position for all intelligence, the NDI (again, currently seven different cabinet officers have their fingers in the terrorism pie) and even the latest intel bill didn't give the intelligence director sufficient access to the president; we give the NDI tasking authority; we create the IIA, our own internal intelligence agency; and we move the FBI out of the way so it can do what it does best. Even after all that, there is more to do.

The Department of Defense is going to be the toughest nut to crack. It has to be brought under control. As I have said, the Defense Department has 80 percent of the intelligence budget and operates in direct conflict with the CIA. Hell, in Iraq the two have been in open warfare. The Pentagon has required the CIA guys to live in the "Green Zone" in Iraq, which was set up as the safe zone for the men in charge. Tell me this: How the hell can they spy from the Green Zone? Simply put, they can't. Both sides are spending so much time badmouthing each other to their bosses and to Congress that they are using up valuable satellite time that would be better used for operational issues. The CIA still refuses to share information with the Defense Department, and in turn Defense keeps important information and plans from the CIA. It is all BS and must stop. You can't have the two most critical agencies in the War on Terror at each other's throats—you want them at the terrorists' throats.

So what do we do with the Department of Defense? First, the department loses all assets that collect nonmilitary intelligence, and the National Security Agency—our top agency for electronic eavesdropping—comes out from under the Defense Department's budget control. From now on the department deals only with strategic and tactical military intelligence. If something relates to terrorism, it goes to the CIA.

Why the CIA? Because it will have a new action arm. This arm of the CIA will be a more robust, competent group and will answer directly to the NDI. Because it's my book, and because I believe that if it walks, squawks, and flies like a duck, you ought to call it a goddamn duck, we will call this group the Terrorist Killing Agency, or TKA.

The Terrorist Killing Agency will be able to move fast—not like anything under our current bureaucracy, which can't do anything quickly. We cannot have a fast-paced, totally focused, agile, and responsive intelligence community giving real-time intelligence to any organization that doesn't have the ability to move *right now*. The type of action I'm talking about is: "The bad guys are over there—go kill them." Currently, even Delta Force and SEAL Team Six, which are very capable, can't move quickly enough, because they are burdened with bosses and their bosses' bosses, who refuse to take the kind of risks necessary to win this War on Terror.

We want the CIA to continue checking the proliferation of weapons, finding nuclear weapons, and tracking rogue nations like North Korea and Syria. Its agents are great at analyzing newspapers, websites, and phone calls. They are even pretty good at getting other countries' government workers to be traitors. This is where they reign. But if it's terrorism, they will hand it over to the TKA.

The TKA will have one mission, one reason for existing: killing terrorists anywhere on God's Green Earth. It will have its headquarters in the United States but have bases all over the world—Africa, Eastern Europe, the Middle East, South America, Central America, or anywhere else terrorists are bred. Each of these bases would be self-contained, complete with its own intelligence, administration logistics, communications, and operators. The TKA would operate in these countries with or without the host countries' permission. Operating without the host countries' permission is not the best way to do this, but it's better than having no presence at all in places that won't give us help, like Syria. It requires the use of local nationals, great care and determination, and a political will to commit to this, since those doing this work will be at great risk.

This is very tricky but doable and necessary. Using people native to a country that hates us is risky. In order for it to work we must pay them a lot of money. We must give their families jobs in Wal-Mart or at Dell. We must do whatever it takes to ensure their cooperation. It goes something like this: Go to Detroit or Portland, Maine, get in a cab, and talk to Abdul. When you're done, you tip him a lot. Then you offer to buy Abdul coffee, do a background check on him, and get him to introduce you to his family. When you discover that Abdul has family back in whatever country you want to set up in, you fly with him to that country, where he makes introductions. Then you do more background checks. You check out everything three times over, and then when you are as sure as you can be, you start your business. There are no guarantees in a plan like this. It is risky. But sometimes it works.

The TKA would not be a large organization—less than five thousand people, including operators, staff, and leadership. This organization's role would be to take the fight into the homes, the bedrooms, the boardrooms, and the bathrooms of the terrorists. The TKA would hunt the terrorists down and kill them and their supporters, wherever and whenever it finds them.

I even have the guy to run this: General Gary Luck. Luck, who was sent to Iraq in early 2005 to assess our efforts there, has commanded the Joint Special Operations Command, which includes Delta Force and SEAL Team Six; he has multiple combat tours in Vietnam; and he is one of the three best leaders I have ever seen, which is why he is beloved by his men. Plus he has no neck and can pick up the side of a building.

In case General Luck has other things he wants to do with his life, I have a couple of other people in mind. The NATO commander appointed in 2003 is a Marine general named James Jones. There may be a better guy currently wearing a uniform, but if there is, I don't know him. He is exceptionally competent, a caring leader, and for a price will speak French.

Another guy who could take this fight to the terrorists is a retired four-star admiral named Snuffy Smith. Snuffy was the first and best commander of all the NATO soldiers, over sixty thousand of them. He's fully capable, and he's currently playing golf, so he's well rested.

(I just recommended two Navy guys and one Marine and I am an Army guy. Fair and balanced, that's me.)

The TKA will have a budget equal to that of a medium-sized country. The NDI will be the don of all the government intelligence agencies. No one will be able to stand in his way. He will have "Hunter/Killer Teams" pre-positioned around the world. These teams will have a standing order to kill terrorists whenever and wherever they find them. There will be no need to ask permission. No "Mother may I?" Just kill them where they stand, sleep, or kneel.

Those who are in charge of these teams will have to be well trained and highly moral, as well as extremely deadly. This is no easy task. In order to get the right kind of people to do this work, we have to recruit the best. The best are those who have already proven they can handle this type of work or have been in similar tense and dangerous situations—like firemen and policemen or those who have already served in the military. To get the best of these types of people we have to pay a premium price—which we are still unwilling to do.

Once you get these people, you must train them in the most realistic and unsafe environment you can find. I mean people have to get really hurt in order to get though this type of training. I've talked about what Delta Force and the SEAL team put their people through; this will be worse. You put these people into situational training environments in other countries. You put them into training with Israeli and South African agents. When it's over, you have well-trained agents, ready to do this very important job. Oh, you give them a serious bonus—if they get through the training. And you keep paying bonuses to keep them.

Even with these "superagents," there will undoubtedly be mistakes. And when those mistakes occur, they *must* be addressed and it *must* be done in public. It must be done in public because "we the people" have to believe in those who conduct this war. We must trust that we are trying to get it right. We need to see that those fighting this war haven't become barbarians or terrorists themselves. We need to know that they are the people defending us the best way they can. We cannot have doubts about these things. Holding people accountable for their mistakes—publicly—is the only way we can ensure that the American people will want to be involved in this fight or will send their sons and daughters into the service. "We the people" are, after all, in charge of our government, and we deserve to be told the truth about this war. We should demand it.

TKA missions and mistakes will be reviewed by a panel of judges, operators, intelligence experts, and a nonexpert civilian. This panel will make recommendations to the NDI, but if necessary, it will have the power to go above him to the president. The purpose of this panel is to provide for public accountability and to present cases for prosecution when warranted.

A number of other groups should be involved in gathering intelligence. Homeland Security is not one of them. We will look at Homeland Security many times throughout the rest of this book because it often offers the best examples of how *not* to do something, but for now it is enough to know that Homeland Security belongs nowhere near the world of intelligence.

Homeland Security is an agency in need of help. Before it gets so far down the track that it builds a five-sided building like the Pentagon and starts inventing its own language like the military, it has to go. It is true that Homeland Security now holds the new TTIC—Terrorist Threat Integration Center—which just means the computer where all the intelligence we gather is stored. Let's move it. Let's put it where it belongs, with the CIA. Combining all the intelligence in one place is a necessity. Putting it under the purview of Homeland Security is a disaster.

We of course need the component parts of the Homeland Security Department—the Secret Service, the Federal Emergency Management Agency (FEMA), the Department of the Treasury, the Coast Guard, and the Transportation Security Administration (TSA). We just don't need the department that now oversees these critical agencies: the Homeland Security Department. What has the Department of Homeland Security contributed to the War on Terror? First, a color-coded alert system that no one understands, and second, duct-tape hoarding.

Look, Tom Ridge, the former head of Homeland Security, is a good guy. He was a poor kid who became a Vietnam vet and got to go to Harvard and then become governor of Pennsylvania. But no one not drawing a paycheck from him thought he or his agency was cutting it. Creating Homeland Security was a knee-jerk reaction to 9/11. It does not have tasking authority, nor does it have the access to the CIA that it needs. Homeland Security needs to go away as we reorganize. In order not to do any more damage to our ability to fight this War on Terror, we must trash this department.

Intelligence is not the job only of federal agencies. Those who live and work in an area will always know more about what is going on in that area than anyone else. They will have better intelligence and better gossip. They will know who is doing what to whom, even if they don't know what it all means. The local sheriff and police officers will always hear things. It's time to put this to some use. We need to give these guys some training so that when pieces of the terrorism puzzle fall into their laps, they will recognize them. We need to make it so these guys start reporting these things to people in a position to understand the information and act on it. In this fight for our lives, we must start looking in our own backyards.

Currently, the CIA is doing some training here in the United States. It is training electricians, exterminators, plumbers, and the like in what to look for when they enter someone's house. A team of more than a hundred former spooks simply teaches the untrained what to look for and whom to tell when they find something. The FBI has increased its efforts in training local law enforcement. I work in a program that works with our nation's chiefs of police, helping these public servants get more up-to-date information on terrorism; this program is free, or at least my part certainly is.

We need more of this. We need everyone looking out for signs of terrorism.

Putting It All Together

As we have seen, we are all screwed up when it comes to intelligence. Yes, it's a mess, but now you know what that mess is and you know what needs to be done to fix it.

There are too many agencies. We need to have a parade, give out some awards, and put to rest at least four national intelligence agencies. We have too many bosses telling too many people what to do when it comes to intelligence. We need one boss, and it should be the national director of intelligence. This boss of bosses must have control of all the purse strings and of those he is in charge of. He must have tasking authority.

We need to create the IIA, to do what needs to be done internally.

We also need to create the Terrorist Killing Agency (TKA). We can call it something else if you like. I am sure many think it is a terrible name, and no one in government would ever go for it. They're too sensitive. At least the name "Terrorist Killing Agency" makes its mission very clear and direct: to kill terrorists anywhere, anytime, starting today. If we are serious about the War on Terror— and we have to be—then we need to create this agency dedicated to killing them.

All of this works only if the NDI does his job. It works only if all of the intel coming from the local cops to the IIA and from the IIA to the TKA is coordinated. This works only if someone is looking at the whole picture. In the next chapter we will look at bureaucracy and what happens when it gets in the way of getting the job done. All the information necessary to stop 9/11 was out there floating around the many parts of our government. It has taken us years since 9/11 to put it all together. If we had put it together and reacted to it before 9/11, there would not be a hole in the middle of New York City.

CHAPTER 5

Who's in Charge?

If we believe that al Qaeda took five years to plan 9/11 (and they did), if we know that countries like Syria, Iran, North Korea, and Saudi Arabia are secretly or openly supporting terrorism (and they are), if we believe that our government is just starting to get its act together when it comes to fighting terrorism (and trust me, we are nowhere near ready), then *change* is required. Perhaps getting our bureaucracy reduced to a manageable size, building accountability into a *new* governmental structure that will allow us to move forward, and insisting on true leadership from our elected officials, and from those they appoint, just might be in order.

In Chapter 4 we discussed how many different cabinet officers have responsibility for some part of the fight against terrorism. We also know now that too many agencies are doing the same thing. We talked about how many steps it takes to get anything going. The sheer size of the huge bureaucracy that makes up our government is one of the central barriers keeping us from winning this war. We simply can't move fast enough because we are bogged down in bureaucratic red tape. This cannot continue.

Too many times in this fight, no one has been in charge. Oh, some have had the titles or the stars on their shoulders that imply authority, but when it comes down to really making decisions, this authority is an illusion. Right now, and in the recent past, the authority figurehead has had to ask for permission to do his or her job. He or she does not have the authority to tell other agencies what to do. Coordination of effort is *not* the rule. Men and women have died, and will continue to die, in this War on Terror because of the impenetrable bureaucratic maze. This maze creates mistakes by bosses who *don't, won't,* or *can't* make decisions. Those in charge must never sacrifice the lives of those fighting this war without good cause. Lives must never be jeopardized because of inept planning, poorly coordinated tactics, or faulty intelligence.

Consider this: Before 9/11 we had forty-seven agencies, congressional committees, and presidential commissions that could, and did, interfere with, exert control over, and generally waste the time of the agencies that were trying to fight terrorism. Once the horror of 9/11 was fully realized, our government went into action—and made itself bigger, more complicated, and a hell of a lot slower to move. Within one short year, there were *fifty-seven* agencies, committees, and commissions that would do the work that forty-seven had been doing. *Unbelievable!*

The bureaucracy is everywhere, but no agency, no bureaucracy, no organization can match our newest one for sheer layering, sheer numbers of staff, and sheer uselessness. I am of course talking about the brand-spanking-new Department of Homeland Security. The government employees who work at Homeland Security are, for the most part, dedicated Americans. The issue is not with them. The issue is with their bosses and their bosses' bosses. The point of forming the Homeland Security Department was twofold: to consolidate federal public safety organizations that could help defend the United States against future terrorist attacks, and to create a public relations tool that the government could point to and say, "Look! We are doing something." Well, it accomplished one of those.

With Homeland Security, the U.S. government consolidated such organizations as the Secret Service, the Federal Emergency Management Agency (FEMA), the Coast Guard, and the Transportation Safety Administration (TSA) into one giant bureaucratic leviathan. This new government arm has managed to amass a workforce of *170,000.* Homeland Security is supposed to help protect us. Well, Homeland Security ain't doin' its job! What it has done, however, is make agencies like the TSA and the Secret Service less effective.

Witness the fact that airport security has been inspecting our grandmothers' underwear while still refusing to profile Arabs. Witness how we protect ourselves during a political convention like the one held in Boston in the summer of 2004; we shut down entire highways, and parts of the city became an armed camp. Those living in a city move out when Homeland Security moves in.

FEMA used to be a nut-crunching, get-it-done-now agency. It became that way after it was restructured and given serious power in the wake of a class-five hurricane named Andrew that devastated Florida in 1992. The federal government looked inept in its ineffective response to the hurricane, since ultimately the Army had to go in to help. Recovering from that embarrassment, FEMA became a shining example of how an ineffective agency can refocus its task and become very good at what it does. It became one of the bright lights of our government.

Well, never let it be said that your government can't screw up a good thing. After FEMA was thrown into the Department of Homeland Security, a test came for the new organizational structure in the form of a class-five hurricane named Charley, which also blew through Florida and left behind a wasteland. The pre-9/11 FEMA would have been all over Charley, but instead we were witness to frustrated families without power, and great young National Guard kids saving the day—again. Hey, folks, if you can't beat a hurricane, good luck with the terrorists.

We see this amassing and layering of staff, useless generation of paper, and incessant need to hold meetings everywhere in our government. During the Kennedy years, the president of the United States was served by about 60 staff members. Care to guess the size of the current staff at the White House? Give up? It is over 1,500; that's a *2,500 percent* increase in forty years. Well, you might say, don't the president, the secretary of state, and the national security adviser need these talented, hardworking Type A's? Not for a minute. The boss needs information for sure, but not filtered through hundreds of eyes. The boss needs to know what is going on, not what his staff thinks is going on. Staffs like to interpret, think for the boss, give their opinions, make names for themselves, and vie for attention. Staffs interpret to the point that day becomes night, rain becomes snow, and weapons of mass destruction . . . well, WMDs are everywhere.

As we saw in the last chapter, many of the problems plaguing our intelligence community—the ongoing turf wars, the obvious intelligence failures—stem from unnecessary bureaucracy. Of course, like all bureaucracies, the intelligence bureaucracy feels compelled to protect and promote itself. That's why we've seen so many officials furiously fighting the changes that need to be made. The Washington establishment isn't looking to protect you and your family; it's looking to protect itself.

Our armed forces have not escaped the contagion of runaway bureaucratic growth either. The military men and women we have serving now are the best in our nation's history, but when you put thousands of staff officers over them, it gets very difficult for these great men and women to do their jobs. Let me be specific: A three-star general in Iraq or Afghanistan will have more than a thousand people on his staff. A thousand-person staff? That means a thousand different people can influence an order that should have gone directly from the guy in charge to the guy who should carry it out. It is important to understand that these thousand staffers do not fight bad guys; they generate paper, plan, and interfere. You have got to be kidding me!

If you ever saw the secretary of defense walking through the Pentagon with ten to thirty officers and civilian aides trailing behind him, or sat in a meeting with a general or admiral and counted the ten to 100 primary staff officers taking notes, you would realize just what a big waste of time, effort, and talent this is. Each of the note takers is boss of his or her *own* large staff of at least a hundred or two hundred hard-charging men and women. Somewhere along the line, we decided that it was better to write papers, take notes, and attend countless meetings than to actually do anything.

Like the intelligence community, our military remains stubbornly resistant to change. And the truth is, no matter how brave and competent our fighting forces are, no matter how advanced our military technology is, our political and military leaders aren't fighting this War on Terror correctly. They're making the same mistakes over and over, refusing to adapt. In the next chapter we will discuss military operations in depth to show just what changes need to be made and how our armed forces have to be bludgeoned into making the necessary adjustments.

Altogether, the Pentagon employs *twenty-five thousand* Americans, civilian and military. Much of the work these employees do is redundant. If we are really serious about winning the War on Terror—not just talking serious, but kill-them serious—then that workforce should be cut in half. *Now.* By presidential decree. No study, no congressional hearings, no televised debate—just send half of them packing. Hold on! I do not propose that we send all these men and women off to the unemployment lines. Rather, we should continue full pay and benefits as we reassign these individuals or retrain them to assume important positions elsewhere in the government or military structure. In fact, if these ousted employees cannot be absorbed into other departments or agencies, then we can continue their pay and benefits—as long as they *leave the Pentagon.* In this way, we will reduce the interference in decision making and the numbers of meetings required before decisions can be made.

This goes for all staffs in our government directly or indirectly associated with the War on Terror: cut them in half, today. Then, in thirty days, cut them in half again. And I mean everyone: the president, the secretary of defense, the secretary of state, the directors of the CIA, the directors of the FBI—everyone. The sizes of their staffs are inversely proportional to the speed at which they can make decisions. If you are a boss and have a thousand people working for you, that's the number of people keeping you from doing your job, whether your job is to catch the bad guys, spy on the bad guys, or kill the bad guys.

By hacking away at the bureaucracy, we'd finally be able to get something done.

"It Ain't My Fault"

The runaway bureaucratic structure has not only prevented us from doing what needs to be done when it needs to be done, it has also created a lack of accountability. It is time to demand accountability of our leadership. We have watched commission after commission study what went wrong. We have officials from every walk of life saying, "It ain't my fault," or "It's no one's fault, it's the system." We even have former government officials stuffing secret documents down their pants!

This story is so farcical, so out there, so unbelievable that you are going to think it has to be a bedtime story. Brace yourself. Once upon a time there was a former national security adviser to the president of the United States. The adviser's name was Sandy "I-Ain't-Going-to-No-Stinking-Vietnam" Berger. The president was Bill "I-Did-Not-Have-Sex-with-That-Woman" Clinton. Mr. Berger's job was to protect our nation's secrets while he advised the president on the most sensitive matters in the world. During his tenure (he spent six years as either deputy national security adviser or national security adviser), he had to read our nation's most classified papers—documents so sensitive that he wasn't even allowed to remove them from his office. Mr. Berger even had to have special telephones that scrambled his conversations in his car, home, and office to protect America's vital secrets. In fact, in this bedtime story it is fair to say that everything Berger did in his professional life was a secret. Now comes the really ludicrous part: Mr. Berger was caught stuffing classified documents in his pants and socks in the National Archives. Could this be true? Yup. You had to wonder, why would this very smart guy do something so stupid as to smuggle out sensitive documents he knew weren't supposed to leave the secure room at the Archives? Maybe because the documents showed that he and his boss had done little or nothing to try to stop terrorism for eight years.

But the truth is, even if Berger did try to cover up his own failures and the Clinton administration's failures, it wouldn't have worked. The reason it wouldn't have worked is that *we all know* he and the Clinton administration screwed up. But they weren't the only ones. They weren't in office when 9/11 happened, of course. No one in Washington says it because everyone there is looking ahead to the next election, but our government screwed up. On September 11, 2001, nineteen Arab men killed more Americans than did the entire Japanese fleet at Pearl Harbor on December 7, 1941. That's a big screwup.

This is not the first time that mistakes have been made. Every administration has had times when bad decisions have been executed and we have paid a terrible price. Remember the October 1983 Marine barracks disaster in Lebanon? A couple of months later, President Reagan received an advance copy of a report on the bombing prepared by a Defense Department commission. The report blamed officers in the chain of command for not ensuring the safety of the troops. According to one of Reagan's key aides, David Gergen, Reagan read through the report and made a beeline for the pressroom. And right then, the Great Communicator told the national media that the buck stopped with him. "If there is to be blame," Reagan declared, "it properly rests here in this office and with this president. And I accept responsibility for the bad as well as the good."

Imagine, a public figure actually standing up and taking the hit! We have not seen that in Washington since then. Our leaders must take a lesson from Reagan. They have to start with what went wrong, stand up and take the heat, and move out smartly. Unfortunately, in the years since the 9/11 attacks, all we've seen in our nation's capital and in the media is finger pointing. Defenders of the Bush administration blamed Bill Clinton's team; Clinton's people said they had warned their successors about bin Laden and al Qaeda. We've heard excuses and, on occasion, apologies. But no one stood in front of the cameras and accepted responsibility, as great leaders do.

Suggesting that those in charge must take responsibility for not being prepared is a radical idea. Yes, I know, as soon as a leader does that, the opposition party will seize on that admission of guilt for political gain. But if enough of our elected officials and government bosses say, "I did it, it's my fault, I made this decision and it was the wrong one, but here's why I made it," maybe, just maybe, we can move forward and fix the damn system that was, and is, still broken. By trying to deflect blame, you spend your time fighting the media, the opposition party, and disgruntled members of your own party. And that's time our leaders should be spending fighting the terrorists.

George W. Bush was the man in the White House when all this occurred. He should have kept Harry Truman's sign on his desk: "THE BUCK STOPS HERE." As president, Bush should have taken part of the responsibility for the debacle and then fired those that had led him down the wrong path. He should have started with George Tenet, the director of Central Intelligence. Tenet was supposed to have been in charge of *all* of our nation's intelligence services, but in the time leading up to 9/11 he didn't do his job. The devastating casualty count on that day stands as testament to his failure. Yet Tenet was allowed to stay in his job for nearly three more years. And officially he wasn't even fired. In June 2004, when three separate committees were about to lay the blame for 9/11 and the lack of good intelligence at his feet, Tenet was allowed to resign, without the disgrace that he deserves. He moved on to a nice consulting job and the lucrative speaking circuit.

What might have happened had George Tenet been fired right after 9/11? Well, maybe the guy who replaced him would have understood that if stuff went wrong, he wouldn't last long as the new head of the intelligence community. Maybe the way the CIA does things might have changed—and maybe we wouldn't have had the embarrassment of the WMD situation in Iraq.

Someone must pay for the incompetence. At the time of this writing, more than 1,200 men and women have been killed in Iraq alone. If we count the deaths of combatants in Afghanistan and the victims of 9/11, the death toll is currently over four thousand. We also have over eight thousand wounded. Incompetence has played a major role in these casualties. This was the incompetence not of the victims but rather of our leadership. For this our leaders should be prosecuted or court-martialed. Our leaders will only view the deaths and maiming of American citizens and soldiers seriously if they have to answer for them. Maybe if we see a few four-star generals and a director of the CIA in front of a judge trying to answer for their mistakes, the system will change.

General John Keane, who was the Army vice chief of staff until 2003, testified in July 2004 before Congress and said, "The Pentagon had planned insufficiently for postwar Iraq"; he also acknowledged that the failure "has cost lives." Hey, General, just a little late, don't ya think? Come on, man, you were there. You had four huge stars on your shoulders. You were the second-highest-ranking man in the Army. You had more than thirty-five years of Army experience. What were you thinking when the secretary of defense was insisting for four months after we took Baghdad that we were *not* in the middle of a guerrilla war? This is just another example of incompetence and just how myopic a bureaucracy can become.

We have to give the general some credit; at least he said it. "We could have done far better for [deployed U.S. forces] if we had properly prepared them for what the reality is we're dealing with," he declared. Only one problem: he was *retired* when he said it. It might have meant much more if he had said it while on active duty. But that would have required the courage that the burdensome bureaucracy sucks out of our leaders. "We have a lot of young folks that paid the price for that lack of foresight. Am I correct?" asked Congressman Ike Skelton of Missouri, the committee's ranking Democrat. "Right, yes sir," Keane replied. How about, *And I am sorry for not doing my job; I am sorry I was not a true leader?*

We didn't demand accountability for 9/11. Not one single government employee has been fired or even reprimanded for the largest loss of American lives on a single day since the Civil War. How is this possible?

Why have we continually refused to hold anyone accountable? The answer is easy: *No one is in charge anywhere in the whole damn government. So no one is responsible!* I can hear the critics now: "Of course someone is in charge. We have directors, generals, cabinet officers, presidents; they are in charge." Sorry, they are not. We have already discussed the fact that until we have someone in our government who can pick up the phone and move the Army, Navy, Air Force, Marines, CIA, FBI, and/or the Coast Guard and tell them what to do, no one is in charge. It may be that the president has this authority, but be assured that if he exercised this power, he would be met with political and bureaucratic opposition. New laws would be proposed, details would be leaked, and the *New York Times* would of course run every piece of minutiae on the front page.

The truth is that even the president can't truly act as ultimate authority, because the necessary information to act is buried under the bureaucracy's multitude of agencies, laws, lawyers, political appointees, and so on. It is impossible to order a timely and necessary action under these circumstances. Any government that forms something as complicated as the United States federal tax code cannot possibly take swift and decisive action. Our government structure in its present form accomplishes only two things: first, it gives lots of people jobs, and second, it absolutely guarantees that no one will be held responsible for bad decisions.

Can You Believe This?

To understand how all the layers of bureaucracy are keeping us from fighting an effective War on Terror, just look at the Pentagon. Two weeks into the invasion of Afghanistan, we had Osama bin Laden's number two man, Ayman al-Zawahiri, in our sights. A Predator unmanned aerial vehicle, a small plane that has cameras and sensors aboard, had been following this evil man and his friends for three hours. Oh, by the way, this plane had Hellfire tank-killer missiles hanging on its wings ready to fire. The Predator pilotless drone aircraft was flying in a high arc around a convoy of al Qaeda sport utility vehicles. The precision cameras clearly showed that the mastermind of al Qaeda's most barbaric acts was in striking distance.

Now, to fully get this, you have to know that the Predator is flown by remote control; the person flying the aircraft was sitting at a desk 120 miles away and using a joystick like the ones our kids use in video games. The controller, a fully qualified pilot, had the button to launch one or all four Hellfire missiles. Given all of this, you would think the mission was clear. There is the bad guy, here are the missiles—shoot the missiles, kill the bad guy. Right? Wrong! In this War on Terror, simple and effective answers are not often available.

The problem here arose because the CIA built the Predator, got the money to deploy it, and developed ways of using it. So the agency owns it, right? Uh, no. Our boys in blue, the United States Air Force, had insisted that they had to be in charge of flying the drone, since the Air Force believes it is the only service that matters in the flying business. Of course our friends in the Marine Corps who fly jets and helicopters took umbrage at the Air Force's supposition. Army pilots also got into this mix. Suffice it to say, after long-drawn-out discussions, the Air Force won this battle of military forces and also won the fight with the CIA by getting control of the Predator—when in flight.

So okay, the Air Force flies the plane, sees the bad guys, and shoots them. Who cares, as long as there are dead terrorists at the end of the day? By this point in the book you probably know it couldn't have worked that easily. You are right. So who screwed it up this time?

The U.S. Army is exceptional when it comes to adding unnecessary bosses and generally slowing progress down. The one thing the Army loves is being in charge. Not to be outdone by the Air Force, the Army said, *We are running this war in Afghanistan.* So even though the CIA owned the plane and the Air Force was in charge of flying the thing, the Army decided that it would control the when, where, and at what it would shoot. Oh, and just to prove to you that the Army has the best in bureaucratic structures, those making the critical decision to fire the missiles would make this call from multiple time zones away.

Officers and staffs in Afghanistan, Qatar, and even Europe were capable of making a fairly straightforward decision to kill a terrorist who had played a major role in 9/11. But not on your life would the Army allow those on the ground, the guys in the middle of the fight, to make that decision—not when it could hold a meeting in Washington or Tampa, to make the decision. When you don't move your headquarters closer to the front lines, but still demand to be making decisions or to be kept "informed," then you force the guys in the middle of the fight to arrange their schedules around you. Too bad we can't get the terrorists to operate on our timetable as well.

General Tommy Franks, the four-star general in charge of Central Command, was at CentCom headquarters in Tampa. He held a meeting and was actually able to watch, in real time, the convoy full of terrorists. According to a source who was in the room that day, all in the meeting said, *Yup, there is the bad guy.* But they also thought that there might be family or nonterrorists in the convoy. So you know what happened? Because of this, the general, or those holding the meeting with the general, or a lawyer in the meeting, or all of them and none of them, decided not to shoot the missiles.

No sir, can't take the chance of hurting anyone but the terror-ist—no bystanders, no terrorist family members. Notice how high the bar is for the good guys? So we didn't shoot the missiles. We just watched as these terrorists rode around planning the next wave of destruction against American citizens. A general in Florida decided for a general in Afghanistan, who decided for an Air Force major flying a CIA plane, not to kill a very bad man. What part of this don't you understand? All of it? Me too.

This is not just bureaucratic bungling of the highest magnitude; it is also a failure of leadership at every level. It demonstrates an un-willingness to make the tough calls. It shows us that our leadership is willing to let polls determine action rather than tried-and-true mili-tary tactics. Our leaders choose concern for their own careers over doing the right thing. In this case, the right thing would have been to kill the son of a bitch while he rode around in the caravan.

Truth is necessary here. We always do our best to save innocent lives and avoid killing or hurting noncombatants. However (and this is a huge *however*), we use sharp objects and explosives and things called MOABs (the Mother of All Bombs); things break and . . . well, innocent people sometimes get killed or badly hurt when we do op-erations. It's unfortunate, but it's unavoidable. The fact this happens does not mean we should not do the operation; it just means we need to be honest and accept the consequences of our actions. But to do that takes real leadership.

Make It Happen

Now it is time for our leaders to do what we elected them to do. We need true leadership from our elected officials, from our military, and from our intelligence community. We need these people to do what holding a job as a public servant demands of them. Without leadership, we have nothing—no defense, no ability to really get at what and who is killing us.

Some people think the 9/11 Commission showed real guts in calling for reform. The commission did a decent job, but as I said before, the recommendations they made—and I do mean *all* of their recommendations—are old news. For twenty years, I and many others with a background in counterterrorism yelled, threw things, and begged for people to pay attention. We pleaded that things be changed. "It could never happen here," "It ain't my job," "You are crying wolf"—those were only a few of the answers we were given. Had politicians been more concerned with our safety, our country, and our lives, and less concerned with their jobs and the money they get from lobbyists, they would have made reforms long ago.

Even more troubling, as soon as the 9/11 Commission released its report, in the summer of 2004, many people started acting as though the report were an end in itself rather than the beginning of a long process of reform. The authors congratulated themselves for writing "the definitive work" on what happened leading up to and during 9/11. But all they really did was put stuff we already knew in a ten-dollar book.

Okay, but at least the 9/11 Commission provided the recipe for change. It doesn't really matter that it is an old recipe; at least now it has been written down for all Americans to see. So let's start making those changes. This is what's going to take leadership. Trouble is, piss-poor leadership is everywhere. It is in the military, in all branches of the services. It is in the intelligence community. And of course it is in our elected officials. How can we look at 9/11 in any other way? It was a complete failure at every level of government.

There are exceptions, of course. To the few leaders out there who actually care about their country and the men and women who serve under them, to those who do their job well and in a self-sacrificing, compassionate, competent way, I apologize for what I am about to say.

If the nameplate on your door says boss, if your title says you are in charge, then lead, damn it. Stop trying to figure out how you can get around an issue. Stop bad-mouthing your political opponents. Stop trying to find out how you are doing in the polls, or how to play an issue to gain a few precious points in those polls. And stop trying to get invited to a good party. We, the American public, demand to be protected. If you are not doing that, you need to be fired. You are no longer a leader, no longer in charge.

One straightforward definition of the term *leadership* is the ability to get people to do something they don't want to do. If you are a true leader, you must always be out in front and you must do the right thing even when it is the unpopular thing. You have to share the danger into which you order others to go. You must never, and I mean *never,* ask someone to do something you are not ready to do yourself. You may not be as good at it as the one you are ordering, but you have to be willing, and those you order have to know that— period. Those under the leader must always know that they are protected by the leader. They also have to know that you as the leader put your men and women ahead of yourself; that's why, in the military, when the food shows up, you are the very last to eat—always. This is tough business, this leadership stuff. It ain't for everyone. In fact, it's really for very few.

If you are a leader, then you know that leadership is never about you. So if you want to get all the credit, if you want to use what you are doing to further yourself, then stay the hell away from anything to do with leadership, *please.*

A leader is in charge of people. You have to care about the people who look to you for the answers. You have to care how they live, eat, breathe, and sleep. Are they happy at home? Do they have a home? If we are talking about combat leadership, then a leader is as scared as his men. They know it. You know it. So a leader acknowledges his fear and theirs. Only an idiot is not afraid going into combat. But your love for your men makes you train them harder than they ever thought possible. You want them to sweat in training so they don't bleed in combat. And you want them to know one another, since it is for one another that they will fight. And maybe, if you are good enough, they will fight for you, but they will always fight for one another.

Our armed forces do extremely dangerous, extremely demanding work. But this is exactly what our soldiers train for, and what most of them live for. The men and women in America's armed services will never quit, never stop, never let you down; they are the best that ever were or ever will be. The only thing they need is leadership. They need leaders to be there when there is real danger, to lead them from the front and not from an air-conditioned office in Washington, D.C.

Soldiers will complain about only one thing: the kind of uncaring, self-serving leadership we see all too often in the military and in the government. In this War on Terror, our military has been challenged as it never has been before, and our soldiers still are not receiving the support they need from our leaders. It's bad enough, as we'll see in detail later in the book, that the military brass hasn't adjusted its tactics to fight an enemy that doesn't ride in tanks or jets or battleships but hides in caves and has cells of terrorists spread out all over the globe planning their next assault on the American people. Much worse is that our politicians and military officers are trying to exploit these brave soldiers for PR purposes. When we see soldiers marching in parades in Baghdad in 115-degree heat wearing Kevlar helmets and vests, this is a failure of leadership. We are in a fight for our lives. We are dying at an alarming rate. It's so dangerous that you can't even take a civilian plane in or out of Baghdad. We are thousands and thousands of miles away from home. Whatever shall we do? I know, let's have a parade!

The only people who want or care about a parade are the officers. I have a message for all those who want to hold a parade: Grab yourself by your own ass and go march! But don't you dare take the little time that a soldier has off in a combat zone and make him go and practice marching for hours and then stand in the heat. Especially if you're doing it because a VIP like a congressman, a general, or a president wants to have pictures taken with soldiers around him.

When we hear that a Navy SEAL team cannot get support while it guards the most important man in Iraq, we have to wonder where its leadership is. In the summer of 2004, the U.S. government decided to take responsibility for protecting the interim prime minister of Iraq, Iyad Allawi. It assigned some of the best combatants in the world to do this job, Navy SEALs. Only one small problem: the U.S. military forgot to give the SEALs all the tools they needed to do their job. They needed everything from gas for their vehicles to money to buy food, and the military couldn't get it done. The SEALs were forced to call back to the United States to their families and friends to get help. I have spoken to people who received such calls; it is no fantasy. This is a failure in leadership.

The SEALs, being SEALs, still got the job done, but come on. They were guarding arguably the most significant guy in the Iraqi government, which should be considered a fairly important job. You would think that the SEALs would get any damn thing they wanted and not have to go around and beg. You can't have the security details to a mega-important person worrying about gas for their vehicles; you can't, but we do. Unfortunately, the SEALs case was not an isolated incident. All over Iraq and Afghanistan, our guys are calling home for help because they are simply not getting what they need to do their jobs. This needs to stop, like so many other things in this war that demonstrate a lack of leadership.

When we hear that a U.S. Army division actually brought a horse to Iraq because the horse is its mascot, we all need to stop and wonder: where is that division's leadership? Look, I am not against horses. They are nice animals. They work hard and run fast. But taking a horse to a gunfight in Iraq, in the middle of a guerrilla war—come on! It takes money and soldiers to look after the horse. It took some rather sophisticated maneuvering and deals to get that horse from Fort Hood, Texas, the home of the First Cavalry Division, to Baghdad. It's just silly and should never have happened. This is a failure in leadership.

Now, how could anyone possibly know about this horse parade?

Because the Army actually put the damn horse on TV. The Fox News Channel was broadcasting when the outgoing head of the Coalition Provisional Authority, L. Paul Bremer, was visiting the headquarters of the First Cavalry Division, and cameras rolled as the horse appeared in the lobby of Division Headquarters to greet the ambassador. This is how acceptable such a practice has become. Nope, nothing wrong here.

Later, when the terrorist city of Fallujah was harboring those who butchered four Americans and hung them from a bridge, our leaders called back U.S. Marine and Army units that had already made it a third of the way into the city. The soldiers had to stand down, and Fallujah remained a safe haven for terrorists until November 2004, eight months later. Or how about the brilliant decision to disband the Iraqi army and police and yet let the militias stand? What a breathtakingly stupid decision.

Parades in 115-degree heat? Mascots? Refusing to go after terrorists? All this is wrong by any measure. No wonder we have problems. No wonder things in this war go sideways. We cannot move with the speed we must in this fight if we have to have so many hands touching each decision to act. Are we ready to change this? If we are not, then more great young Americans will die. They will die because we aren't focused on the prize. We need to be focusing on the death of terrorists and not on some damn general's idea of fun.

As frustrating as all this is, fixes can be accomplished fairly quickly if we concentrate only on those things that will help us win this war: cut the bureaucracy, make people accountable, and instill real leadership in those who are in charge. We can be successful. But the only way we are going to be truly ready for this fifty-year fight is to get it right at the beginning. Hope is not a method. Making these things happen cannot be merely a wish. Making things happen is an absolute necessity.

As I write this, a full three years after the 9/11 attacks, Osama bin Laden is still at large, Iran is playing the nuclear card, North Korea is defying treaties and world opinion, and Syria continues the pretense of friendship with the West. We don't have enough Special Forces in Iraq, our soldiers are still dying and getting wounded, and we lack the leadership necessary to make the hard decisions necessary to correct these problems.

The fix is a simple solution: the strongest leadership from all levels possible in order to defeat our enemy. Well, as the captain of the starship *Enterprise* would say, "Make it so."

CHAPTER 6

Are We Ready to Wage War?

So now you know how we can begin to fix our intelligence problem, and how we need to focus on three main problems within every organization of our government: lack of leadership, lack of accountability, and excessive bureaucracy. We needed to start yesterday to be there now, but we didn't start yesterday and we aren't even close yet. Every day that we don't fix it—and I mean oiled, lubed, and put away—we are simply making the next 9/11 more probable. We have been forced into this war by a mass murder. If 9/11 hadn't happened, we would still be slashing our counterterrorism budgets; our military would still be getting cut; our intelligence services would still not be talking to one another; and Americans would still be getting killed with impunity by the thousands. It took a catastrophic event to finally wake us up. So again, late being better than never, it's time we take a hard look at ourselves and ask, *Are we ready?*

Are we ready to wage war? What do you think? We are definitely *not* ready to fight this war. But we can be.

So what can be done? What, if anything, is there left to learn?

What difference will it make? The last question we can answer right now. The difference will be whether or not our children and our way of life survive.

As discussed, we have to use every weapon at our disposal. We have to look at everything with a new eye and come up with new weapons, new ways of defeating terrorism. We must get out our terrorist toolbox, which contains the Terrorist Killing Agency, the director of national intelligence, the Internal Intelligence Agency, more military, more spies, more money, and less bureaucracy. But we need to add much more to our toolbox. Our enemy, the terrorists, may be murderers, but they are not stupid. They have stuff at their disposal too. Stuff like madrasses, the killing manuals, and nut-job jihadists. So guess what we have to do? We have to close the madrasses, burn the killing manuals, and kill the fascist jihadists.

We also have to target banks. Yup, banks. Why concern ourselves with banks in the War on Terror? The answer is simple. The answer is one trillion dollars. According to news reports, an estimated one trillion dollars is the amount of dirty, illegal, corrupt money that floats around the globe annually. A substantial part of this corrupt money can quickly find its way into the dirty pockets of terrorists. You can't fly a plane into a building if you can't afford the ticket! Since 9/11, it has dawned on our government that although money may not be the root of all evil, it is definitely one of the operational pillars. There's a quick solution: If a bank allows its computers to be used by terrorists, it should lose its license, its investments, everything. We must *kill* the bank.

So what are we, the most powerful nation in the world, doing about the problem of dirty money getting to terrorists? So far we have reacted in typical fashion: we have formed another governmental agency. In other words, we added another layer, another somebody in charge, another set of people calling for meetings. This, of course, is exactly what we *don't* need.

This new agency is called the Office of Terrorism and Financial Intelligence and is responsible for tracking and stopping the flow of the terrorists' funding. In three years this agency managed to collect more than $200 million in bad-guy money. This is good. We should all be happy that this amount has been taken out of the hands of the bad guys. But wait! Hold the cake and cookies. Don't do a little dance just yet, because when you remember that there is over one *trillion* dollars a year floating around the world in illegal funds, much of which will wind up in terrorists' hands, $200 million isn't a whole lot.

Dirty Money

We already know that in this fight for our lives, intelligence is our most important ingredient. For the terrorists, *money* is at the center of their needs. Terrorists need training, guns, explosives, poisons, plane tickets, and pilot licenses. All these things cost money. Unfortunately for us, the terrorists seem to have no problem getting money. A lot of the funding comes from dirty sources, from corrupt commercial and criminal endeavors like drug dealing, slavery, embezzlement, and financial fraud. That doesn't mean that only organized crime or illegal cartels are the source of funds. Terrorists also receive generous contributions from corrupt politicians and governments. Many times the terrorists are given funds that were designated for poverty relief but were diverted by these corrupt politicians. These sterling leaders steal from the treasuries within their own countries and become the benefactors of their terrorist friends. The dirty money goes into a bank in another country or is invested in a legitimate business. In both instances, the money comes out the other end as "cleaned money."

Terrorist organizations obtain and transfer money in numerous ways. We are going to look at the main types of transferring funds, because it's important to know how something works before you can figure out how to stop it.

In Islam, *zakat* is the giving of money and gifts to the needy. It is at the core of Muslim religious participation. Most Muslims give *zakat* through state-sponsored collection agents or to organizations that distribute the money to a number of charities. The well-meaning Muslim has no input or control as to whom or where his money winds up. This is a problem. What the very generous Muslim man has unwittingly done is provide direct aid to terrorists, because much of the money is diverted, skimmed off, or provided to groups for the purchase of weapons and explosives or used for operating costs of terrorist training camps.

Now, get ready! Our favorite state sponsor of terrorism, the oil-rich kingdom of Saudi Arabia, is smack-dab in the middle of this mess. Of course, we don't complain. Saudi Arabia has more than 40 percent of the world's oil and they are our *friends*. It wouldn't be polite to complain—not even a little. Take a deep breath. Go get your medication.

Saudi Arabia collects *zakat* through a government agency similar to our IRS. It then distributes the money to "recognized" charities. The Saudi Ministry of Finance and National Economy estimates that Saudi collections exceed $10 billion a year. The CIA and FBI estimate that more than 40 percent of this charity money winds up in either the Saudi royal family's golden pockets or the hands of terrorists. Did I mention that these *zakat* charity funds are distributed by Islamic banks? These Islamic banks, by the way, are owned by the Saudi royal family. Damn, this family is making a lot of money on this deal; they are skimming off the top and getting a percentage of what the banks charge to handle the money. *Deceptive, criminal,* and *duplicitous* are some of the adjectives that come to mind when talking about the Saudis and the money they make from *zakat* and what they do with that money.

The Islamic banking system has been a mystery to most businesses and governments in the West. Islamic banks by law cannot charge interest on loans. This means that an Islamic bank must make its money through investments. Many Muslims send their *zakat* through Islamic banks. Even though this process is legal, the giver cannot be assured that he has funded a legitimate charity. *Zakat* funds deposited in Islamic banks are taken off the books and "disappear" because they are not considered part of the banks' assets or liabilities. Therefore, these funds are not reported. The bank has served only as a collection agent. The *zakat* can then be transferred, without regulation, to "worthy" charities as determined by the bank.

Western-style accounting and auditing practices that monitor what those investments truly involve have only recently been implemented, and monitoring remains haphazard at best.

Now, here comes the really complicated and insidious part of all of this. Some of the largest Islamic banks have their headquarters in Switzerland. The Swiss banking philosophy involves secrecy and a system of complex governmental regulations that add another layer of crap we need to wade through in order to trace the terrorists' money. This isn't anything new. This is the same banking system that was complicit in hiding billions in Jewish funds that the Nazi regime stole during the Holocaust. *Hey, Switzerland! How would you like all your snow melted?*

Calm down. I am not advocating going to war with Switzerland. But this issue underscores how difficult our job is. Fighting the War on Terror does not mean just killing terrorists and stopping countries like Saudi Arabia from supporting terrorism; we will have to go after other nations like our *friends,* the Swiss. We need to make them understand. We need to make them stop. Later on, we will discuss the different methods we should be using to convince our friends and allies to help us, but for now it is enough to know that this war should not be fought in Afghanistan and Iraq alone. It needs to be fought on all fronts, in all nations, including our own.

In 1999 the United States uncovered a big money-laundering scandal involving the Russian mafia. You remember the Russian mafia? They are the guys that will sell anything and everything to pretty much anyone who can pay, including terrorists. They are the guys who look good doing this because they are sanctioned by the Russian government. So where, pray tell, were the bad guys washing their billions of dollars in dirty money? Right here in the United States! The Bank of New York laundered money for the Russian mob. Some of that money might have gone to the bad guys who blew a hole in lower Manhattan. We'll probably never know, because after years of investigation, almost nothing has been done about it.

Lucy Edwards, a vice president of the Bank of New York, and her husband, Peter Berlin, pleaded guilty to money laundering, immigration fraud, and other federal crimes in February 2000, but as of this writing they have never been sentenced and never spent any time in prison. Indeed, the only person who was actually sent to jail in connection with the scandal was a low-level secretary, Svetlana Kudryavtsev, whom Edwards and Berlin paid about $500 per month compensation to monitor some of the accounts—accounts from which Edwards and Berlin laundered a reported *$7 billion* from Russia. And Kudryavtsev went to jail for a whopping two weeks!

Did we kill the bank? Uh, no. According to the *New York Times*, regulators at the Federal Reserve and the New York State Banking Department "formally sanctioned the Bank of New York for 'deficiencies' in its anti-money-laundering practices." The newspaper conceded, however, that "the move, known as an enforcement action, did not include monetary penalties against the bank and fell short of a more serious 'cease and desist' order that regulators could have imposed." In reality, the Bank of New York's agreement with the regulators compelled the bank only to abide by money-laundering laws—something that the bank was *already* required to do.

You'll be happy to know that the Bank of New York's chairman and CEO, Thomas Renyi, did not lose his job. But he was punished: In 1999, after the scandal broke, he received "only" a bonus of $5.73 million, $850,000 in salary, $167,819 in other compensation, and 500,000 stock options—this down from 1998, when he received a $6.53 million bonus, $850,385 in salary, $166,150 in other compensation, and 500,000 stock options. Some punishment! This was done in the open with hardly a whimper from anyone, at any time, in any position of authority. And you ask whether we're ready. Asked and answered.

If we can't stop banks within our own borders—hell, within the confines of the very city that lost hundreds of brave firefighters and courageous police officers and thousands of citizens—how can we get our act together to shut down banks on the world scene that are trafficking in illegal funds that wind up with terrorists? And how the hell can we expect our government to get at the banks in countries like India, Russia, and of course Saudi Arabia? Remember, *zakat,* since it is based in the Koran, is carried out all over the Muslim world. So this illegal funding of terrorism can be found from Turkey to Pakistan and from the Philippines to Morocco. The word *pervasive* does not even come close to covering the landscape on this subject. This is a particular problem because few countries outside of the United States even bother to regulate or check charities, and even we didn't do anything until 9/11. Our State Department could have addressed this almost total lack of worldwide control over charities and their funding of terrorism and other illegal activities. Here's a surprise: it still doesn't.

Every good cop will tell you that when you want to catch a crook, or break up a criminal element, you need to follow the money. The same is certainly true with terrorism. Trouble is, moving up and down the money trail of terrorism requires us to take a different approach. Wherever we find a bank, a person, a business, or a government connected to terrorism, it must be taken out of the mix—one way or another.

The Muslim practice of *zakat* accounts for the biggest share of the money used to finance evil, but there also exist ways of distributing smaller amounts of money around the world in a safe and totally unrecorded manner. It is called *hawala* (*hawala* is Arabic for "transfer"). It is the Muslim world's best-known informal funds-transfer system. *Hawala* is basically an organized system of moving cash from friend, to family member, to friend, without accounting for the money to any government. It is a promise to pay—an IOU. It requires no recordkeeping of transmitters or receivers, no taxes to be paid, no custom duties to be levied. It is, according to an unclassified government briefing on the subject (found in Appendix B), "secure, trust-based, paperless and generally untraceable." The system was designed to allow the disadvantaged to receive money from churches, their families, and their friends without allowing governments to steal it from them.

And *hawala* accounts for massive sums of money, even if the individual transactions tend to be fairly small. Interpol estimates that India alone conducts $680 billion in *hawala* transactions annually. According to estimates from the International Monetary Fund (IMF), as much as $2 trillion is laundered through the *hawala* system every year. This is a huge amount of untaxed, unaccounted-for money. This is all done in the open. Although this practice is illegal in many countries, including the United States, numerous banks in both Islamic and Western countries use the system.

We learned about *hawala* after the 2001 attacks on the United States. Seems that much of the money the attackers used for apartments, food, and plane tickets was transferred by *hawala*.

If we are at all concerned with the concepts of *zakat* and *hawala,* and we must be, then we have to get at the charity industry. I am not advocating more regulations for regulations' sake, but I am insisting on getting serious about charitable organizations that are nothing more than fronts for terrorist organizations. If we put a few heads of charities in jail for supporting terrorism, we might get the attention of others. If that does not do it, then we might want to expel the foreign nationals that are here collecting for these charities and using the good intentions of Americans to fund pure evil. We have to be ready to do *anything* to win this war.

The Assassination Answer

The terrorists' ability to secure dirty money to fund their bloody agenda should reinforce our conviction that the War on Terror needs to be fought on a global scale, that it can't be won simply on the battlefield. We must change the way we think if we are to win this war. We must understand that it's not just the terrorists themselves who need to be taken out, it's also the people and institutions who prop up the terrorists. The charities that funnel money to the terrorists are a prime example. Other bad guys include the heads of state who sponsor or give safe haven to terrorists. These leaders are not just obstacles in our pursuit of the enemy; they are the enemy themselves. We have to deal with them, immediately and emphatically.

Here's how we need to start thinking: If a government gives safe haven to terrorists, it can then give safe haven to some cruise missiles. If a country gives money to a terrorist group, maybe we should take over its oil fields. And if a head of state supports terrorism, he can take a dirt nap. I strongly support killing those who would try to kill us. If it means Kim Jung Il of North Korea goes the way of the dodo, we do it. And if it means, dare I say it, assassination of someone who supports terrorists and refuses to stop state sponsorship of terrorism, let's get to it. Let's get it right.

Did I really use the word *assassination?* Absolutely! We need to have the mechanisms, capability, people, and political will to do targeted killings of those who would kill us. That means not just individual terrorists like Osama bin Laden and Ayman al-Zawahiri are targets, but also the leaders of countries that refuse to stop supporting the guys who kill us. The main argument against assassinations has always been that it opens your own country's leaders to assassination. Well, gee, I think flying planes into the White House, as the original 9/11 plot called for, might constitute a form of assassination. The point here is that the terrorists have changed the rules.

I know this assassination thing is troubling for many of you—an unacceptable tactic. But it is a nuance that must be appreciated. What would you have done to stop 9/11? That is exactly how you need to think about the War on Terror, because we must do everything in our power to prevent more 9/11 attacks—which is exactly what the terrorists are planning.

Then you need to realize that we *turned down* opportunities to take out at least one key al Qaeda leader *before* 9/11. According to a high-level foreign intelligence source I spoke to, in 1997 Ayman al-Zawahiri, the number two man in al Qaeda, was in Lebanon getting his face changed—you know, to go incognito. The Israelis informed us and offered to help us make Dr. Death a martyr for his sick cause. I don't want you to misunderstand what I am telling you; the Israelis offered to help us assassinate Zawahiri. The Israelis would provide the surgeon with a poison that would be injected into Zawahiri along with the anesthetic for his surgery. Two days later, Zawahiri would be dead—of a heart attack. Maybe 9/11 would not have happened. But we said no. *What the hell were we thinking?*

This is not pretty, but I never promised pretty. I promised answers. We have tried to fight terrorism by bringing these murderers into our court system, or by ignoring them altogether, or by buying them off—as we did with the Iran-Contra disaster—and none of this worked. I can hear some of you crying foul. I can hear the cries of "We can't do this" and "The terrorists have rights." Yes, terrorists do have rights. They have the right to die a death as violent, primitive, and ignominious as possible.

Clearly, we must be careful with the use of assassinations, and there must be—here's the key word again—accountability. All assassinations would be reviewed by a panel chosen by the National Director of Intelligence (NDI). It would be secret, of course. The panel would have a representative from each of the three branches of the government, plus the military, the intelligence community, and a private citizen. The panelists would sit for a term. They would be paid; it would be a job. They would get to review everything involved in the assassination to ensure that the benefits would outweigh the negative consequences if the operation went bad. If abuses happened, then those responsible would have to be held accountable. The Israelis got to try this type of retribution after their athletes were murdered at the Munich Olympics. We cannot lose sight of the fact that we are a nation of laws. But our laws, our Constitution, and our Bill of Rights are not suicide pacts or weapons to be used against us.

They are the protection of Americans' civil liberties. Terrorists are bent on denying American citizens the freedoms that our founding fathers hoped to secure when they created those documents. We are in a war our founding fathers never conceived of, and we have to make adjustments for our own survival.

And the fact is, the prospect of assassination brings fear and dread into the hearts of terrorists—two emotions we want them all to experience, all the time. Assassination is an invaluable tool to use against terrorists, and it is 100 percent necessary. Just look at how the Israelis have used the tool in their struggle for survival. In 2004, an Israeli helicopter in the Gaza Strip fired missiles at the "spiritual leader" of Hamas, Sheik Ahmed Yassin, killing him. Israel had targeted other leaders of the Palestinian campaign of terror, but Yassin was definitely the big boy. As leader of Hamas, he had been giving the thumbs-up to suicide attacks on innocent Israeli women and children for years, and he hadn't ever paid a price. Well, finally he did. Did Israel's killing of Yassin piss off a lot of people around the world? You bet. But was it effective? Absolutely.

Are we ready to do it? Probably not. Hell, most won't even say the word, so this assassination business is going to take a while before it is adopted. We aren't even willing to swallow our pride and admit we need help.

Some people say assassinations are illegal. And yes, in 1976 President Gerald Ford issued an executive order forbidding U.S. personnel from assassinating foreign leaders. President Reagan extended that executive order in 1981 to include hired assassins. But the president could overturn the decision today with a stroke of the pen.

Getting the Help We Need

Is it really possible to win the War on Terror without the full involvement of our allies, especially our European allies, including France and Germany? I don't think so. We need our allies' intelligence services, our allies' bases, and sometimes our allies' forces. It is a fact, Jack! Our CIA, FBI, National Security Agency, and armed services do not have even 10 percent of the Arabic speakers we need to really get at this fight. It will take another three to five years, without any bureaucratic holdups—which happen every minute of every day in this country—to get this deficiency corrected.

So what do we do in the meantime? We beg, borrow, and steal other nations' intelligence agents who do speak the languages and also have the skills we need. *Okay, but how?* you're probably wondering. Some of these countries don't like us, and they sure as hell don't want to help us. Well, that's true, but one thing can overcome a lot of sore feelings: money. We offer to forgive a nation's debt if they can help us. We pay for the help, for crying out loud. It is the height of arrogance and stupidity to not go and ask the South Africans, the Moroccans, even the much-hated French—who by the way have a great intelligence service as well as excellent special forces—to lend us a hand. We are naked, and without this help we can't get at the terrorists in dark caves.

Look, I get that the French, Germans, and Russians have been real asses when it comes to Iraq. They are selfish, sometimes even criminal, jerks for not helping us so far. So what? We need help. They can help. So go ask them. We cannot let pride get in our way. If the pompous French could help us stop another 9/11, why in God's name would we not ask for it, or pay for it? Come on! Figure this out. Stop talking about fighting and let's really get at this. All of Europe owes us. Hell, most of the free world owes us. It is time for them to pay up. Let's make a sign that says: *The United States of America will take any and all help fighting and killing terrorists.* Now let's hang it on the front door in every language. Of course, we will probably have a little difficulty finding enough linguists to make the signs.

Truth is, we don't have enough of anything.

In May 2004, we told close to seven thousand servicemen and women who have served their nation honorably and left the military that they had to go back into service. They had no choice in the matter. Oh, and then we told those who had been serving with such honor and distinction in Iraq and Afghanistan for more than a year that they would be staying—for as long as we wanted them to stay. You know what? This sucks. These young men and women are our best and they deserve to be treated with a hell of a lot more respect than that. This is outrageous, shortsighted, asinine, and just plain wrong. It is not the way to fight this war.

Allow me to explain. During the past twenty years we have managed to reduce our armed forces to the point that today, right now, the U.S. Army has only thirty-three active-duty maneuver brigades. These, the infantry and tank units, are the heart and soul of the Army. Right now, those thirty-three organizations are going to Afghanistan or Iraq, coming back from Afghanistan or Iraq, or getting refitted from their last job. There are no more soldiers to do this fight. This means that we cannot fight anywhere else unless we just bomb the bad guys, which, by the way, has never worked.

Our government's answer to this problem has been to use the Reserve forces. These are great men and women, but they train only one weekend a month and two weeks a year. That is 47 days a year versus the 365 that the active forces get to practice. Our very brave soldiers in the Reserves are actually serving longer in Iraq and Afghanistan than are their active-duty brothers and sisters. There is no comparison between the two types of unit, and there was never meant to be. But since thousands of these citizen soldiers have been deployed in the combat zones of Afghanistan and Iraq, and others are engaged in missions against terrorism overseas and at home, the differences must be addressed and addressed now.

The bottom line is that we are short two Army divisions, a total of about thirty thousand soldiers. We can't get to the winners' circle without them. Got to have them and have them now. We have known this for over three years and have done nothing. Our government does not even talk about this need. To talk about it would be to talk about the money it would cost—$30 billion. We also don't talk about it because to do so would be admitting that we need help and that we were not ready for this fight. It is about arrogance and pride. But you know what? We have no time for either of those things.

Hell, if our president went on TV and said, "I need you to help fight this war," we would have what we need standing in line in a day. They would be trained and in this fight in a year. It is an expensive and politically charged decision. So what? We seem to be willing to screw those in the service now with such things as Stop/Loss. This is the policy that says you can't get out of the military when you are supposed to because your tour has been involuntarily extended. We use Stop/Loss and use the Reserves until they dry up. So we need to institute a mandatory national service program, which I'll talk about more in Chapter 8. One of the ways young people may choose to serve their country is in the military. We need more soldiers; there is no ducking that. If everyone is required to serve his country in some way, we will get the numbers we need. I happen to agree with those who argue that some form of the draft will be needed. But what is not needed is the kind of draft we had forty years ago, when there were so many exceptions that for years only one segment of society was really eligible for the draft. No, in this new world of the War on Terror, no exceptions—all of a certain age must be eligible.

The U.S. Marine Corps is regulated to around two hundred thousand Marines. We need more, and now. So change the law. Does anyone really think that Afghanistan and Iraq are the last places we're going to have to fight? Sorry, this war is going on for at least the next fifty years. Get the new soldiers up and ready now, before it's too late.

Oh, and while we're putting more active-duty soldiers and Marines in this fight, we have to figure out how to better use our very talented and brave Reserve forces. Oh sure, we're using them, but we're not using them *correctly.* At this writing, more than 40 percent of the force fighting and dying in Afghanistan and Iraq is from the Reserves and the National Guard. Soldiers from the Guard and the Reserves clocked a total of nearly *63 million* days on active duty in 2003—a fivefold increase from the 12 million duty days recorded in the late 1990s.

Selling America

Here is something else we can do: get at the hearts and minds of our enemy. *Hearts and minds? Has the colonel gone touchy-feely on us?* No, not at all. The point is, we have to use every tool available to us to get at the bad guys. We need to play with their minds by using our psychological-operations guys. Playing with the bad guys' minds is an old trick, but we have to use it even more than we are now.

Psychological operations are designed to affect people, governments, and events. But the difference between psychological operations and almost all other operations is that the psy-ops troopers do their deals with computers, leaflet drops, television advertisements, radio spots, and education manuals. They do their work in hospitals, in movie theaters, in schools, on street corners, at sporting events, and in churches and mosques—anywhere people can be reached. In order to be effective, these operations have to be part of the overall attack plan. That means *before* we attack, not after we attack.

It is called preparing the battlefield. It is the same type of tactic as bombing before we attack on the ground to lessen the number of bad guys our troops will face. In psychological operations we get inside the bad guys' heads. We trick the government we're attacking into believing that we're *not* going to attack or menace them in advance when we *are,* which seems to be the current M.O. We get the other guy to leave the battlefield before we even get there, or we get him to worry, or he looks the other way, or we get the different factions mad at one another by planting fake stories in their newspapers. Hell, we do what the Republicans and Democrats do to each other every election year. We spin!

In order to do this first, we have to get inside the places that are causing the Muslim world to hate us as much as they do. I know that the politically correct crowd is throwing this book out the window now. But come on, who does not know this? Admitting it is one thing, writing about it is even worse to them. Sorry, but it is mostly Muslims who are trying to kill us. So we have to descend on the countries, cities, and villages within the Muslim world and we must get at their books, their teachers, their religious leaders, and their religious schools. We have to get on the prayer rug with them and market our message that we are the good guys.

We have to counter the al-Jazeeras of the world. We will have to say up front that we are going to refute their ideology and then do it. This will require a commitment of money and talent. We have the necessary ingredients to fulfill this commitment; all we need now is the will. We can't allow the Islamofascists to continue to dominate the airwaves with anti-American rhetoric.

We have to sell America and all that is good in American society to the rest of the world. We have to advertise on television stations in the Muslim world, or at least ones that reach the Muslim world, and tell of the many great things that "we the people" have done for Muslims all over the world. Hell, we need to start in our own hemisphere by doing some broadcasting to the Canadians, who actually allow al-Jazeera on their cable network but will not allow us to send Fox News.

We have saved, and continue to save, thousands of Muslim children. For example, we have inoculated the children in Iraq against disease. That is a huge accomplishment, one that the citizens of Iraq should hear about and be reminded of daily. We need to have many Arabic radio stations blaring good news, and there are many good-news stories. We have to do things that are subtle but effective, from candy bars with slogans to prayer rugs bearing an American flag. The selling of America will have to involve many different projects, and as in any commercial enterprise, we must be ready to dump what does not work, fix what needs to be fixed, and increase those projects that yield success. Unlike selling the hula hoop, selling America to the Muslim world will not be an overnight success. It will take time and patience to achieve our goal, but we must be prepared to stay the course for as long as it takes.

Another part of psychological operations is parting with our money to help the people we are invading. How about fixing sewer systems and building roads, schools, and hospitals as we are doing in Iraq? We have to announce to people that we want to help, and that when the United States becomes an ally it keeps its promises—the water will be clean and the hospital will be built. These are the messages we have to put out every minute of every day to the people we just invaded. Their lives can be better. The terrorists made their life miserable but we will help them make it good.

The campaign to sell America will also help us get the assistance we need from other countries. The sad truth is, it ain't going well so far. We've been embarrassed by countries refusing to lend a hand to this global campaign against deadly enemies—for instance, when Turkey made our soldiers sit in boats while the U.S. State Department fruitlessly tried to get them clearance to use the country as a staging base. Hell, Turkey is a democracy and we *still* could not convince them. Time to get energized or cattle-prodded, to get other countries to fully engage with us in this war.

And you know what, we also have to end one of the key sources for the hatred and anti-Americanism within Islamic countries: the unresolved Israeli-Palestinian situation. Whether or not people want to admit it, the fact is that many who practice the Muslim religion view the United States as an enemy exactly because we support the Jewish state. It is no accident that Islamofascists call us the Great Satan and call Israel the Little Satan. This is not to say that we abandon Israel—far from it, in fact. But it *is* time now for us to become the honest broker in the Arab-Israeli conflict. Why? Because a peaceful solution to conflict in the Middle East is another tool in our anti-terrorist toolbox. With the sudden death of Arafat, this is the best opportunity in sixty years. If we resolve that conflict, we can steal at least some of the hatred from our enemies. This is clearly easier said than done, but without a peace between the Palestinians and Israel, we'll all continue to pay the price of terrorism. This will take the total commitment of more than one world leader, and for sure the leadership of the president of the United States will be the key ingredient.

Doing What It Takes

We have barely scratched the surface of what this country can do in support of the War on Terror. George W. Bush's ever controversial secretary of defense, Donald Rumsfeld, figured this part out pretty quickly. In 2003, when the Army had to replace its outgoing chief of staff, the defense secretary looked at all the hundreds of generals in the Army and said, *Uh, no, ain't going to pick any one of you.* Instead Rummy reached back four years and picked a retired guy named Peter Schoomaker, a former Delta Force commander, to be the boss general. Big Pete, as he is called behind his back, came out of retirement to lead the entire Army; he was beholden to no one. So what happened? Did he come in and make big changes? Nope. Hasn't happened. Not yet. Schoomaker could have gone out and tortured the Department of Defense, he could have fired and hired, changed the way the generals and colonels are selected, changed the way we fight; he could have done so much when he came in. But he didn't. It seems the government bureaucracy can be quite alluring. Still, I have hope that Big Pete will find the fix necessary to rejuvenate our military.

So one guy coming out of retirement to save the day did not work, but maybe he might be able to pull it off if he was joined by a few hundred, or a few thousand, proven combat veterans. These guys will come back voluntarily because we tell them we need them, we give them the authority to do their jobs and get things done, and we pay them really well. Let me be clear, these retirees are not going to take any current positions. They would be *additional* troops— troops that have actually done some of the harder tasks required in war. And many of those who have been successful could become ad- visers. They could go out and see what is going on and report back. They already know which things don't work, because they've lived with them. They could warn us off the mistakes we have made in the past and therefore make us more successful in the future. We have retirees that can do as well as, if not better than, those on active duty.

Right now, we have more than twenty thousand private security guards in Iraq doing a spectacular job. It was private security guards who guarded L. Paul Bremer, the head of the Coalition Provisional Authority, in Iraq for almost a year without incident. We have many more of these retirees who could easily serve for a few years and would welcome the call. They will have to be paid more than they were, but thousands of those men and women are available.

And finally, here is a radical idea: If this really is World War III, if this really is a war for our survival, if we really are going to invade sovereign nations that support terrorism, then how about we make it official, for crying out loud? That's right, how about we ask Congress to actually *declare war*? Why not declare war on terrorism just the way we declared war against Japan and Germany? Hell, then the president gets real wartime powers. We get to count who voted for the war and who did not. The nation really gets it. There isn't any more ambiguity. This isn't a law enforcement issue; it's not an issue for the courts. This is a world war, plain and simple. Declaring war seems to me to be the first thing a sovereign nation should do when some nation or some entity attacks it. You know, sometimes truth is the real tool, the most powerful one in our toolbox.

Our tactics must continue to evolve in this war. We are dealing with an enemy that uses any and all means to connect with its vast network of operatives spread around the globe. We are dealing with nations that tell us they are our friends and give millions of dollars to our enemies. We have to have tools that we never used before, never dared use, and were afraid to use. The bad guys sure haven't been afraid to use any of their new tools. They have used our own planes to kill and disrupt our way of life. In Iraq, they have killed Americans using roadside bombs placed inside of dead animals, abandoned cars, plants, and garbage. Yup, the bad guys have a few tricks. We need to be better. We can be better, period.

CHAPTER 7

Guerrilla Warfare

The War on Terror is, of course, a new kind of war that requires new approaches and new tactics. But in some ways it's a very old kind of war too. It is a guerrilla war, the ugliest, nastiest, most unnatural and unholy fighting you can do. Each time we decide to fight terrorism in another country, we will face the conditions we have faced in Afghanistan a little and continue to face in Iraq a lot. The fighting in Iraq has become nothing less than a full-scale guerrilla war, and it quickly got bloody.

These guerrillas have shot our soldiers and burned their bodies. The *New York Times* and *USA Today* have printed pictures of the charred remains of our sons hanging from a bridge over the Euphrates River, in a town called Fallujah. Those mutilated men had been assigned to guard food for the same people that killed them.

In another incident, a mullah named Muqtada al-Sadr openly called for the death of Americans, commanding his insurgent force to "terrorize your enemy." By the spring of 2004 the militia was taking out brave Americans. So how did we respond to this radical Shiite cleric? We responded with words. Gee, think that stopped him? Twice between April and September 2004 our military forces had him cornered, the first time in Sadr City, then later in Najaf. We backed down both times because Shia leaders put pressure on our State Department, and State caved in. We backed off so as to not piss off the religious leaders like Ayatollah Ali al-Sistani, who told his people to cooperate with us—for now—and threatened to rescind that cooperation if we went in later. Then our troops surrounded and took control of the city of Najaf, al-Sadr's stronghold. We launched our jets from an aircraft carrier off the coast and dropped 500-pound bombs on the city. We used our tanks. We used our helicopter gunships to subdue the enemy. We even wounded al-Sadr. And then we stopped our advance to negotiate.

This is not how you fight a guerrilla war.

A guerrilla war sometimes seems to defy logic. In Iraq we began building hospitals and schools, but there were riots in the streets, and snipers and bombers threatened the lives of employees working on the construction projects. In the Iraqi city of Basra, our British allies similarly faced riots, roadside bombs, and terrorist attacks despite the fact that they did a spectacular job of helping the local population and had the city under control. The threats multiplied. Terrorists and guerrillas have put bombs in the carcasses of dead animals and among the garbage that lines the streets. They have blown up our vehicles, our men, and our women. They have blown up innocent Iraqi bystanders.

We are looking straight in the face of guerrilla warfare. This is an insurgency. The guerrillas did not recognize us as liberators; they saw us as occupiers.

Unfortunately, our leaders refused to acknowledge this fundamental truth. You might remember—because I sure do—that Secretary of Defense Donald Rumsfeld said that this was not a guerrilla war, that there was no insurgency. In a 2003 press conference, Rumsfeld talked about "looters, criminals, remnants of the Ba'athist regime, foreign terrorists who came in to assist and try to harm the coalition forces, and those influenced by Iran," and then insisted, "That doesn't make it anything like a guerrilla war or an organized resistance. It makes it like five different things going on [in which the groups] are functioning more like terrorists." He continued to say this for more than four months.

We need to be intellectually honest here. The fact is, when you invade a country, 100 percent of that country might not like being helped/conquered; they may eventually come to like you, but probably won't like you at first. And if you can't admit to a problem, you certainly can't plan for how to cope with that challenge. We have lost hundreds of soldiers and seen thousands wounded because we had no plan for coping with the guerrilla warfare we now face—and that was because we were unwilling to admit to the reality of the situation. This was a major failure. But as with the intelligence community, no one in the Pentagon got fired for this one. No sir!

In this War on Terror, we will continue to fight guerrilla warfare. We had better figure this out. Let's look at what we're up against and the resources we have available to really fight this kind of a fight.

Taking the War to the Insurgents

In a traditional war, such as World War II, the bad guys lined up on their side and the good guys lined up on their own side. Each side had its own uniforms, tanks, planes, boats, and soldiers. They met in the middle and killed each other. Good guys always win these wars.

But we aren't fighting a traditional war. In a guerrilla war or an insurgency, the bad guys never line up. They never stand and fight. They don't have the recognizable uniforms, tanks, planes, boats, or soldiers. The bad guys use children, women, and some men to do their fighting. They shoot the good guys or blow up the good guys in restaurants, cars, and buses. Organizations that fight guerrilla wars couldn't possibly compete with their opponents in a traditional war.

Look at the North Vietnamese: They couldn't have fought us toe to toe, in the air, on the sea, or full up on the battlefield, so they fought us with their surrogates, the Viet Cong. And over the course of more than a decade, they killed thousands of great American young men and women who were for the most part not trained to fight the guerrilla war confronting them.

The French became successful guerrilla fighters when Germany occupied their nation in World War II. Many argue that the insurgents in Iraq have enjoyed the same type of success against us. Why would they want to fight this way? Because it's the only way they can.

The problem we face is the same one the Germans faced in France: it is the way we are fighting. We still have the uniforms, the tanks, the planes, the boats, and the soldiers. We still line up to fight like we would for the other kind of war. We need a lesson in guerrilla tactics.

In the past fifteen years, oil companies in countries like Mozambique have actually hired private armies like the South African firm Executive Outcomes to recapture equipment lost in an insurgency. And in 1995 Sierra Leone's government contracted Executive Outcomes to fight the rebels from the Revolutionary United Front (RUF), who were terrorizing the country and threatening to topple the government. With 150 to 300 former Special Forces fighters, Executive Outcomes kicked the crap out of the RUF, driving the rebels back into Liberia. After stabilizing the capital of Freetown, these highly qualified professional soldiers set out to recapture the diamond-mining areas from which the RUF terrorists prosecuted their illegal war. Executive Outcomes had a three-month plan to capture these areas; the campaign actually took three *days*. Sierra Leone was able to hold elections for the first time.

Then the government terminated Executive Outcomes out of an unfounded fear that these soldiers for hire would take over the country. Once the contract was canceled, the rebels came back; within ninety days the country had fallen to the same terrorists that Executive Outcomes had defeated. The UN sent in a peacekeeping force of 8,000 troops, but this huge force—which swelled to more than 20,000 soldiers—only made the situation worse. In fact, the RUF took some of the peacekeeping troops hostage.

Executive Outcomes achieved tremendous success employing guerrilla tactics; the UN's much larger force suffered major setbacks because it relied on more traditional fighting or "peacekeeping" techniques. Let me say this again. To successfully counter insurgencies, we must be willing to fight a guerrilla war.

Our magnificent military took both Afghanistan and Iraq extremely quickly, and we will have similar success wherever the fight against terrorism takes us. If we attacked Iran, for example, we would kick the Iranian army's butts as easily as we did the opposition in Afghanistan and Iran. But the Iranians would of course mobilize a guerrilla force in the cities and in the mountains, just as we've encountered insurgencies in Iraq and, to a lesser extent, Afghanistan. (And by the way, the Iranians have actively supported the insurgents in Iraq.) The same scenario is likely anywhere within the Middle East. This does not mean we should not attack the next country that is supporting terrorists, but it does mean that we need to be better prepared for the inevitability of guerrilla warfare after we win the traditional war. We have to be able to win the war and win the peace.

Our brave and dedicated soldiers are not the problem; our political leaders need to adapt. We blew our chance to defeat the guerrillas in Vietnam. We had the military skill but lacked the political will that would have been necessary to win. We killed the enemy every way possible, but we never got the fact that they did not care how many of them we killed as long as eventually we left. We left, so they won. And because of our unnatural fear of the Russians and Chinese, our politicians were never willing to take the war to Hanoi. We bombed them, yes, but we wouldn't invade. We were defeated in Vietnam because of a lack of political will and an inability to understand the nature of our enemy.

We can't do that again in Iraq or Afghanistan or wherever else the War on Terror demands we go; we have to get it right this time. Sadly, the early results have not been encouraging. Politicians interfering with the fight in Fallujah and Najaf—this is the same interference that cost us the war in Vietnam. If we don't figure it out against the terrorists in Iraq and Afghanistan, we will encourage guerrilla outbreaks throughout the Muslim world. Our very survival depends on our ability to fight this war the way it can be won. Let's fight it there, not here; our enemy, if not defeated on his home turf, will hit us here.

Special Operations

So how do we stop the bad guys? We stop them, or at least slow them down, by going into towns like Fallujah and eliminating the terrorist resistance. Let me put it simply: *Kill them all.* Kill every mother's son who is making roadside bombs, who threatens to kill our sons and daughters, and then deal very harshly with countries like Iran and Saudi Arabia, who have been funding them. Attacking the terrorists and then immediately backing away will never solve the problem. This is what we first did in Fallujah. We got a third of the way into the city, kicking serious ass, only to be pulled back by politics. We didn't touch Fallujah at the beginning because we knew it was going to be a very hard city to take. So instead of facing it head-on, we bypassed it so we could claim a quick victory and send good news back home. The plan was to go back later and take control of it. We delayed the confrontation until four Americans were killed, burned, and hanged, but by then it was almost too late. The Sunnis were in control of the city. We thought they were on our side but we were wrong. Fallujah remained a hotbed of terrorism, and no one did anything about it for months. Finally—*finally*—in November 2004, the politicians let our guys loose in Fallujah, with great success. Sure, we had to counter the wishes of the ever-so-helpful Kofi Annan and the United Nations, but we got the job done. Only it should have been done much earlier.

In a guerrilla war you don't usually get the big victory, the large body count, the city captured, or the government toppled. In a guerrilla war you get drips. *Drip*—one soldier is killed by a roadside bomb. *Drip*—the rail bridge has been blown up. *Drip*—the water is poisoned. *Drip*—the local police chief is killed by a sniper. Soon you are fighting in all directions at once, and support for your efforts is diminishing at home. Yup, lack of home support is a clear sign that you are up to your armpits in a guerrilla war.

To fight this kind of a war requires flexibility, swift maneuvering, and the best damn soldiers in the world. We've got all that. But for some stupid reason we're not taking full advantage of our resources. When the war against Saddam Hussein's regime began in 2003, we had more than 10,000 Special Operations soldiers (Army Special Forces and Navy SEALs) in or around Iraq. They, along with the great Army and Marine tank units that ran to Baghdad, did a spectacular job of taking Iraq away from Saddam. That's no surprise. Earlier I called our Special Forces supersoldiers, and that's exactly what they are. They are Olympic athletes with guns. They jump out of airplanes at thirty thousand feet carrying hundreds of pounds. They train with tribesmen in Uganda and spend weeks in ice caves in Norway. They are comfortable being shot out of a submarine's torpedo tube or protecting foreign dignitaries. They can train a new army in Afghanistan or Iraq.

All the branches of the military except the Coast Guard—Army, Navy, Air Force, and Marines—have Special Operations forces. The most important for the purposes of fighting the War on Terror are the Army's Special Operations Command and the Navy SEALs. The members of the Air Force's Air/Sea Rescue, or Pararescue, unit endure an extremely demanding training regimen, but they are usually only seen or heard of when they pull a mountain climber off the highest point of Mount McKinley or rescue a downed pilot in the North Atlantic. The Air Force also has the Special Operations Wings, which fly gunships and electronic eavesdropping aircraft. Meanwhile, the Marine Corps got into the Special Operations business later than the other services did; in the late 1980s it formed the Marine Expeditionary Units (Special Operations Capable). The Corps basically trains infantry soldiers in basic Special Operations techniques before they go out for their six-month deployments so that these Special Operations units will be available if any trouble arises.

As well trained as the Marine and Air Force Special Operations forces are, the Army and Navy units remain most crucial to the War on Terror. The Army Rangers are one kick-ass group—the finest light infantry unit in the world, period. They conduct what is called "direct action missions," or raids (such as the one made famous in *Black Hawk Down*). In World War II, these were the guys who climbed the cliffs during the Normandy invasion. Incidentally, the Rangers used to wear black berets, but we had a general who thought hat color and shape were important. Isn't that just the type of "brilliance" we have come to expect from a general? "I'm the new boss. Let's see, what should my first order of business be? I know: Everyone change his hat." You can't make this kind of stuff up. So now the Rangers wear brown berets and the rest of the Army wears black berets, except the Airborne, who wear maroon berets, and of course the Green Berets, who wear . . . well, green berets. Okay, enough about hats. But you get my point?

And what about those Green Berets? These are the United States Army Special Forces, the only organization trained and equipped to defeat guerrillas. Hell, some in the Army think the Special Forces guys are guerrillas in uniforms. So how many Special Forces did we keep in Iraq to deal with the deadly full-scale insurgency? *Fewer than 1,500.* Hello! What am I missing? I'm missing the head of the idiot who made the decision to minimize the presence of the Special Forces in this war. Instead of putting these guys into the thick of the action that they're rigorously trained for, the Army bosses sent Special Forces to home bases like Fort Bragg and Fort Campbell. Some were sent to Africa, some back to Afghanistan, but most were sent home. Idiotic.

You have to understand, an Army Special Forces recruit will first be tested as if he were going to be a brain surgeon. He will be given aptitude tests, IQ tests, a personality test, a physical-aptitude battery, and, of course, the infamous Physical Fitness Test. The potential candidate has to do a prodigious amount of push-ups and sit-ups and also run like a deer. Then he must put on a sixty-pound rucksack and cover twelve miles in less than four hours. During the recruit's year-long training cycle, he is taught history, political philosophy, intelligence operations, and guerrilla and counterguerrilla operations. Although the other branches of the military provide their recruits with difficult training, it does not compare in intensity with Special Forces training.

The Navy, of course, has the SEALs, who are arguably our nation's most flexible force. SEAL is an acronym for "Sea, Air, and Land," which is entirely fitting, since they carry out operations over all three. They conduct raids the way the Army Rangers do, serve as bodyguards for top government officials, as they have been doing in Afghanistan and Iraq, and work for our nation's intelligence agencies. There are only ten SEAL platoons, with each platoon made up of about thirty-five of some of the world's finest warriors. Each of the U.S. military's four-star commanders gets a SEAL platoon to help fight the bad guys. SEALs are what we call a "force multiplier," which means that they are worth more than the sum of their parts— especially in guerrilla warfare or fighting terrorism, where a platoon of a few dozen SEALs can be as effective as five hundred or even a thousand infantrymen.

Look at what the Army Special Forces and the Navy SEALs did after we invaded Afghanistan in 2001. With air support from the U.S. Air Force, a combined force of fewer than two hundred Special Forces, SEALs, and CIA Ground Branch operatives took out the Taliban and captured Afghanistan in less than a month.

So if these are the guys who are most equipped to conduct guerrilla warfare, why don't our leaders have all of them out there fighting the guerrilla war we're actually in?

Part of the problem is that their direct commanders won't release them to fight on the front lines of the War on Terror. According to sources within the Navy SEAL community, both General Tommy Franks and his successor as CentCom commander, General John Abizaid, asked the commanders of SEAL units to give up these platoons for a while. You know, so the United States could use them in the fight against terrorism. What do you think the answer was? You guessed it—*no*. These geniuses in uniform would rather have our finest warriors getting tanned on a beach in Hawaii than hunting or killing terrorists. I don't know about you, but this really makes me want to smash something.

Our leaders need to stop messing around and send these elite troops, the best guys we have, to go deal with the insurgents. Our Special Operations soldiers will prove critical to fighting the sort of guerrilla campaigns that are, and will continue to be, a huge part of the War on Terror. Unfortunately, the Pentagon brass hasn't figured out how to conduct this war properly. Our government hasn't woken up to the fact that executing a counterguerrilla campaign goes against all the traditional battlefield rules and training. There are no battle lines. Death can come from virtually any angle. That's why we need to use those who have been trained to defeat an insurgency.

Because our decision makers simply aren't used to this kind of fight, they need to turn to the experts for advice. So, Mr. Secretary of Defense, Mr. Secretary of State, and even you, Mr. President, ask the people who know. Ask the experts, damn it! When the political and military leadership in a guerrilla war won't ask for help, you get a strategy that is doomed to fail. You get very tough and competent tankers driving huge M1A1 Abrams tanks into a city of five million while trying to fight guerrillas. You get Special Forces guys in the weight room looking good but not helping.

We'll never win if we keep making the same mistakes.

Failed Leadership

Using Special Forces works. We have proven that it works time and again. These guys go into villages where Americans have never been before; they ask permission of the village elders; they bring medicine with them and help establish order where only warlords ruled; they live, eat, and sleep in the village; they grow beards because all the men in the village have beards; they don't wear uniforms or even helmets so they can blend in; they make friends. And they get information. They make a difference and it works. This is how the Special Forces do things fighting a guerrilla war.

So why don't we keep doing it? A big problem is that we are still fighting ourselves. Here is the perfect example: In September 2002, insurgents in Afghanistan tried to assassinate the leader of the newly formed Afghan government, Hamid Karzai, but the security detail charged with protecting Karzai, members of a special Navy SEAL unit, fired back at the gunman, killing him.

The SEALs put their lives on the line to save Karzai, and in fact one was wounded in the firefight. These brave men prevented the insurgents from dealing a devastating blow to U.S. efforts in the War on Terror. The United States had just kicked the Taliban and al Qaeda out of Afghanistan, and having Karzai's steady hand at the helm of the new government was a key part of the rebuilding strategy. Not being able to protect the new president of a country we supposedly were in control of was not the kind of news our government was looking for.

So those who saved this very important individual were richly rewarded, right? They were given a knighthood, maybe a weekend in Las Vegas, a tickertape parade in New York City, a promotion, a pay raise, a letter of appreciation? Uh, no. I know, they were at least given a pat on the back, an "attaboy," or a thank-you? Someone at least said thank you for saving our collective bacon, right? Again, no.

The SEALs certainly weren't looking for any reward, but for sure, they didn't expect what they got. The head guy in charge of the security detail, the guy who was wounded in the firefight that saved Karzai, got a message from his bosses back in the United States, several time zones away. The message he got said, *Get a haircut.*

It turns out that the Pentagon brass saw news photos of the Special Operations forces who had protected the Afghan leader. The *New York Times* had run a front-page photo of the slightly wounded SEAL standing with an M4 carbine and a hand grenade hanging from his belt, and the idiot general who penned the order didn't like the scruffy, bearded look. He said he was "concerned" with the "image" of the Special Operations soldiers. You've got to be kidding me! The guy had just been wounded saving the life of a very important person.

I can't say this enough: The jerk who gave this order is not the exception in our military senior leadership, he is unfortunately the norm. Ask the SEALs, ask the Special Forces guys, ask the tankers, ask the infantrymen. They will tell you the deal, and the deal is that we are in a hurt locker without a key.

Here is another example of our military's failure to understand what we need to do to defeat the insurgents: The Green Zone in Iraq is the supposedly secure/safe zone where the men in charge meet and sleep. In Baghdad in July 2004, a knife-swinging terrorist attacked and severely injured an American soldier within the Green Zone. Now, you would think that this was hardly a fair fight. An American soldier in Iraq has lots of guns at his disposal. The terrorist would be three shades short of smart to go after a soldier who's carrying a loaded weapon. He would be, except the soldier was not carrying a weapon. Those in charge ordered that when in the Green Zone, soldiers would not be allowed to carry their weapons. What drug are these people on? Whoever gave that order needs to eat more fruit, as the left side of his brain is in desperate need of fiber. Our soldiers were being attacked between seventeen and twenty-five times a day. We were in the middle of a guerrilla war, the very nature of which was that you didn't know where the next attack would come from, and some idiot said, "No guns." No guns? *No guns?* That's the height of stupidity!

Even if we solve the problems plaguing our military leadership, we'll have other issues to deal with. The biggest is that if we were to get all our Special Operations troops doing what they should be doing—killing terrorists and guerrillas—we still wouldn't have enough to win the war. We definitely need to find more of these guys and train them, even though that's not the only solution to our current shortfall in qualified Special Operations forces. To employ the other options will require real political leadership, however. It will also require us to lose our arrogance. The United States is not the only nation with great Special Operations soldiers; others can help us defeat the terrorists and terrorist sponsors who are out to kill us. In fact, some countries, like Poland and Britain, have already allowed their Special Operations teams to fight with us. But (and it seems in this fight against terrorists there is always a *but*) plenty of other sovereign nations have talented Special Ops that we aren't using at all. For example, we're in desperate need of soldiers who speak Arabic. Guess who has an entire army that is fluent in Arabic and are also superior soldiers? Israel. Guess how many within the Israeli army are working with us in this war? Working with us in, say, in Iraq? Oh, I don't know . . . try *none*. Why is this happening? Well, some of the people in Iraq and in the rest of the Middle East might not like it. Gee, why is that? Could it be anti-Semitism? Yup, you bet. So our government hasn't asked the Israeli government for help for fear of antagonizing the Muslim world—that is, *further* antagonizing the Muslim world. Why are we so concerned about this when so many in the Muslim world already hate us? We're fighting for our lives here, as are the Israelis; it would only make sense that these warrior nations would combine efforts to defeat those who would try to destroy us.

The Israelis aren't the only ones who can help. The South African army has had a great deal of experience fighting terrorists and has soldiers with unique language skills. But we are not even considering asking them for help. Can you guess why? Political correctness! It seems that some members of our government think it would appear a bit off for us to be openly working with a military that was involved in apartheid. And we don't want to be seen to be asking for help. We don't want to appear as if we can't go this alone. This is beyond arrogance on our part. It is suicide. We may actually lose this war unless we open ourselves up to the help that is available.

The French, Germans, Italians, and Moroccans all have spectacular intelligence services, and their Special Forces range from adequate to exceptional. We are not even talking to them. We have to talk to them. We have to use them. We have to ask them for help—damn it, we need it.

The New Rules of War

In order to win this war, we have to have an "out-of-government" experience, which is like an out-of-body experience but a whole lot rarer.

Governments, militaries, and even elementary schools run on rules and regulations. The guerrillas do not answer to rules. They make them up as they go along. Our leaders in the government and the military must adjust from the tradition of fighting armies that have doctrine and history to fighting ragtag groups that have no uniforms, use kids and women to hide behind, carry messages by camel, and kill indiscriminately. We need to adapt.

In a guerrilla war you have to get in bed with those you normally don't even say hello to. Here is a news flash: Nice people don't join guerrilla armies. Your typical, well-educated young professional is not normally going to go gunrunning or drive a supply truck for the bad guys. Scum-sucking, bottom-feeding slugs are what you normally get in guerrilla armies. So guess what, the friends and families of these clowns are probably not going into the priesthood either. If we want to infiltrate a guerrilla army, we are going to have to get into the pigpen and wrestle.

We must infiltrate organizations that are run on family ties. If we can get inside the bad guys' tent, all things are possible. Being able to speak the language of those we're helping seems like a no-brainer. Up until now, it has not been. It is a must. If you are in Afghanistan up in the mountains speaking Pashto with a Brooklyn accent, you are going to kind of stick out. So maybe we want to think about using anybody who will help us while not sticking out.

We should set up whorehouses for intelligence gathering, using both men and women. Hell, the governments of Saudi Arabia and Yemen import women to act as prostitutes, so yeah, setting up whorehouses to gather intelligence is a must. We should have medicine that does not work delivered to the guerrillas. We should spread some fake money around. We need to get to those who are supplying the guerrillas and stop them. We need to cut off other governments from helping the bad guys and punish those who do not listen. Most important, we must be willing and able to react violently and immediately to threats. We can't take any crap from anyone.

Those in charge have to listen to people that they normally don't even see—civil affairs people, psychological-operations experts, media experts, infrastructure experts, and emergency aid experts, to name but a few. These types of people normally don't get in front of the boss. The jobs they do are not cool or sexy.

Insurgencies are won by frontloading operations with things like civil affairs teams to help with new governments, laws, traffic control, and psychological operations teams. All of these can be used to help design effective public relations programs to get the government's message out and counter what the guerrillas are attempting to spin. You have to have absolute control of the public communications system if you want to even begin to defeat an insurgency. Television, radio, and newspapers all must be controlled by the good guys. The government must be able to immediately get the honest, always correct, message to the people who are in the middle of the insurgency. Rumors can be deadly to a movement or a government. Controlling the airwaves gives a government a fighting chance against the insurgents. Get the people's attention and tell them what you want them to know.

All wars are ugly, but guerrilla wars are particularly ugly. They are not for the weak of heart. They require us to play by the new rules. And here are those new rules: There are no rules except winning. If you want to win in an insurgency, you must think like a guerrilla fighter. The only thing that the Geneva Conventions are good for in a guerrilla war is prosecuting war criminals after the conflict has ended. They matter little during the fight. Our soldiers have to be given the freedom to move now, shoot now. They don't have that authority right now, and the result has been the tragic loss of life we have witnessed in Iraq.

Killing is a major part of a guerrilla war, but it has a twist. You always have to think how each of the killings will help your cause. You have to have a psychological plan for every time you decide to take aggressive action. If we understand that guerrilla wars are won in the mind as well as with violence, then killing and maiming must have a purpose. Sometimes not killing will have a more powerful effect than using a bullet. We have to be willing, on occasion, to let bad guys walk in order to turn them and use them for our own purposes. Kill them later.

Counterguerrilla campaigns sometimes require us to employ methods as sickening and soul-destroying as those used by the guerrillas. This will take moral men and women in the extreme, who know the price they are paying and do it anyway. One tactic is to kill guerrillas but then plant clues to make them think they are being offed by those inside their own organization: notes, pieces of clothing, fingerprints, and so on. A more insidious trick is to leave bullets around that explode in the guerrillas' guns. Poisoning the guerrillas' water supply works well too. And then there are snipers. You kill a few people carrying guns on a street, and no one knows who killed them except you and your sniper team. I guarantee you, no one will go on that street for a while. Hell, no one will go near the neighborhood for a while. The message is clear: "Don't come out of your holes or we will kill you." We want the guerrilla crapping-in-his-pants scared.

If we agree that guerrilla wars are won in the mind—and I assure you, they are—let's figure out what the guerrilla needs, uses, and believes in. Then let's use all these things against him. Take the fight directly to him. Kill a religious leader while he is preaching hatred or advocating killing soldiers. This is not a free-speech issue; it is a survival issue. When one of your own is killed or injured and someone claps, laughs, or wants to dance in the streets, shoot the son of bitch where he or she stands, sits, or kneels.

Guerrillas need money to work. Much if not all of their funding comes from crime. Take away the ability to carry on the profitable criminal activity and you take away the guerrillas' ability to wage war. The drug trade is pervasive throughout the Muslim world, but we do know a couple of things. To make heroin you need poppy. Care to guess who produces more poppy than any country in the world? Afghanistan. In fact, Afghanistan accounts for three-quarters of the world's poppy production. A friend of mine who returned from there in 2004 told me that he drove for four hours across just one poppy field. *Four hours*—that is some serious produce. We have controlled Afghanistan since late 2001. So if we know that guerrillas are using illegal drug money to support their operations, and we know that Afghanistan is the largest producer of an illegal substance, you would think that we have put a huge dent in the bad guys' ability to make heroin. You would be mistaken. Poppy production has shot up since we took that country back from the Taliban and al Qaeda in 2001. Our own State Department admitted in the fall of 2004 that it expected poppy cultivation to increase 40 percent from the previous year. And according to the Drug Enforcement Administration, opium production in Afghanistan more than doubled from 2002 and 2003.

You may now stand up and throw large objects at the wall, because this is outrageous and it must stop now. We need to drop an incendiary bomb on a poppy field. Hell, we need to drop bombs on all the fields. We should do it now and do it often.

When it comes to supporting an insurgency, money is the root, the soul, and the epicenter of all evil. Jesus Christ and all the saints in heaven, get the money out of the hands of those who would do us harm—dry it up, steal it, move it by computer, drive a truck to the back window and hook up a rope to drag the safe down the road, or whatever else it tales. If we do this, a couple of things will happen. The guerrilla will now be forced to slow down. The terrorist now has to go find more money, and while he is doing that, he will not be able to harass us. We might even get lucky when he is trying to get more money; because we are smart and can figure out how he operates, we might catch or kill him in the act.

A guerrilla war may be the most dangerous kind of war we fight; so many things can go wrong! Turn on your TV sets. Pick up a paper. Watch and read what happens when you don't prepare for a guerrilla war. In Iraq, at the time of this writing, no fewer than twelve cities are in flames, and we have just lost thirty-two American lives and more than a hundred Iraqis in a single day. And this is a typical daily news report from a country where we won the war more than a year ago. We have well-trained Marines dying in ambush by the hands of guerrillas who are hiding in cemeteries and in mosques. There are more than 2,500 attacks on coalition forces a week. This is now. This is real and it must stop.

We have to strap on the all-day feedbag. We can and must learn how to win a guerrilla war. But it takes real political courage, unconventional military thinking, and a citizenry that is fully informed and supportive. When you are in a guerrilla fight, you have to be brutally honest with your citizens. Because of the unpredictable nature of a guerrilla war, the good guys will have bad days. An engaged press corps and an ethically centered government will have prepared its citizenry for these bad days. If our government doesn't tell the truth about the challenges we face, and if the guerrillas achieve some success, our leaders could find themselves watching from the sidelines, paying consultants to figure out what an eighth-grader knows—that lying is one thing, but lying and getting caught . . . well, that is time to find a new job.

Guerrilla wars are in our present and our future. As we take this current fight for our existence to those who would kill us, we are going to see guerrilla fighters again and again. Applying the principles in this book guarantees that the other son of a bitch dies for his beliefs and that you don't die for yours.

CHAPTER 8

What Can *We* Do?

I do a lot of traveling, and wherever I go, those who recognize me from the Fox News Channel ask, "Colonel Hunt, how did we get in this mess?" "What is the game plan?" "What should I really be afraid of here at home?" "How can we catch the bad guys and still safeguard our civil liberties and the American way of life?"

But I'm struck most by another strain of questions that always comes up: "What can I do to keep my family safe?" "How can I help?" "Is there anything I can *really* do that will make a difference in this war?" Most Americans have been asking questions like this, but so far, answers haven't been forthcoming. Right after 9/11, Americans went to their local blood banks to give blood, gave money to the Red Cross and other charities, and did whatever else they could to pitch in. Most of us didn't know what else to do, especially since our leaders told us the best thing we could do was to go back to living our normal lives.

But there is something you can do to help us win this war. You can do it starting right now. You've got to know up front that it's not exciting stuff. It's not sexy. No one will ask you for your autograph or want your picture. It does not involve carrying guns or jumping out of airplanes in the middle of the night in some foreign land. But what you can do is every bit as important as all those things. It will require real thinking, real commitment, and some sacrifice and pain.

Face Reality

The first thing you have to do is to face the facts. I demonstrated in an earlier chapter that the United States did little to nothing before 9/11 to counter the growth of terrorism. Our inaction gave the terrorists opportunity to build. So the bad guys have really had decades to hide weapons, establish cells, and buy off entire countries. Therefore, all thoughts of a quick and easy fix during this war need to be forgotten. To be in a position to affect this War on Terror, you have to accept the fact that we are fighting a war unlike any we have ever fought in the past and that this war will be part of our lives for many years—for the next thirty to fifty years, if not longer.

We got tired of war in Vietnam, in Korea, and in two World Wars. Vietnam was so different because of the view we had every night on our TV. It almost broke our spirit to fight at all, even when war was our only avenue. This war we fight now is far worse than Vietnam. Why? Well, first, we got clobbered here at home, and second, our communications are so good that we are watching battles in real time, right now. Real-time war on American TV is like viewing a car chase on steroids. And this fight will only get uglier. People are going to die; many will be bad people, but some will be our soldiers and spies. The terrorists are using fourteen-year-old boys and girls with explosives strapped to their bodies. We have to be able to accept this evil and fight it to the death—their death. We must develop a stomach for the ugliness. We need to learn how not to flinch.

We need to understand the central premise of this war: the bad guys are not going to stop unless we kill them, right now, over there on their own turf. Our mind-set has to be tuned to this central premise and it must remain there for the long haul. This is not a television war; it is a real war. Real wars are long and unpredictable.

Become Informed

Why have we remained almost completely ignorant of these Islamic terrorists and the reasons for their jihad? There is a glut of information available. We know who the leaders of the terrorist organizations are; in fact, we know so much that people have written full-length biographies on them. We know how these religious fanatics interpret their religious doctrine, the Koran. We know the fighting tactics that these zealots will employ; we have their manual. So lack of information is not the problem. But the way we, the American people, receive this information leaves a lot to be desired. Much of what we are told comes to us in the form of thirty-second sound bites. Our media asks for answers and allows the expert to make his/her argument in nine seconds—usually while the guy conducting the interview is yelling over what the expert is saying. If you want to help, if you want to ensure success against the bad guys you can't rely exclusively on this sort of superficial information. We can all agree that 99.9 percent of us are not going to be involved even in the slightest way in catching a terrorist. So the least we can do to support the guys and gals who parachute into enemy territory or take on radical insurgents is to get off our asses and do the basics: read, watch, and listen. Become informed.

Okay, I can hear you saying, "What the hell does that all mean?" It means pick up the damn newspaper. Watch the news. Read, read, and then read some more. Pick up the *Economist,* the *International Herald Tribune,* the *Christian Science Monitor;* in other words, read as many publications with as many different points of view as you can. Read those things that offer a more in-depth explanation than the thirty-second explanations we are used to. Become informed.

Talk, argue, ask questions, and get involved with this. The War on Terror is, after all, the most compelling and critical subject of our day. If we do this, it is a way we can influence our very survival. You think I'm overstating it a bit? The hell I am! This is World War III. Become informed.

We must pay attention to our world. Our citizens are some of the most uninformed on the planet. Most of us when given a map of the Middle East couldn't identify one of the countries located in the region. In a recent survey, only 52 percent of those questioned knew who Yasser Arafat was. Seems to me this means we are in trouble. Hell, just yesterday I saw a report on TV that said when six people were asked to name the vice president of the United States, they couldn't do it. Come on, people! We are better than that, or at least we should be. We cannot stand in the face of the storm waiting for someone to tell us to come in from the damn rain. We must demand that our elected officials protect us. In order to do that, we will, at a bare minimum, need to know who they are. As a nation we must change on this note; we can't remain ignorant, because our destiny requires that we become informed.

Get Angry

Get angry! Stay angry! Anger is the fuel that you and I need to accomplish what we have to do. We need to feed ourselves with this fuel. Don't forget what the terrorists did to us—ever. You must remember how you felt. I am suggesting that the war against terrorism cannot be won without all of us feeling a bit uneasy, a bit afraid, and a whole lot angry.

You must be pissed at the very thought that we were attacked. Attacked? We weren't merely attacked, we were slaughtered by the thousands. A bunch of religiously fanatical Arab men—fifteen of whom were from Saudi Arabia—used our own airplanes to kill us. They murdered our fathers, mothers, sons, and daughters. You re-

ally have to stand up and scream when you remember the murder of
our brave policemen and firemen whose only desire on 9/11 was to
save lives. They actually ran into a bombed-out building while the
survivors ran for their lives. Dead, so many dead.

Remember the funerals for the firemen and policemen, the funerals at the Pentagon and in Pennsylvania, the faces of their children, their mothers, and their fathers. Remember how they played
"Taps"; that always gets me—it is the sound of a river of tears. Remember all of it; don't let it go. We will need this anger and past
heartache to keep up this fight, to do what will be necessary for a
long time: killing terrorists.

Demand Accountability

How about we demand accountability from our leaders? Because
those in charge are politicians, who by their very nature are some-
what self-serving and want you to reelect them, they need to know
that this stuff matters to us. They need to know that we won't send
them money, won't vote for them, and won't like them if they don't
do their jobs. They need to know that our safety and well-being are
more important than their jobs. Don't just tell them; write to them,
e-mail them, and yell—yell a lot. This squeaky wheel needs oiling,
and it needs oiling now. We have the power to do this.

Those of you who donate money to parties, candidates, and
causes can do what every lobbyist and every large corporation does:
Demand. Demand access to the decision makers. Demand participation in decisions. I know, I know, the politicians will say, "It ain't so,"
or "No one buys me." But we all know how politics really works.
Money and blocks of deliverable votes buy things, end of story. So the
next time someone asks you for a $10 or $10,000 donation, tell them,
No, not until you sit down with us and answer some questions. And you
don't necessarily have to be a big-pocket donor to make a difference.
These guys have staffs that tell their bosses when people are upset.

When enough of us get going and make a lot of noise, they have to respond. When you have their attention, ask the real questions and expect honest answers. If you're not satisfied, keep asking the questions—and don't let go of your money. Ultimately, we're demanding safety, competence, and protection.

Hell, our tax dollars are paying for all the things that ensure the safety of senators and congressmen and their families. Who is protecting *your* family? Well, politicians would tell you that the police department and fire department and hospitals are. They'd say that the federal government, the Army, Homeland Security, and the CIA are protecting the American people. Damn it, demand to be as safe as our political leaders. It's our money, and we're supposedly the ones the government is protecting. That should count for something. Do you feel protected? My God, ride any train in this country—any train—and see how vulnerable we are. Penn Station, South Station, Union Station—these are all huge targets and extremely open and vulnerable. We have spent billions since 9/11 trying to upgrade security on our failing airlines, and another few million on protecting our railroads. Are these places safer? No, not much. It is still possible for someone to take control of a plane and fly it into a building.

And those aren't the only places where we're vulnerable. Ask mall security why they let cars park so close to the building. Ask why there are not metal detectors or bag checkers in large public gathering spots. What do you think would happen to our economy if ten two-person teams of terrorists walked into ten upscale malls in ten different cities in ten different states and blew themselves up? How about ten more teams of terrorists then going into ten grocery stores in ten more cities in ten more states and blowing themselves up? Do you think you are going to want to go shopping for baby food the next day?

These are real problems that our leaders aren't addressing. We need to demand answers. When we leave politicians and bureaucrats to their own devices, they hold hearings, generate paper, line their pockets, act important, ride in limos, hold press conferences, and spend our money. They won't do what's necessary without the American people questioning, prodding, and threatening them with the loss of their jobs. We can and should ask these and other questions. Our lives are in danger, and when we have questions, we should ask them with great clarity and emotion.

Questions about what the government is doing to protect us aren't the only ones you should be demanding answers to. Step back and ask the next logical questions: "Is this War on Terror going well? Are we doing all that we should? Are we doing it the right way?"

One of the many things we are learning from various sources is how much we still don't know. For example, why did Mohammed Atta and his terrorist buddy drive to Portland, Maine, from Boston, Massachusetts, then get on a plane back to Boston, where the 9/11 suicide flight mission to New York City departed from? We don't know. After three years and numerous investigations, we don't know. This is inexcusable and wrong. Atta didn't go to Portland for fun. Maybe he met with someone. Maybe he passed information. Maybe someone there helped him. Maybe whoever he met is still here. This is a sign that things are not going well. Those who did the investigation are not at fault here. The investigators are the very best in the world at what they do. The fault clearly lies with the terrorist supporters. We don't know because of an almost total lack of cooperation the FBI and our government received from Saudi Arabia during their investigation.

I am going to remind you of some things we learned earlier in this book. I know you won't be shocked. When the guy who is leading the war against us, Osama bin Laden, is roaming around in some cave in a country that has professed to be our ally, it ain't going well. It will go better when that son of a bitch is dead.

It is not going well when our country sends its soldiers to war without the equipment that they need to survive. Remember, that is what we have been doing with our great Reserve forces. Until recently, fewer than 60 percent had the proper body armor or vehicle armor. No sir, not going well there at all.

When things aren't going well, "we the people" must respond. We need to stand up! Maybe we can even throw something. We can scream. These are our sons and daughters, our fathers and our brothers, our flesh and blood. Demand an accounting of how they died. Never accept an answer that doesn't make sense. Call the newspaper in your town. Write letters, make phone calls, conduct Internet campaigns, yell at your congressman, call in to talk radio shows, jump up and down until someone pays attention. Keep at it until things change. We can help. We must help. We can make a difference.

A Couple of Rules

There is nothing un-American or unpatriotic about asking—hell, demanding—answers from our government. The people who will accuse us of being *un*-this and *anti*-that are the same people who did not do their jobs and allowed 9/11. These are people who would rather insult and belittle us than answer the damn questions. It's far too simplistic to say that we all should rally 'round the president, the government, the flag. What about when things are going wrong or when we are not sure whether they're going right? As I've said, when necessary, we need to demand change.

But there is an important distinction to draw. Yelling about a war is great. Actually, it is necessary before a war. The yelling helps us focus on the justification for our actions. It helps solidify support. It helps formulate policy. Yelling after a war is equally important. It allows us to explain our strategies. It helps us learn by our mistakes. It provides us with the forum necessary for accountability. But yelling during a war is not always the best tactic. War is hard work for the troops on the ground. In this war, our troops are suffering in 130-degree heat while wearing sixty pounds of gear and a damn uncomfortable helmet; they're getting shot at daily. Maybe under these circumstances, you want to shut up. Although we're talking about yelling at our policymakers, not at the brave people on the front lines, yelling at our leaders—no matter how justified—can be misinterpreted by those fighting our battles for us as well as by our enemies. Our enemies don't understand the concept of a free society that will support its military forces while criticizing its leadership.

And our troops deserve our support. Their work is keeping us safe. Their job is protecting us. They have plunged themselves into the middle of hell so that the terrorists don't come here. When we yell about the war while the soldiers are in a fight, it sounds as though we are yelling at them. Soldiers need letters from home, a cold beer, a place to sleep, the knowledge that their peers respect them.

So here is the first rule: When the bullets are flying, shut up. Bullets stop flying, start yelling. Demanding answers is essential, and questioning our leadership's effort is fine as long as we are careful to couch our remarks in words that show this is not about those soldiers fighting.

Here is rule number two: When it is absolutely necessary that you yell while the bullets are flying, you never yell at the soldiers. First off, they have real guns and can hurt you. But more important, they are fighting for you. So shut up or say thank you. And if you have to yell in the middle of a war, yell at the politicians all day, but never yell at the soldiers.

And here is something else you can do to make sure we keep this war on the right track, and again it is not easy stuff. We have to be very careful not to turn against our own country in this fight. Doing this will not stop the terrorist attacks that surely are being planned against us. I know Muslims attacked us. I know this is a religious war. But those in this country legally, those *American citizens* who look "different," are not the enemy just because they look the way we imagine Arabs or Middle Easterners look. Turning on them can cause us to lose valuable assets in this war and gets us nothing except divisiveness within our own population. As Americans we cannot tolerate bigotry and discrimination against fellow Americans; if we do, we weaken the things that make this country great.

The Patriot Act

I've made a big point in this book of screaming about how we can't shy away from this fight, how our leaders can't worry about hurt feelings and must do everything in their power to achieve a single objective: killing the terrorists. And that's all true. Our government must be focused on the critical tasks at hand; our leaders need to be watching for the right opening to strike, and when it presents itself, strike hard. But at the same time, we have to remember that we can't sacrifice what makes the American system great—the rights and liberties our founders ensured us.

This brings us to the topic of the Patriot Act and civil liberties. We have to use the Patriot Act to make our country less vulnerable to attack, but all of us should have problems when it comes to the act. While our police did need some help with the bad guys, we went too far and made it more complicated for Americans to maintain their rights. Read the Patriot Act. I did. It is monkey-butt ugly and would piss off any and all of the founders of American democracy. The basic credo of American democracy can be found in our Constitution and the Bill of Rights. The men who fashioned these documents made sure they were written to be understood. In contrast, the politicians who authored the Patriot Act made sure that their language was so convoluted as to be indecipherable. The Patriot Act is written in such a way that only a lawyer with a thesaurus in each hand can understand it. It was a deliberate attempt to circumvent our freedoms.

The Patriot Act is confusing and open to far too much interpretation. Plus it gives all the power to one side. I understand that we are in war and we want to kill the bad guys, but we cannot lose that which makes us Americans, that which makes us great—our civil liberties. Surely we want to make the job of the police one that can be accomplished. Untie the cops' hands, absolutely. Make it possible for them to do their jobs, yes. But the Patriot Act in its present form *must* be modified to protect the civil rights of Americans and to target those from other countries who have not earned the protections of our Constitution. You only earn those protections through citizenship. We'd best adjust this document so that we don't lose more in this war than we already have. When one of our citizens, no matter how bad, does not get treated like an American, we are already sliding down the slippery slope to becoming just like our enemies.

We should not be putting citizens of this country in jail without access to a lawyer and without formally charging them. But that is exactly what we did in the case of Jose Padilla, under the auspices of the Patriot Act. Padilla, an American citizen, was arrested in May 2002 and as of this writing has been incarcerated for well over two years *without being charged*. I get the fact that Padilla was picked up at O'Hare Airport in Chicago after returning from Pakistan and that he was allegedly planning to set off a dirty bomb sometime in the future. He could be a very bad guy. Well, okay. Then why didn't our government say so? Why didn't it prosecute him? Padilla is, by right of citizenship, entitled to a trial. Prove his guilt. And then execute his ugly ass. Holding Padilla in a Navy prison without charging him has made us look petty and guilty of civil rights violations. We are a noble country with morals and ideals; we have laws that obligate us to be the best, even when we don't want to. We need to act noble even in this hour of need. Once again, Padilla may be the devil incarnate; if he is, then let us try him, convict him, and send him to burn in hell. But don't forget the fair trial by a jury of his peers. (Interestingly, our courts do not seem to be indicating support for the act. As this is being written, courts are overturning arrests similar to Padilla's.)

I understand what drove our government to adopt the Patriot Act. We are scared. Better safe than sorry. I got that part. But what if the next guy in office decides that blue-eyed blondes need to be detained without a lawyer, or the next attorney general does not like Catholics or Southern Baptists? Not possible? Well, we didn't think it was possible to wake up one morning and watch planes fly into buildings. Our government, in its best effort to protect us, has started to take away things that make us Americans, and we are okay with it because they are only arresting minorities, Muslims, other people. Hey, wake up! Arresting is okay. Prosecuting is okay. When we find an American guilty, throwing him or her in jail is great. Executing his or her sentence with extreme prejudice is terrific. Hell, if we have terrorists in jail, I'll be happy to pull the trigger when it is time to kill them. But only if you follow the steps we just outlined. I didn't invent this; it is American law and cannot be circumvented at the whim of a sitting administration.

If you are angry, or a little afraid, because our government officials did not protect us on 9/11, why on earth would you give the same government more power and access to your life without at least questioning it? Don't allow the government to deny any American his rights without a fight. We cannot turn inside, against one another. Turn outside. Turn against the murderers. Commit to being mad-dog ugly about "them" over there. We must preserve us, this life and this country. Pay attention—this is the only chance we are going to have to get this right. I may not know much, but I know this is important.

Frankly, there's an even more practical reason to consider the Patriot Act a problem: It has created an unneeded distraction at a time when our government can't afford any diversions. Here are some simple rules to live by: Don't piss on Superman's cape, don't spit into the wind, don't pull the mask off the old Lone Ranger, and don't distract a bureaucracy when it is in a fight. In the War on Terror, we must have all government offices focused on two things: protecting us and killing terrorists. They *cannot* be screwing around with controversies involving our own countrymen. If we have American citizens in jail being denied due process, our leaders constantly have to answer questions concerning the apparent violation of rights. That is a foolish and unnecessary distraction from the main tasks in the War on Terror, and it must stop. And look at what happened in the Jose Padilla case: Our former attorney general, who should have been fighting the fight against terrorism, actually called in from Moscow to hold a press conference in which he took credit for catching a _suspected_ terrorist. We need to stop having press conferences declaring some arrest or victory that might not even be a victory for all we know. That's another needless distraction.

Besides, when we're assessing the Patriot Act, we need to understand that we already have most of the laws we need to fight terrorism in the United States. The laws in this country when printed would fill up a football stadium. We need our laws simplified, not made more complicated. So if a bad guy has three phones, one warrant should cover them all; we should not have to stand in line to get three separate pieces of paper signed. That is just plain stupid and a huge waste of time. Streamline the process and cut through the bureaucracy. We also need to enforce our laws better. We need more training, more money for our police, and better leadership from the guys in charge. We need courageous leaders.

Giving the Proper Support

What else can you do? In addition to demanding answers from our elected officials, we also must demand that our underpaid firefighters, police officers, and emergency medical personnel receive the proper equipment and training for this new war. They are not receiving it. They must be—now. Here is why. If the fireman coming to help you goes down from a chemical attack because he does not have the right chemical suit, then you are not going to be helped. You are going to die. The same thing goes for all of those brave Americans who first respond to a crisis. Again, stand up, make noise, contact the local officials where you live and work.

We should be very proud of our government employees. Another way you can help is to say thank you to a cop or a fireman. You can write a thank-you letter to a soldier fighting overseas, and provide him with some of the stuff that makes his tour a little easier: send him phone cards, start a fund to help his family, whatever. All of this counts, all of this matters. I know, from being on the receiving end of such gestures during my years in the military. These little things make a huge difference to men on the front lines.

Many towns have websites that are being used to talk to soldiers serving in Iraq and Afghanistan; get on them and support the guys. Get your kids' school to support a specific unit; ask them what they need and then have a drive to gather this stuff, and mail it off. It beats the candy bars and wrapping paper that the schools usually peddle, and it allows all of us to participate in this fight even if we're not in the military. Go to your local police and fire stations and see what they need. You will be surprised and so will they that you asked.

We can let a few things go to make room for this next fight. One of those things is old wars. We have to be able to forgive ourselves, our servicemen, even our politicians in order to get at the next fight. In the 2004 presidential election we witnessed renewed controversy over Vietnam. All that the attacks on both sides of this issue did was separate and divide us again. We seemed unable to focus on terrorists as we once again debated our performance in Southeast Asia. With such disputes we create imagined enemies where none exist. We need our vets working together, using their collective experience in this new war, not fighting one another.

The Ultimate Commitment

Something else we can do is accept a form of national service, as mentioned in Chapter 6. This idea has been around for a while. It goes like this: Everyone, and I mean everyone, between the ages of, say, eighteen and twenty-one, must serve his or her country. The service can be in many forms, not just military (despite what many opponents of this concept suggest). National service can be two years in Appalachia teaching school, or in Boston working at a homeless shelter, or working in the Peace Corps, or building a road in West

Virginia, or working at a veterans' hospital. You could choose how you would serve, but serve you must. Many, of course, would choose military service, and this national service program would address our shortage of soldiers. This service would be for men, women, those in wheelchairs, those with medical conditions, and everyone else; a few exceptions might be necessary, but there would be absolutely no deferments.

If we institute such a national service program, young men and women will finally understand what citizenship means, what sacrifice means, what working together toward one goal means. We will get a generation that understands what this country means. This one is the most difficult commitment we can make, but it is also the most meaningful. National service would bring us together as nothing else could. It would guarantee our success. A nation that has all its citizens committed through demonstrated service would be invincible. It is one of the most important reasons that Israel has been successful against such overwhelming odds.

Do You Care?

There was a time in our history, not so long ago, when we would have known what to do when faced with an enemy. We would have done all the things I have mentioned here and more. We would have banded together and fought to protect our country and our way of life, and we would have done it unquestioningly. But we have become lazy. We have become a nation of fast food and the nine-second sound bite. We have become complacent—accepting easy answers because the more difficult ones require effort and hard choices.

Well, the road ahead is filled with only tough choices. There are no easy ones in this War on Terror. We will have to make sacrifices. Our sons and daughters will go to places on the other side of the world to pick up a gun and fight, and some will not come back. Our taxes will go up, because this fight will not come cheap. Our way of thinking will be challenged at every turn and we will have to look inside and take a stand without fear of what the rest of the world might think.

We are the greatest nation in the world. We are a great people. When things go well for too long, we sometimes lose sight of the fact that the things we have, the things we take for granted, are those things that people around the world are routinely denied. September 11 was a reminder to us that we cannot take our freedoms, our rights, or our responsibilities for granted.

You and I are "we the people." We must actively participate in the decisions that we will face in the coming days, weeks, and years. The decisions that will determine the outcome of this war. The decisions that will determine how many will die here at home, and how many will die in foreign places. The decisions that will determine whether we remain the leader of the world or take our place among those nations that offer less to their citizens.

So yes, there are things you can do to help win this fight. There are things you can do to protect your family. You have made a start by picking up this book. Now it's time to take the next step.

The next step is to determine what the hell you care about. Are you okay with the fact that the organization created to make our airports safe, the Transportation Security Administration, has laid off security officers? Do you care that you still can't take a piss when your flight is thirty minutes out from Washington, D.C., because you could be a terrorist? Do you care that the same flight is probably not protected by an armed sky marshal because we don't have enough of them?

Do you care that we sent guys to war in Iraq without the right flak jackets or armored protection in their humvees? Do you care that National Guard and Reserve forces were assigned to twenty months' fighting in Iraq right after getting back from thirteen months straight in Bosnia? Do you care that we have sent guys from all the branches of armed services back to Iraq and Afghanistan for a third tour? Do you care that no one has been fired for not seeing 9/11 coming or for missing the WMD issue in Iraq? Do you care that Afghanistan is allowed to produce 75 percent of the world's poppy even while we control the place?

I think you care. I think most Americans care. I think together we can right these wrongs.

We have had more than a dozen different congressional committees—six for the House, seven for the Senate—investigating, questioning, and commenting on 9/11. We had commissions, twenty months of testimony, and more than nine hundred witnesses. Clearly that was not enough. We seem to think we need more talking before we do anything. Anyone care about that? We have senators announcing sweeping changes to our national intelligence community on Sunday television shows. They threaten the dismantling of the CIA. They offer this quick fix without a consensus of their fellow senators, or the White House. Do you care about this?

In the middle of our nation's fight against terrorists on many fronts, we descended into another full-throated debate about Vietnam, a place that won't let us go. We can't do both; we have to let one go to get at the other. How is that one for an attention getter?

Now you know what you can do. Now you know what needs to be done. So get up off the couch, grab a congressman by the tie, and get going.

CHAPTER 9

We're Still Not Getting It Right

After all you've been through in this book, after all of the things you've heard and been able to picture in your mind's eye, it is reasonable, as we approach the end, for you to want to know if we are getting it right. So what do you think? How are we doing in this fight? Since we were attacked in 2001, we have gone on the offensive in Afghanistan and Iraq, and at least three separate committees have investigated to death the question of how we got here. So, as my teenage son would say, "What's up?"

Even after all that has happened, even after we have learned a great deal, sadly, we're still getting a boatload of things wrong. "How do you know that?" you might ask. Fair question. Let's take a look.

One of the major issues with security in this great nation is how we accept or process visitors, and specifically, how we prevent bad guys and others from illegally entering our country. The key question is, How can our nation prevent terrorists from using our borders, our airports, and our seaports like a turnstile? We of course have to use our intelligence agencies and police organizations to determine who the killers are, who the bombers are. Our intelligence agencies do their homework, and we check our information and say, "Yup, he's a bad guy, put him on the list."

Simple enough, especially with our technology today, which could track a fly as it buzzes around the world. But despite our extraordinary technical capabilities, we don't seem to be able to get our heads out of our asses when it comes to watch lists. Thanks to— here we go again—ridiculous government bureaucracy, the whole process starts to go to hell. We might be able to figure out that we want to put a bad guy on the list of people we don't want to let into this country, but our government keeps no fewer than *twelve watch lists* that we can choose from. Mind you, not one consolidated list; that would be too easy. No sir. That would be *twelve*. Truly unbelievable.

It's not that the bureaucrats haven't made promises. In his National Strategy for Homeland Security, published in July 2002, President George W. Bush said, "We will build and continually update a fully integrated, fully accessible terrorist watch list." In April 2003, then–Homeland Security director Tom Ridge told the Senate that his department was "accelerating consolidation of watch lists." Almost a year passed, and then Ridge told the Senate Governmental Affairs Committee that merger of the watch lists would be completed by the end of the summer of 2004. Summer came and went, and the lists still had not been combined.

At the very least we could expect the twelve watch lists to be consolidated within one agency, such as the U.S. Citizenship and Immigration Services (formerly the Immigration and Naturalization Service) or its parent organization, the Department of Homeland Security. But even that hasn't happened. In September 2003, President Bush ordered everyone to work together to create a master list of "known and suspected terrorists." Well, more than a year passed, and it still hadn't been done. Even individual agencies kept multiple lists.

Look, this is not hard. Carry the damn list to the other offices.

Copy the other lists. Send an e-mail. Write it in holy script or rent a plane and write the names in the air, but for crying out loud, get this one right.

At the same time we can't check the list for actual terrorists, we are preventing well-known senators from boarding planes. In 2004, Ted Kennedy, senior senator from Massachusetts, encountered hassles when ticket agents refused to allow him onto a plane that he had been taking back and forth between D.C. and Boston for forty-two years. Why was he prohibited from flying? It turns out that a suspected terrorist was using the name Edward Kennedy as an alias. Okay, so checking everyone with the name Edward Kennedy makes sense, but at some point the ticket agents should have been able to confirm that this was in fact the long-tenured Democratic senator, especially after he said, "Look, I am Senator Edward Kennedy. Here is my ID. Here is my fat face. See, it is me." You can imagine what happened after Kennedy got stopped at the airport. The senator's staff jumped on this, and the Homeland Security Department was flooded with e-mails, threats, and letters. Tom Ridge, the director of Homeland Security at the time, called the senator and apologized, as did Asa Hutchinson, Ridge's number two guy. Hutchinson assured the senator that they would take care of the problem immediately.

But the problem wasn't fixed immediately. In fact, it took weeks for the Department of Homeland Security to clear up all the confusion with the senator and the watch lists. Airlines screwed with Kennedy on at least four other occasions over a period of a few weeks. And Kennedy is a very powerful man in D.C. He has clout. He has money. He has a huge staff. And he is, after all, a *Kennedy*. How come he got screwed like this? If a Kennedy can't get this type of problem fixed, care to guess how you or I would fare if that happened to us?

So for those out there who say that the watch list issue is being fixed, tell them about Teddy. What happened to Kennedy is just plain wrong, and it highlights the problems of bureaucratic incompetence in our government. Not surprisingly, this major screwup occurred under the Department of Homeland Security, which has become a disaster area.

Embarrassments

One of the things that we seem to be most proud of since 9/11 is that we have improved our airport security operations. I mean, we now have long lines, two-hour waits, and more metal detectors, so security *must* be better, right? Well, the Transportation Security Administration employees are clearly a cut above the former private security guards that were everywhere in our airports before 9/11. But the bad news is that our security still has too many gaps in it.

You can rest assured that we are still not getting it right when it is against Transportation Security Administration policy for an airline to have two people of the same ethnic background interviewed simultaneously. This regulation exists because to pull two Arabs out of line might be perceived as discrimination. Discrimination? *Discrimination?* Arab extremists have been killing us for more than twenty-five goddamn years and we can't interview two passengers that have the same ethnic background? But we *can* keep Teddy Kennedy from boarding a plane? Tell me, how the hell does that make sense?

You can also be pretty sure we are not getting it right when people begin to play politics with the War on Terror. Listen, we have a 500-page report that took twenty months to finish, from a committee that heard testimony from more than nine hundred witnesses, recommending changes that *must* be made to our intelligence community. So what did our government do? The officials in charge of our security did what every damn institution does when faced with a demand for action. They formed yet another committee, but this time they called it a task force. The task? To study the report. So ten more government workers and political appointees have been taken from their day jobs for twenty more months, and when they are finished they will prepare . . . *another report*! This is business as usual. It didn't work before 9/11 or before the Iraq War, and it sure as hell is not working now. You do not *study* terrorism; you fight it. Only those who don't want to do anything form task forces or committees to study another committee.

This is bad enough, but I'm afraid it gets worse. The 9/11 Commission recommended changing the committee structure within Congress to deal with our new terrorist threat. Since these changes would result in certain people losing power and influence, Congress rapidly circled the wagons. Concerning instituting these changes, congressmen said that they didn't want to move too fast—as if that were possible. So naturally they decided to hold fifteen separate hearings, sponsored by six different committees, then had a recess to figure out what to do.

Hey, Congress, pay attention! The 9/11 Commission already told you what changes need to be made. Don't study it; do it. Don't sit back now that you've passed a half-assed bill. Go for it. Have courage. In the end, it's not just your jobs that are at stake; it's people's lives. We are fighting an enemy that moves quietly but strikes with deadly force. We are not going to beat these guys by holding a damn meeting! All this talk about protecting the integrity of the bureaucracy makes me wonder: if a bureaucracy is so important, why don't the damn terrorists have one?

Now, of course, we have higher standards than the terrorists do. We are a nation of laws, so sometimes we do have to put the bad guys on trial rather than simply kill them. How well have we done when we've caught terrorists and brought them to trial? We have had the Patriot Act, which was supposedly designed to enable us to actually accomplish something when we put terrorists on trial. We have had righteous indignation on our side. We have had the full might of the U.S. government on our side. It should have been a slam dunk. We win—well, only sort of.

In February 2004, a federal prosecutor in a major terrorism case in Detroit took the extraordinarily rare step of suing the U.S. attorney general. Assistant U.S. Attorney Richard Convertino filed a whistleblower lawsuit in federal court alleging that the Justice

Department interfered with his prosecution of four alleged terrorists and compromised a confidential informant. He also claimed that there was "gross mismanagement" in the Justice Department's terrorism unit.

Ladies and gentlemen, can you believe that our government *sued itself*? We are at war with terrorists, and one arm of our government sues another over how some bad guys are prosecuted. Lack of cooperation was one of the key reasons cited as to how 9/11 happened. Almost three thousand people died, and we still can't work together. The embarrassing lawsuit in Detroit points to a huge gap in our fight against terrorism. Here we were, beating the bejesus out of our intelligence agencies for not talking to and not cooperating with one another, and yet at the highest levels of our government the U.S. attorney general was apparently screwing up a terrorist prosecution! The attorney general simply cannot get in the way of his own people. Those are the people trying to win the War on Terror. My God! Mr. and Mrs. America, get out the bug spray—the room needs to be fumigated.

The results were predictable. In the original Detroit case, three of the four men Convertino had prosecuted had been convicted—two on charges of supporting terrorism, the third on charges of document fraud. But several months after Convertino filed his whistleblower suit, a federal district court judge threw the convictions out. The Justice Department had actually asked the judge to dismiss that trial victory, saying that the prosecution had made mistakes in the case—in other words, blaming Convertino. As of this writing, Convertino himself is facing a criminal investigation for his handling of the case.

Whatever the outcome, the whole sordid saga proved to be a tremendous embarrassment to the United States. The Detroit convictions had been upheld as a great victory for the U.S. government in the war against terrorists. At the time, Attorney General John Ashcroft proclaimed, "Today's convictions send a clear message: The Department of Justice will work diligently to detect, disrupt, and dismantle the activities of terrorist cells in the United States and abroad." Suddenly, not much more than a year later, we were admitting that we screwed up.

So does that indicate to you that we're getting it right? I didn't think so.

Stupidity and Screwups

Good God, what else could go wrong? A lot, as it turns out. How about the color-code terror alert system? When your government is trying to appear as though it is accomplishing something, it can be amazingly creative—and amazingly stupid and counterproductive. This is a game you learn when you take a job in government; you learn to play Cover Your Ass. But at no time in our history has the U.S. government been more creative or more ridiculous than when it decided to use a color-code system to tell us if the bad guys are coming.

As you probably already know, this was the brainchild of Homeland Security. The color-code system tells us at what state of alert we are—or in plain English, it is designed to tell us how likely it is that the terrorists will attack today. We go to "heightened" stages of alert depending on the color given by our government. There is absolutely no point to this exercise, with the possible exception of employing someone's nephew and giving the rest of us migraines. Nothing within this color-code system will make me safer, or more aware of anything except the damn color. I'd feel safer knowing that my government has decided to go after the terrorists hiding in northwest Pakistan. Instead, I get the daily bulletin on the color of the day. This is like our government in the 1950s telling us to hide under our desks in the event of a nuclear attack. Colors, duct tape, and wooden desks don't stop 10-kiloton bombs or terrorists.

So what does having a color of the day bring us? We get a series of press conferences where some government official stands up and tells us not to be afraid but we are moving to a higher level of alert because credible intelligence indicates we should do so. We get governors, mayors, police chiefs, cabinet secretaries, and others telling us that they have information; then in a quieter voice they tell us that the information is not specific enough for them to tell us what we should do about it.

In August 2004, Tom Ridge held a press conference. He said there was information specific enough to lock down three major cities and warned us that the terrorists were planning an attack to disrupt our election. Then a day later, we were told that the information was old—years old—but very specific. This is not the way to run a railroad, let alone a country in the middle of the War on Terror. We need to stop the press conferences and throw the color-code system out the window now.

Our intel guys do good work finding out information about potential threats, but our government should be focusing on getting any sort of *specific* intelligence to the public safety officials who might be affected and who can take action—police, firefighters, hospitals, and of course the military. The rest of us don't need to be subjected to countless hours of press conferences and assurances from officials who can't back up what they are telling us. We just need to know people are doing their jobs. Scrap the damn color-code system; spend the money on training and more spies. Stop the madness.

Neither the British nor the Israelis change colors. They don't even have color codes. They don't take the risk of telling the bad guys what they have learned by holding press conferences the way we do. Both Britain and Israel, which have been fighting terrorists longer than we have, spend their time and use the intelligence they gather to hunt the terrorists. They actually protect their citizens with action. Our government spends its time making it *look like* it is doing something. We don't need illusions. We need action. We need competence. We will get them when and only when we see bad guys dying in caves, rather than our people jumping to their deaths from one hundred stories up.

Even when we do have successes, our government often finds a way to blow it. For example, in the summer of 2004 the good guys—that would be us—recently captured two bad guys in Pakistan. These two clowns had information on them that confirmed al Qaeda was checking out buildings in New York City; Washington, D.C.; Newark, New Jersey; and San Francisco. This was a great intelligence get. Nice going, guys! Take a bow . . . great, now get back to work.

Unfortunately, when U.S. government officials decided to hold a pile of press conferences, they forgot to make sure everybody was on the same page. During one press conference, the U.S. attorney general talked about Mohammed Naeem Noor Khan's arrest. Khan was an al Qaeda computer expert who represented a gold mine of information on the terrorist network; we were using him to trap other al Qaeda killers and feed al Qaeda false information. In other words, we had "turned" him to work for us. Khan was a double agent. In this kind of war, having a Khan working for us is a big deal. But by releasing his name, our government threw away this major asset. It seems the guy giving the press conference didn't get the memo that said Khan was working for us. Thanks a lot.

Piss-Poor Leadership

Throughout this book I have pointed out that since this is a different kind of war, we have to alter our way of thinking. I have also said over and over that we need to use our Special Forces more, get aggressive, and get the fight over with. Well, goddamn if we did not do both those things. We decided to secretly install Special Forces inside our embassies overseas. These guys have the language skills, the operational savvy, the maturity, and the shooting skills to get at terrorists in Morocco, Zambia, and many other places. The State Department, the Department of Defense, the CIA, and the Special Operations Command held a meeting, and for once they all said, "Yup, let's do it." So we did. The idea behind this operation was and still is brilliant. Your government did a good job. Nice going, guys!

Now, as Paul Harvey would say, "And here's the rest of the story."

According to news reports, when the Special Forces got to the embassies and started to set up shop, some of the ambassadors decided they didn't like it and weren't going to allow it. Independent of the decisions made by their bosses in Washington—cabinet-level bosses, mind you—the ambassadors decided that these "killers," these soldier spies, were not going to operate in "my country." Can you believe this crap? Well, believe it. Our Special Forces are not even being allowed to leave the embassy grounds, let alone go out in the dead of night to cut the throats of al Qaeda terrorists.

The reasons for this are appalling. The ambassadors said no out of fear—fear that the Special Forces soldiers would upset the ambassadors' comfortable life of parties and trips and influence. The embassies operate on a "get along" principle. The Special Forces were there to spy and kill. Plus, they were working for Defense, not State. It was another turf war where politics and perks got in the way. These are all BS reasons. We are at war. We need all our guys doing their jobs, all the time; they shouldn't have to worry about some State Department weenie getting his pants in a twist.

My God, we finally get it right and some pencil-necked State Department slime bucket says no. This is our government in gridlock. Cabinet officials approve and coordinate a program and some ambassador gets to say no? He shouldn't get to say no. He should have to find a new job. After the things we have been through, I don't understand how we can have ambassadors who are not ready to do everything within their power to help with this fight. Unless we get the highest officials in our land to fix a simple matter of disobedience or insubordination, we are doomed to failure.

I can hear some of you saying, "So what?" or "That's how the government works." Listen, it is not just that we have incompetence at the highest levels; it is that these examples of stupidity are happening during our most dangerous time, war. You cannot simply accept that the government is the government and that the nature of the bureaucracy will never change; that attitude is a death sentence.

While bureaucratic incompetence hurts War on Terror efforts in all parts of the government, it's particularly devastating in the military. We certainly can't allow our armed forces to run this way. In an in-depth article about the war in Afghanistan based on internal Defense Department investigations, Elaine Grossman, senior correspondent for the weekly publication *Inside the Pentagon,* writes, "A new analysis of a hotly debated 2002 battle in Afghanistan contends a 'sloppy' chain of command set up by Army Gen. Tommy Franks, then the top warfighter in the region, made combat failures in 'Operation Anaconda' almost inevitable from the start. Senior Army commanders have been widely criticized by their air and naval counterparts for not coordinating effectively across the services in the days and weeks of ground-force planning that led up to Anaconda."

You might remember Operation Anaconda. We knew that Osama bin Laden and his band of murderers were holed up in Afghanistan and that the repressive Taliban regime was backing them up. So it was a no-brainer to attack Afghanistan; it was the logical first step in our war with terrorists. We thought this operation would allow us to capture or kill Osama bin Laden. Well, we didn't capture him; we let him escape. Still, our soldiers, airmen, and SEALs, along with Canadian snipers, performed miracles despite inept planning and coordination by their bosses. Grossman recounts that during a battle in Afghanistan's Shahikot Valley, "1,400 American ground forces encountered 10 times the 150 to 200 enemy troops originally anticipated" and that the "plan to use Afghan troops as the vanguard force fell apart in the opening days of the campaign when they encountered heavy resistance." The Army commander had initially been "convinced he could wrap up the fight in just a few days using ground forces with little external support" but then had to "issue an emergency appeal for air support and logistical assistance." Grossman cites a paper by an Army Special Operations officer who wrote that "ambiguous command structures established on an ad hoc basis and approved by U.S. Central Command created conditions that inadvertently excluded the Air Force from the planning of Anaconda." The Special Operations officer added, "In the rush to conduct combat operations in Afghanistan, CENTCOM lost sight of two age-old principles of war: unity of command and unity of effort."

In other words, we lost good men in this operation because our military leaders didn't talk to one another. Once the battle started and it was clear that the intelligence was wrong, the military could not react quickly enough. Once again, it was brave soldiers who made the difference, as they always do.

So what? We won, did we not? So what's the big deal? The big deal is that the officers who did not plan this operation correctly were the same people who a few months later were involved in the planning for Iraq—or rather, the lack of planning. We did not plan for an insurgency after our initial invasion of Baghdad. We did not give our soldiers the proper equipment to go into combat, like flak jackets and armored humvees; even today we have unprotected truck drivers running three hundred miles of roads lined with mines and booby traps. This isn't politics; this is life and death. Soldiers have called their families—hell, soldiers have called *me*—to ask for help. They've spent hundreds of dollars of their own money to buy stuff before they go off to war. We had soldiers training in the snow at Fort Drum who were about to deploy to Iraq, where the chances of snow are really not that high.

Partly because our leaders did not plan properly—because they didn't have the right units, the right money, and the right equipment ready—more than 1,200 soldiers have died and thousands of others have been wounded.

To understand how poor the planning was, consider the situation involving the explosives in Iraq. Explosives became a big news story (briefly) right before the 2004 election, when it was reported that 370 tons of explosives had walked away right under our noses. But that it turned out to not be quite right. In fact, we probably destroyed some of the supposedly missing explosives, but no one seemed to know how much or which stuff. After the election, the issue disappeared. But it shouldn't be gone. The truth is that Iraq had more than a million tons of explosives—and that's just the stuff we knew about. As of this writing, we have destroyed 400,000 tons—but what happened to the rest? Seems we still don't know. When preparing for the war, our leaders should have had plans in place to guard and destroy this stuff. But again, bureaucratic bullshit got in the way. We didn't secure it then, and now we won't even own up to the explosives we haven't eliminated. This stuff is killing our guys.

We had a truckload of decisions being made by a general named Franks who was seven thousand miles away. I don't think it's too hard to see why that was a problem. This and other problems have not been fixed, which explains many of the difficulties we've experienced in Iraq. As noted earlier, we folded under political pressure and pulled out of the terrorist stronghold of Fallujah even after our forces had gotten a third of the way into the city; we had to go in again eight months later. We disbanded the Iraqi army and police only to discover that we needed them to maintain security. We allowed religious nut jobs like Moqtada al-Sadr to have standing armies; then to our surprise, we wound up fighting these same armies. We kept Reserve units for almost two years straight in combat zones while we rotated the regular units out after one year. Our Defense Department and the CIA have not shared information; in fact, those in the field say that it has become open warfare between the two agencies. The war in Iraq perfectly captures the many problems that continue to plague us in the War on Terror: bureaucratic incompetence, intelligence failures (we hadn't had spies on the ground in Iraq since *1998,* which helps explain why our intelligence community screwed up so badly on the WMD issue), lack of political will, military screwups, and much more.

And Iraq hasn't been the only place where we've encountered setbacks. Within a couple of years of our initial success in Afghanistan, we were allowing the warlords to rule whole areas of that country, and it even appeared that both the Taliban and al Qaeda were creeping back in. Then, of course, there is the heroin and opium problem we discussed in Chapter 7. Because we haven't fire-bombed the poppy fields, poppy production in Afghanistan has sky-rocketed since we began occupying the country. Not good. We could bring to a halt the production of 75 percent of the world's opium pretty damn easily, but we haven't. Instead we let the drug trade flourish, thereby lining the pockets of the bad guys. All this reflects poorly on military and civilian leadership.

Our armed services, along with the national intelligence community, represent the very tip of the spear in the War on Terror, but as long as we keep seeing the kind of poor leadership and lack of planning that we have witnessed in Afghanistan and Iraq, they will continue to suffer. Of course we are winning, but we need to understand that we have a long way to go. We also can't forget that we have suffered thousands of casualties. The brave men and women who have sacrificed themselves deserve better than they are getting from our leaders.

Our military guys and gals deserve better than the stupid, limp-wristed, totally incompetent planning and decision making that we've witnessed. The troops have a name for leaders who are more comfortable at staff briefings than they are in combat: "PowerPoint Rangers," since they are really good at giving presentations using PowerPoint slides. Unfortunately, our military promotes a lot of PowerPoint Rangers—people who have political connections or who get their jobs by taking tests. But the very reason leaders exist is to serve their soldiers, to ensure that they are well trained and perfectly equipped. That ain't the case here—not by a long shot.

Conditioned to Fail

You really know you are having trouble when your own soldiers are responsible for killing or torturing prisoners. That's what has happened in Iraq. Now look, we had thousands of prisoners to look after in both Afghanistan and Iraq. We were swamped, and it is reasonable to assume that mistakes will happen. But we're talking about almost one hundred mistakes here—prisoners either tortured or murdered. Such mistakes are not reasonable.

When this story broke, we were shocked. Some of us still are. The *New York Times* ran more than forty-five front-page stories on this subject. (One questions the *Times*'s motivation here.) We have seen naked prisoners being attacked by dogs or being led about on leashes, and prisoners placed in sexual positions and photographed with a U.S. female soldier. These outrages occurred in the same prison that Saddam Hussein used to kill and torture his own people for thirty years. Abu Ghraib prison was a symbol of Saddam Hussein's worst atrocities, a place feared by every Iraqi citizen. The fact that Iraq's liberators committed such immoral acts is not ironic, it's criminally stupid.

In order for Iraqi prisoners to be molested, raped, and murdered, American soldiers had to have lost their moral compass. But the real scandal of Abu Ghraib is that the soldiers' leaders failed them. Understand, in the U.S. military, commissioned and noncommissioned officers are the people who are totally responsible for everything their soldiers do or fail to do. This is the basic tenet, the bedrock, of the military. In no time in our nation's history have there been more officers and NCOs to supervise soldiers than there are now. So we have a ton of "leaders" who should endure jail time for what we witnessed in Iraq.

More damning, at least three government investigations have indicated that the Abu Ghraib prison scandal can be traced at least in part to the lack of planning for the guerrilla war that we are fighting. Unprepared for the strength of the insurgency or the length of the postinvasion guerrilla war, for months we had only one prison guard for every seventy-five prisoners. The prison was, therefore, a terribly stressful environment. Stress unchecked can become very ugly. And here it did.

That is not to excuse the behavior of the American soldiers who abused prisoners. But if their leaders had been doing their job and sharing the danger, experiencing the same stresses and the same fears as their men, they would have fixed the conditions and made the problem go away. They would have allowed their troops to do their jobs. Instead we had uncaring, incompetent, and criminally negligent leaders. Amazingly, although the military operates on the principle that officers must take responsibility for their soldiers, we have had no officer who ranked above the Abu Ghraib prison guard stand up and say, *This was on my watch. I am responsible.* Not a goddamn one. Believe me, every minute of every day in those prisons, someone was in charge. And therefore, if something bad happened on that watch, whoever was in charge owns it. Let me tell you, if something good had happened—like, say, the guards had gotten some key intelligence from prisoners—you can bet your mother's drawers that these same poor excuses for leaders would have stood up and taken credit.

The failure of leadership occurred even at the highest levels. The investigations into Abu Ghraib reveal that senior officials like Secretary of Defense Rumsfeld "set conditions" that led to this disgrace. Gee, ya think? When you don't allow your people to say "guerrilla war," never mind to plan for a guerrilla war; when you disband the forces that can help you keep the peace; when you are so closed off from the people who work for you that no manner of discourse crosses your desk; when you take the two-star general from Guantánamo Bay who conducted extremely aggressive and highly questionable interrogation techniques and bring him to Baghdad to be in charge of the prisons; when you start hearing about atrocities being conducted by American soldiers and you do nothing about it—when all these things happen, you are setting yourself up for failure.

We need senior officials to "set conditions" that lead to killing terrorists, not harassing or killing prisoners. The prison scandal does not represent what this country stands for—*not at all.* But it does show how much work is ahead for us in the War on Terror. If we can't be organized enough, have competent leaders, have a working system of checks and balances, have a strong moral compass, and have an effective plan for something as simple as running a prison, how the hell can we hope to win this fight with organizations like al Qaeda? Or how can we handle countries with a record of duplicity like Russia? I'll tell you. We can't.

So how do we take care of the Abu Ghraib travesty? Easy one: blow up the damn prison and put the leaders who allowed this on trial—and not just low-ranking soldiers who behaved badly, but also the leaders who allowed this to happen. And in the future, in the next war, we need to remember what can happen when we don't adequately plan for things like guerrilla war and prisoners of war.

Never Give Up

In the fall of 2001, we all had flags flying from our cars and trucks, our lapels were full of American symbols, songs were written, records were made, and the television and radio were blaring patriotism. But by 2004, we had political BS—finger pointing over 9/11 and the bizarre distractions of a political campaign that focused more on what candidates did thirty years earlier than on the war in front of us. Today, soldiers are dying and bleeding, firemen are being laid off, cops are not getting contracts. And what are we doing about these things? We're not even watching. We seem not to care.

Is this us? Are we saying we give up? Are we saying we don't care anymore? Where is our fire, our rage? It is not going well when we are lethargic and passive. The terrorists are still out there. In fact, if former secretary of the Navy and recent 9/11 Commission member John Lehman is to be believed, "For every jihadist we kill or capture ... another fifty are being trained in schools and mosques around the world."

We got a tragic wake-up call on 9/11. Or we should have, anyway: I'm not sure we are heeding it. We need to be aware and just a little afraid, but never, and I mean never, complacent. We have to be up to the task of winning this war or we might as well get out the prayer rugs and figure out where Mecca is, because that will be how we will be praying if we don't win this one. Those of us who survive, that is.

I am not suggesting that this fight is hopeless. I am suggesting that we have to get up off our asses, stop figuring out if the critic is a Republican or a Democrat, and fix the problem. Our families' lives are at stake. Stop talking about the problem and get around to the getting at it. For me this is not about being right or wrong, left or right of political center. This is all about my family's safety and my country's success in the War on Terror.

It is not enough to pat ourselves on the back and say we have not been attacked in the years since 9/11 and then go put our heads in the sand again. Our ports are as open as the Mojave Desert, our trains and subways are an invitation for disaster, every mall is a potential Ground Zero, terrorists are still operating all over the globe, Iran continues in the process of building nuclear weapons, and numerous countries are supporting the terrorists. Wake up and smell the cordite. This war ain't going away. If we don't want to go away with it, and I for one don't, then we need to fix every damn problem mentioned in this book, and then fix the next ones.

Part of me wants to say sorry for yelling at you for all these pages, but I won't. You are too smart to fall for that ploy. Part of me even wants to pat your head and say, "It's okay, it will be a better day tomorrow." But nope, we're not going to have any of that either.

Here is what can be said: We are the greatest people in the greatest nation that ever was or ever will be. And we can be thankful that we have so many hardworking, honorable, brave, intelligent, great Americans who are protecting us every day. There are not enough of them, and there are certainly not enough of them in positions of power and influence. But we can be hopeful for the future.

Besides, we are getting some things right, and those things need to be acknowledged. For example:

- The city of New York is great news. Not only did it not give up after 9/11, but it got very aggressive and hired intelligence and military experts for its already great police department.

- The Department of Defense got it right and rebuilt, in record time, the destroyed sections of its five-sided building that some people call the Puzzle Palace but the rest of us know as the Pentagon.
- We formed the Transportation Security Administration in record time and at least began the long process of making our airports more secure.
- We immediately attacked Afghanistan and destroyed all of the al Qaeda and Taliban we could find there.
- We had the guts to tell the world that we have not found weapons of mass destruction in Iraq, even though we had partly justified the attack by saying Iraq was actively developing WMDs. Other nations would have tried to hide these facts to save themselves from embarrassment.
- We began to change our intelligence community with the passing of a new bill at the end of 2004.
- We are staying the course in Afghanistan and Iraq, not cutting and running.
- We have finally correctly identified the French and Germans as countries not to be trusted.
- We changed the face of the Middle East. Afghanistan now has more than 9 million registered voters, over 40 percent of them women. The Iraqi people, after suffering under a dictator for decades, are now picking their own government—something seen clearly by people in neighboring countries who also endure life under dictators. Hell, the Iraqi soccer team even competed in the Olympics, when a year earlier they were being tortured for losing a game.
- The world finally knows that the United States means what it says.

And that just scratches the surface of what we have accomplished so far. And remember, for all the bickering and name calling and blaming that's gone on in our country, we are united on more things than we are divided on.

We are a passionate and compassionate people.

We are givers more than takers.

We accept more than we reject.

And we love more than we hate.

We can accomplish and have accomplished almost anything we have tried. Our military is clearly the dominant force on the planet. We have defeated tyranny in two world wars. And we can win this great victory as well.

I am and always have been an optimist when it comes to this nation. We and only we can win this fight. No doubt, we will need a little help from our "friends." But in the final analysis, in the final battle, it will be as it always has been and, with the help of whatever God you believe in, always will be with this great country. After 9/11, we woke up and said to the terrorists, "This will not go unpunished." We have to be sure we meant it. It is my belief that if we fix the things we've talked about, the bad guys won't get the chance to whack us again. Many fixes are difficult to accomplish, but all of them are doable.

If we do these things, there we will be at the end, standing tired, bloody, yet unbowed. And under our feet will be the lifeless head of the last terrorist we killed.

AFTERWORD FOR THE PAPERBACK EDITION

Do They Get It Yet?

They Just Don't Get It was first published in April 2005, more than three and a half years after September 11, 2001. I wrote this book because I was frightened and, frankly, pissed off. Why was I upset? Because during those three and a half years we as a nation had made few significant changes in the way we dealt with terrorism. The truth is, we were no safer the day this book hit stores than we were on September 10, 2001. Because I have some experience in the terrorism business, and because I am lucky enough to be on Fox TV and radio, I hoped that the book would remind us what we *should* have learned on 9/11 and would prompt some changes. In fact, I hoped that by the time this paperback edition appeared—a year later—I would be able to say that most, if not all, of the things that I wrote about would be well on their way to being fixed.

Tragically, I was wrong.

Look around. We have spent $177 *billion* on Homeland Security since the department's inception, and yet most cities and regions haven't truly gotten their act together. What more do they need? For us to say "pretty please"?

Washington, D.C., the nation's capital, is shockingly unprepared. Washington was, of course, one of the main targets for the 9/11 terrorists, and you can be pretty damn sure terrorist groups still think it's a juicy target. So what has D.C. done? Consider this: Since 9/11, more than a hundred small aircraft have violated restricted airspace over D.C., and one huge mother of a 737 (with a governor onboard) did the same. Many of these flights have strayed within two miles of the Capitol and the White House. Pretty much every time it happens, the Capitol police run through the halls of the U.S. Capitol telling people to run. They never say where the evacuees should run *to* or what they are running *from*. Apparently, D.C. authorities feel that protecting the city constitutes whipping Congress into a frenzy and sending senators and congressmen, as well as innocent civilians, scurrying into the street. Watching Ted Kennedy run is scary, but it isn't going to stop the terrorists.

The bottom line is this: You can't just wake up one morning and be prepared to fight and kill terrorists. The terrorists have billions of dollars at their disposal and all the time in the world to plan to kill us. They use our own freedoms to kill us and have "friendly" governments helping them. If you try to fight terrorists this way, you aren't going to do anything but go to the funerals of your loved ones. Every city needs to prepare.

But after this much time and this much money, surely we are, at the very least, prepared at the federal level, right? Wrong again.

When the Federal Emergency Management Agency (FEMA) was needed most, when it should have been demonstrating the total preparedness of the U.S. government to care for its citizens in a time of disaster—whether natural or man-made—it failed. The whole world witnessed the weakness and total incompetence of FEMA— part of the useless Department of Homeland Security. Hundreds of our poorest citizens died; thousands went without food. FEMA could not even drop a bottle of water to the people in need. The government had five days' warning that Hurricane Katrina was coming and still was totally unprepared. News crews could reach those in need but the government couldn't. Can you imagine what would have happened had we been attacked by terrorists? Terrorists don't give a warning. There is no excuse for what we saw; no explanation that will suffice. Our government, at all levels, failed.

While New Orleans was a case study in failure, New York City is the opposite. New York City has done a remarkable job preparing for the inevitable. When terrorists bombed London's subways in July 2005, New York leapt into action. Leaves for municipal law enforcement personnel were cancelled, the night shift didn't go home, and a cop was put on every train. Behind the scenes, many others were working just as hard to sift through incoming intelligence and working sources—listening to the street.

New York's police commissioner, Raymond Kelly, is one of the best "top cops" in the country. Kelly has the best overall operation because he has the experience and expertise (he served as police commissioner under Mayor Rudy Giuliani in the early to mid-1990s), and also the money and the authority, to do what needs to be done. His men and women were ready to react because reacting is about preparation and leadership.

Kelly had hired his force outside of the traditional police world and made a former CIA guy one of his deputy chiefs and a former Marine another. Top Cop Kelly then went to the Israelis and said, "We need your help." The Israelis gave him access to real-time intelligence, armed tactical training for the New York City SWAT team, and training in terrorist profiling for New York detectives. Kelly also established liaison teams of New York City police officers who had lived in Israel, London, Paris, Moscow, and other hot spots. These teams can feed foreign intelligence and police information directly to the New York Police Department when there is even a hint of a terrorist strike against their fair city. Commissioner Kelly also had officers fluent in Arabic and other languages assigned to computer teams to check the Web for any sign of "chatter" indicating an attack.

Simply put, New York City has become the model for how to combat terrorism. There are some other top cops of Ray Kelly's caliber, such as Jon Greiner of Ogden, Utah, who has created the best community-active police department and formed one of the most professional mid-size city SWAT teams; William Bratton, who has proved his worth as police commissioner in Boston, New York City, and now in Los Angeles; and Kathleen O'Toole, the first woman police commissioner in Boston, who is respected by the rank and file as well as by her peers. But after that, we're looking at community after community—probably including *your* community—that just hasn't gotten it yet, despite all the money we've poured into Homeland Security. Will they ever get it?

Stupidity

So where is the $177 billion in Homeland Security money going? It would all be worth it if we were actually making our country safer—except we haven't done that. Congress, in its infinite wisdom, as well as its own self-interest, stipulated that the Department of Homeland Security's budget must be equally distributed among all U.S. states and territories. So, in 2004, the state of New York received $5.41 per capita, while that hotbed for terrorism, Wyoming, received $37.74 per capita. Every Wyoming police officer has his/her own NBC protective suit—that is, protection against nuclear, biological, and chemical radiation. But the first responders in places more likely to be hit by terrorists have one suit for the whole department—if they are lucky. Quick! Everybody move to Wyoming!

Some of the Homeland Security port-security money went to six locations in Arkansas. In addition, grants were made to Oklahoma, Kentucky, and Tennessee. Sounds good! Port security is important. Except, these states are *landlocked*! Yes, sometimes ports are on rivers, but since the ports in California and Massachusetts aren't even close to becoming secure, maybe—just maybe—we want to direct our resources to some of these places before we secure Lake Podunk in East Arkansas.

We have a new director of national intelligence. This guy was supposed to be *the* Man, *the* Boss, *the* Guy in Charge—but he isn't. He briefs the president daily, which is nice—but he doesn't have tasking authority. Why is tasking authority so important? Well, as I explained in Chapter 4, a director who doesn't have this authority can't move assets around as he needs them, doesn't control the hiring and firing of personnel, and doesn't control the money. So what does our DNI, John Negroponte, have? A fancy title, and that's all.

If that wasn't bad enough, in the summer of 2005 our CIA director, Porter Goss, said something that made us wonder whether he gets it at all. In an interview with *Time* magazine in June, Goss was asked whether he knew where Osama bin Laden was. He responded: "I have an excellent idea where he is. What's the next question?" No, I am not kidding; Goss actually made this profoundly idiotic statement! Worse, he added, "When you go to the very difficult question of dealing with sanctuaries in sovereign states, you're dealing with a problem of our sense of international obligation, fair play. We have to find a way to work in a conventional world in unconventional ways that are acceptable to the international community."

I'm not even sure what that means, although I'm pretty sure it means we don't want to piss off Pakistan by going in and killing the guy who orchestrated the 9/11 attacks. If Mr. Goss really knows where the murdering bastard is, then, by God, he should send our guys to kill the son-of-a-bitch and tell us after he has bin Laden's head on a plate. But if he is a bit tired, overwrought, under a ton of pressure, or just plain stupid, then he should shut the hell up. He is not being helpful.

How could we go more than four years after 9/11 and *still* not find a 6'4" Arab who walks around in the mountains with a portable dialysis machine and who often appears on television to tell his Islamo-Fascists where and when to strike next? We are the most powerful nation on the planet and we are allowing one guy to give us the finger.

One guy we did manage to find was Mohammed Atta—two years *before* 9/11. Only we didn't do anything about him.

Atta and three other 9/11 hijackers were identified two years before they helped kill three thousand Americans by a data-mining project code-named "Able Danger." The guys responsible for Able Danger identified four people who they determined could be a terrorist threat, dubbed them the New Jersey Cell, and recommended to the Pentagon that the information be turned over to the FBI. The higher-ups in the Pentagon decided not to share the information with the FBI and ordered most of the documentation destroyed.

Four years later, when the 9/11 Commission was investigating the colossal failure of intelligence that allowed Atta and his terrorist friends to fly planes into buildings and murder innocents, the Able Danger guys came forward and told the Commission staffers what they knew. The 9/11 Commission ignored the information and published a thousand-page report that included no mention of Able Danger.

The U.S. government, instead of pinning medals on the three competent officers who ran this program, threatened their jobs and careers and revoked their security clearances. The feds put a gag order on these guys, ensuring that they couldn't tell the press or Congress what they know. Why? For no other reason than that they would embarrass a few senior officials. Our government did this to its own, in a war in which we desperately need the type of competence and bravery demonstrated by the Able Danger guys. There are no words, no way to say this, except that we are being led by small-minded, incompetent bureaucrats who care more about their careers than the safety of this nation.

We continue to make the same stupid mistakes.

Ongoing Problems

We attacked Iraq, saying Saddam Hussein had weapons of mass destruction by the tons—only he didn't. We should all be very upset that the intelligence was so incredibly wrong. But however it happened, the president has now said that Iraq is the central front for the War on Terror. Well, okay then. We need to win in Iraq. Our guys deserve that, and if it is truly the central front of the War on Terror, then our way of life depends on it. But the unfortunate truth is that we are not doing what needs to be done in Iraq.

Don't get me wrong; we have done some great things. Our great servicemen and women have inoculated every child in Iraq. They have built thirty schools and forty hospitals. They have cleaned and revamped a sewage system that services Sadr City—a two-million-person slum. They have helped put the broken economy of Iraq back on track by making it possible for the Iraqi Stock Exchange to open again. They allowed the first free elections in that country's history. They have suffered more than 2,000 casualties and over 17,000 wounded. As I write this, the bravest men and women in the world are wearing more than sixty pounds of gear and a four-pound Kevlar helmet in 125-degree heat. It isn't the soldiers who aren't getting it done; it is the political and military leadership that refuses to do what is necessary.

While our servicemen and women are doing their thing, what pray tell are their "leaders" doing? I will tell you what they are not doing. They aren't talking about this war in religious terms, which is stupid, considering that the terrorists undoubtedly are. They haven't even *declared* war on terrorism! How do you declare war on something like terrorism? Simple: Go after any country that is supporting terrorists. Sounds crazy, maybe, but it's no crazier than the way we are acting now, where we dance around the subject and ignore the real culprits. Look at our failure to deal directly with Saudi Arabia, Syria, or Iran, who are collectively killing and maiming our men and women with impunity, and then tell me we're fighting this War on Terror correctly.

Many of the terrorists who are killing our guys are foreign fighters, not Iraqis. These bad guys sneak across the Syrian and Iranian
borders and blow up our men and women with IEDs and shoot
down our helicopters with RPGs. They kill our soldiers anyway they
can. The Saudis represent up to half of the foreign fighters in Iraq.

So naturally, we have had a meeting with King Abdullah and
told him that he needed to stop his people from doing this, right?

Well, we had a meeting. The trouble was, our president had to
wait thirty minutes for the late-arriving Saudi king. That's right, the
leader of the free world was made to wait for the ruler of a country
whose citizens are killing our soldiers and whose state-sponsored religion says, "Kill Jews, kill Westerners, and kill any Muslim who as-
sociates with a Westerner or a Jew." *This* is how we're going to win
the War on Terror?

Okay, so Iraq hasn't gone great, but at least Afghanistan has been
a rousing success . . . oh wait, maybe not. Up until the summer of
2005, we all thought we had won in Afghanistan. Supposedly, everything was under control. Then reports started to appear that the Taliban hadn't really been defeated; they had just disappeared into the
mountains, where they licked their wounds and put themselves back
together. Then we got shocking reminders that our fighting forces
are still at risk over there. In late June, a four-man Navy SEAL team
went missing in Afghanistan. The SEALs were doing what reconnaissance teams do: staying hidden and reporting back on the bad
guys. This SEAL team got in a fight and radioed for assistance; when
the response team arrived, its helicopter was shot down, killing all
onboard—eight members of a Quick Reaction Force team plus eight
Army Special Forces Night Stalkers.

So we lost sixteen great Special Operations guys trying to save
the four SEALs—three of whom we later found dead. We learned
the hard way that the Taliban have not given up, nor have they run
away. The Taliban might be a primitive people in a primitive
place—there are only two roads in the whole damn country—but
they have a history of not being conquered. With our technical help,
they have beaten one of the three most powerful armies in the world

(the Soviets), and they did so without owning an airplane. They are tough and they like to fight. They melted into the mountains for a while, but they are back and ready to fight, and they will fight well.

The Will to Win

The ongoing troubles in Iraq and Afghanistan should remind us that victory in the War on Terror has never been a simple proposition and that we must have the stomach to fight the necessary battles.

Remember, the War on Terror is a war that will take at least a generation to win. I am talking about thirty to fifty years of war. Sometimes we will fight in the shadows. Sometimes the front will be in the open, as it is in Afghanistan or Iraq. Nevertheless, it will take thirty to fifty years of nasty killing, maiming, and treacherous war to achieve victory. Here it's been less than five years and many Americans—and many leaders—seem to have lost their will to keep forging ahead. We must remember what our objective is: stopping countries from sponsoring or even tolerating terrorism. When the Saudi Arabians, the North Koreans, the Syrians, the Iranians, and the Palestinians stop using terrorism as a means to their misguided ends, victory will be achieved. When we have made these governments and the terrorists stop, then, and only then, will we have done what is necessary. When the terrorists cannot find help or a place to hide, they will be defeated.

That's a tough task, considering how many terrorist groups are flourishing around the world. Here is a list of active terrorist organizations:

Abu Sayyaf Group (ASG)
Al-Aqsa Martyrs Brigade
Ansar al-Islam (AI)
Armed Islamic Group (GIA)
Asbat al-Ansar
Aum Shinrikyo (Aum)

Basque Fatherland and Liberty (ETA)
Communist Party of Philippines/New People's Army
    (CPP/NPA)
Continuity Irish Republican Army (CIRA)
Gama'a al-Islamiyya (IG)
Hamas
Harakat ul-Mujahidin (HUM)
Hizballah
Islamic Movement of Uzbekistan (IMU)
Jaish-e-Mohammed (JEM)
Jemaah Islamiya Organization (JI)
Al-Jihad (AJ)
Kahane Chai (Kach)
Kongra-Gel (KGK)
Lashkar e-Tayyiba (LT)
Lashkar i Jhangvi (LJ)
Liberation Tigers of Tamil Eelam (LTTE)
Libyan Islamic Fighting Group (LIFG)
Mujahedin-e Khalq Organization (MEK)
National Liberation Army (ELN)
Palestine Liberation Front (PLF)
Palestinian Islamic Jihad (PIJ)
Popular Front for the Liberation of Palestine (PFLP)
Popular Front for the Liberation of Palestine-General
    Command (PFLP-GC)
Al-Qaeda
Real IRA (RIRA)
Revolutionary Armed Forces of Colombia (FARC)
Revolutionary Nuclei (RN)
Revolutionary People's Liberation Party/Front (DHKP/C)
Salafist Group for Call and Combat (GSPC)
Shining Path (SL)
Tanzim Qa'idat al-Jihad fi Bilad al-Rafidayn (QJBR)
United Self-Defense Forces of Colombia (AUC)

And that list is incomplete. For example, it doesn't include the group that attacked London in an extremely well-planned, well-financed, and brilliantly coordinated attack in July 2005. That group is new. At the time of the bombing, we had never heard of them before.

These terrorist killers have the total support of many foreign governments. In many cases, these governments are considered by our government to be *friendly* states. Yet the kings, princes, intelligence agencies, armies, and state-sponsored religions of these nations are supporting the terrorists who are currently planning and executing operations within our borders. Some of the groups are living and working directly north of us—we now know that more than fifty of these groups have an active presence in Canada. Their members can easily walk across our borders. We have done nothing to secure our Canadian borders to keep them from crossing. When we catch them crossing, we often set them free inside the United States and ask them to show up in court for a hearing. Not surprisingly, very few of them show up.

We have to take this stuff seriously. For years we have been hearing "we are taking the fight to them," "there is no place for them to hide," and one of my favorites, "this will not stand." We can no longer allow our government officials, be they elected or appointed, to get away with these disingenuous comments about terrorism. I heard these comments from my friends for thirty years leading up to 9/11. No more of this. Stop talking and start killing or you are fired.

The terrorists are not going away. The pace of terrorism recruitment and activity is not slowing down. If anything, it is speeding up. New camps are being established every day and the money is still flowing to these groups.

Another thing we must realize is that other countries that should be on our radar are not. Iran won't tell us which high-ranking al-Qaeda guys are living there. For all we know, Osama could be sitting pretty in Iran eating bonbons. North Korea is also completely off our radar screen. Both these nations have nuclear weapon capabilities.

This book was written as a case for change, but the truth is that almost nothing has changed. We are still pouring billions of dollars into our intelligence apparatus, but we haven't solved the problem of interagency cooperation or communication. I have actually had senior government employees say to me that change takes time and we, or I, should be patient. Patience my sagging ass! Must we have another 9/11 in order to light a fire under the desks of power in D.C.?

The year 2006 brings the fifth anniversary of 9/11, and we are no safer than before. If history is any indicator, al-Qaeda will strike again. And if the estimates are true, we can expect a biological, radiological, or chemical attack sometime within the next ten years. You might want to stop right now and think about what our leaders are doing to prevent this and also ask yourself, do they really get it?

APPENDIX A

The Manual of Death

Winning the War on Terror—at home and abroad—is the most difficult and important task facing us as a nation. Think about our opponents in this war: they are desperate to kill us. In case you doubt how severe this threat is, in case you think sanctions, diplomacy, and law enforcement are the way to go, in case you think we are not dealing with an evil enemy, just take a look at the manual al Qaeda has used to train its terrorists.

British forces discovered this manual during the campaign in Afghanistan, and as the translated portions shown in the following pages make abundantly clear, the manual's sole purpose is to teach killers how to kill better—to serve the ultimate goal of bringing down the United States of America. The manual also reveals that the terrorists consider *all* ways to kill us, and think deeply on how to perfect their methods.

Scary? Yes. But you need to know the truth.

The table of contents for al Qaeda's training manual tells you all you need to know about these killers. The manual contains chapters on kidnapping, assassinations, explosives, knives and guns, and torture, among other things.

UK/BM-3 TRANSLATION

[E] 19/220

In the name of Allah, the merciful and compassionate

PRESENTATION

To those champions who avowed the truth day and night ...
... And wrote with their blood and sufferings these phrases ...

-*- The confrontation that we are calling for with the apostate
regimes does not know Socratic debates ..., Platonic ideals ..., nor
Aristotelian diplomacy. But it knows the dialogue of bullets, the
ideals of assassination, bombing, and destruction, and the diplomacy
of the cannon and machine-gun.

*** ...
Islamic governments have never and will never be established through
peaceful solutions and cooperative councils. They are established as
they [always] have been

by pen and gun

by word and bullet

by tongue and teeth

To understand the nature of our enemy, you have to understand what they believe.
And to do that, you need to look at their guiding principles. These opening passages
make it crystal-clear what, and who, the terrorists are fighting for. "In the name of
Allah," they have pledged to slaughter us, to annihilate us.

APPENDIX A

UK/BM-5 TRANSLATION

Pledge, O Sister

To the sister believer whose clothes the criminals have stripped off.

To the sister believer whose hair the oppressors have shaved.

To the sister believer who's body has been abused by the human dogs.

To the sister believer whose ...

Pledge, O Sister

Covenant, O Sister ... to make their women widows and their children orphans.

Covenant, O Sister ... to make them desire death and hate appointments and prestige.

Covenant, O Sister ... to slaughter them like lambs and let the Nile, al-Asi, and Euphrates rivers flow with their blood.

Covenant, O Sister ... to be a pick of destruction for every godless and apostate regime.

Covenant, O Sister ... to retaliate for you against every dog who touch you even with a bad word.

UK/BM-6 TRANSLATION

In the name of Allah, the merciful and compassionate

Thanks be to Allah. We thank him, turn to him, ask his forgiveness, and seek refuge in him from our wicked souls and bad deeds. Whomever Allah enlightens will not be misguided, and the deceiver will never be guided. I declare that there is no god but Allah alone; he has no partners. I also declare that Mohammed is his servant and prophet.

[Koranic verses]:

"O ye who believe! Fear Allah as He should be feared, and die not except in a state of Islam"

"O mankind! Fear your guardian lord who created you from a single person. Created, out of it, his mate, and from them twain scattered [like seeds] countless men and women; fear Allah, through whom ye demand your mutual [rights], and be heedful of the wombs [that bore you]: for Allah ever watches over you."

"O ye who believe! Fear Allah, and make your utterance straight forward: That he may make your conduct whole and sound and forgive you your sins. He that obeys Allah and his messenger, has already attained the great victory."

Afterward,

The most truthful saying is the book of Allah and the best guidance is that of Mohammed, God bless and keep him. [Therefore,] the worst thing is to introduce something new, for every novelty is an act of heresy and each heresy is a deception.

UK/BM-12 TRANSLATION

Principles of Military Organization:

Military Organization has three main principles without which it
cannot be established.

1.   Military Organization commander and advisory council
2.   The soldiers (individual members)
3.   A clearly defined strategy

Military Organization Requirements:

The Military Organization dictates a number of requirements to assist
it in confrontation and endurance. These are:

1.   Forged documents and counterfeit currency
2.   Apartments and hiding places
3.   Communication means
4.   Transportation means
5.   Information
6.   Arms and ammunition
7.   Transport

Missions Required of the Military Organization:

The main mission for which the Military Organization is responsible
is:

The overthrow of the godless regimes and their replacement with an
Islamic regime. Other missions consist of the following:

1.   Gathering information about the enemy, the land, the
      installations, and the neighbors.
2.   Kidnaping enemy personnel, documents, secrets, and arms.
3.   Assassinating enemy personnel as well as foreign tourists.
4.   Freeing the brothers who are captured by the enemy.
5.   Spreading rumors and writing statements that instigate people
      against the enemy.
6.   Blasting and destroying the places of amusement, immorality, and
      sin; not a vital target.
7.   Blasting and destroying the embassies and attacking vital
      economic centers.
8.   Blasting and destroying bridges leading into and out of the
      cities.

Al Qaeda views itself as a paramilitary organization. It is waging war, even if we
refuse to participate. Just look at the missions it lays out for its terrorist operatives:
kidnapping, assassinating, blasting, and destroying.

UK/BM-15 TRANSLATION

Necessary Qualifications fro the Organization's members

1- Islam:
    The member of the Organization must be Moslem. How can an
    unbeliever, someone from a revealed religion [Christian, Jew], a
    secular person, a communist, etc. protect Islam and Moslems and
    defend their goals and secrets when he does not believe in that
    religion [Islam]? The Israeli Army requires that a fighter be of
    the Jewish religion. Likewise, the command leadership in the
    Afghan and Russian armies requires any one with an officer's
    position to be a member of the communist party.

2- Commitment to the Organization's Ideology:
    This commitment frees the Organization's members from
    conceptional problems.

3- Maturity:
    The requirements of military work are numerous, and a minor
    cannot perform them. The nature of hard and continuous work in
    dangerous conditions requires a great deal of psychological,
    mental, and intellectual fitness, which are not usually found in
    a minor. It is reported that Ibn Omar - may Allah be pleased
    with him - said, "During Ahad [battle] when I was fourteen years
    of age, I was submitted [as a volunteer] to the prophet - God
    bless and keep him. He refused me and did not throw me in the
    battle. During Khandak [trench] Day [battle] when I was fifteen
    years of age, I was also submitted to him, and he permitted me
    [to fight].

4- Sacrifice:
    He [the member] has to be willing to do the work and undergo
    martyrdom for the purpose of achieving the goal and establishing
    the religion of majestic Allah on earth.

5- Listening and Obedience:
    In the military, this is known today as discipline. It is
    expressed by how the member obeys the orders given to him. That
    is what our religion urges. The Glorious says, "O, ye who
    believe! Obey Allah and obey the messenger and those charged with
    authority among you." In the story of Hazifa Ben Al-Yaman - may
    Allah have mercy on him - who was exemplary in his obedience to
    Allah's messenger - Allah bless and keep him. When he [Mohammed]
    - Allah bless and keep him - sent him to spy on the Kureish and
    their allies during their siege of Madina, Hazifa said, "As he
    [Mohammed] called me by name to stand, he said, 'Go get me
    information about those people and do not alarm them about me.'

Among the fourteen "necessary qualifications for [al Qaeda's] members" the manual establishes, first and foremost, is that the terrorist "must be Moslem." Note also Requirement Number 4, which mandates that each al Qaeda member "has to be willing to do the work and undergo martyrdom for the purpose of achieving the goal and establishing the religion of majestic Allah on earth."

UK/BM-47 TRANSLATION

Prior to dealing with weapons, whether buying, transporting, or storing them, it is essential to establish a careful, systematic and firm security plan that plan deals with all stages. It is necessary to divide that task into stages: First Stage: Prior to Purchase; Second Stage: Purchasing; Third Stage: Transport; Fourth Stage: Storage.

1. Prior to Purchase Stage: It is necessary to take the following measures:

   a. In-depth knowledge of the place where weapons will be purchased, together with its entrances and exits.

   b. Verifying there are no informants or security personnel at the place where purchasing will take place.

   c. The place should be far from police stations and government establishments.

   d. Not proceeding to the purchasing place directly by the main road, but on secondary streets.

   e. Performing the exercises to detect the surveillance.

   f. One's appearance and clothing should be appropriate for the place where purchasing will take place.

   g. The purchasing place should not be situated in such a way that the seller and buyer can be seen from another location. To the contrary, the purchasing place should be such that the seller and buyer can see the surrounding area.

   h. Determining a suitable cover for being in that place.

   i. The place should not be crowded because that would facilitate the police hiding among people, monitoring the arms receiving, and consequently arresting the brother purchasing.

If you're worried about terrorists like al Qaeda getting weapons, you should be: they've spent lots of time perfecting the process for purchasing, transporting, and storing arms, as Lesson 7 reveals.

UK/BM-48 TRANSLATION

j. In case one of the parties is unable to arrive, it is essential to prearrange an alternative place and time with the seller.

k. Selecting a time suitable for the purchase so that it does not raise suspicion.

l. Prior to purchasing, the seller should be tested to ensure that he is not an agent of the security apparatus.

m. Preparing a place for storage prior to purchasing.

2. The Purchase Stage:

a. Verifying that the weapons are in working condition.

b. Not paying the seller the price for the weapons before viewing, inspecting, and testing them.

c. Not telling the seller about the mission for which the weapons are being purchased.

d. Extreme caution should be used during the purchasing operation in the event of any unnatural behavior by the seller or those around you.

e. Not lengthening the time spent with the seller. It is important to depart immediately after purchasing the weapons.

3. The Transport Stage:

a. Avoid main roads where check points are common.

b. Choose a suitable time for transporting the weapons.

c. Observers should proceed on the road ahead of the transportation vehicle for early warning in case of an emergency.

d. Not proceeding directly to the storage place until after verifying there is no surveillance.

UK/BM-49 TRANSLATION

e.   During the transport stage, weapons should be hidden in a way that they are inconspicuous and difficult to find.

f.   The route for transporting the weapons should be determined very carefully.

g.   Verifying the legality of the vehicle, performing its maintenance, checking its gasoline and water levels, etc.

h.   Driving the car normally in order to prevent accidents.

4.   The Storage Stage:

a.   In order to avoid repeated transporting, suitable storage places should be selected. In case the materials are bombs or detonators, they should be protected from extreme heat and humidity.

b.   Explosive materials and detonators should be separated and stored apart from each other.

c.   Caution should be exercised when putting detonators in the arsenal.

d.   Lubricating the weapons and placing them in wooden or plastic crates. The ammunition should be treated likewise.

When selecting an arsenal, consider the following:

1.   The arsenal should not be in well-protected areas, or close to parks or public places.

2.   The arsenal should not be in a "no-man's-land."

3.   The arsenal should not be in an apartment previously used for suspicious activities and often frequented by security personnel.

4.   The arsenal should not be a room that is constantly used and cannot be given up by family members who do not know the nature of the father or husband's work.

UK/BM-50 TRANSLATION

5.   The apartment selected as an arsenal should be owned by the
     Organization or rented on a long-term basis.

6.   The brother responsible for storage should not visit the
     arsenal frequently, nor toy with the weapons.

7.   The arsenal keeper should record in a book all weapons,
     explosive materials, and ammunition. That book should be
     coded and well secured.

8.   Only the arsenal keeper and the commander should know the
     location of the arsenal.

9.   It is necessary to prepare alternative arsenals and not
     leave any leads in the original arsenals to the alternative
     ones.

UK/BM-65 TRANSLATION

An Example of a Security Plan for a Group Mission (assassinating an important person)[3]: Assassination is an operation of military means and basic security. Therefore, it is essential that the commanders who establish plans related to assassination give attention to two issues:

First Issue: The importance of establishing a careful, systematic, and solid security plan to hide the operation from the enemy until the time of its execution, which would minimize the losses in case the executing party is discovered.

Second Issue: The importance of establishing a tactical plan for the assassination operation that consists of the operational factors themselves (members, weapons, hiding places ...) and factors of the operation (time, place). In this example, we shall explain in detail the part related to the security plan. The part related to operational tactics will be explained in the lesson on special operational tactics.

Security Plan for the Assassination Operation: The security plan must take into account the following matters:

    A.   The Commander: The security apparatus should not know his whereabouts and movements. All security measures and arrangements related to members of the Military Organization (soldiers, commanders) apply to him.

    B.   The Members:

       1.   They are elements who are selected from various provinces and are suitable for the operation.

       2.   During the selection process, members should not know one another. They should not know the original planners of the operation. In case they do, the commander should be notified. He then should modify the plan.

---

[3] It is possible to also say "kidnaping an important person." All security measures and arrangements in assassination and kidnaping are the same.

This excerpt from Lesson 9 lays out precautions to be taken to protect the secrecy of a "Group Mission," which is defined as "assassinating an important person."

3.   They should be distributed as small groups (3 members)
     in apartments that are not known except to their
     proprietors. They should also be given field names.

4.   During the selection process, consider whether their
     absence from their families and jobs would clearly
     attract attention. We also apply to them all security
     measures related to the Organization's individuals
     (soldiers).

C. Method of Operating:

1.   The matters of arming and financing should not be known by
     anyone except the commander.

2.   The apartments should not be rented under real names. They
     [the apartments] should undergo all security measures
     related to the Military Organization's camps.

3.   Prior to executing an operation, falsified documents should
     be prepared for the participating individuals.

4.   The documents related to the operation should be hidden in a
     secure place and burned immediately after the operation, and
     traces of the fire should be removed.

5.   The means of communication between the operation commander and
     the participating brothers should be established.

6.   Prior to the operation, apartments should be prepared to
     hide the brothers participating in it. These apartments
     should not be known except to the commander and his
     soldiers.

7.   Reliable transportation means must be made available. It is
     essential that prior to the operation, these means are
     checked and properly maintained.

4.   Interrogation and Investigation: Prior to executing an operation,
     the commander should instruct his soldiers on what to say if they
     are captured. He should explain that more than once, in order to
     ensure that they have assimilated it. They should, in turn,
     explain it back to the commander. The commander should also sit
     with each of them individually [and go over] the agreed-upon
     matters that would be brought up during the interrogation:

UK/BM-67 TRANSLATION

1.   The one who conceived, planned, and executed this operation was a brother who has a record of those matters with the enemy.

2.   During the interrogation, each brother would mention a story that suits his personal status and the province of his residence. The story should be agreed upon with the commander.

3.   Each brother who is subjected to interrogation and torture, should state all that he agreed upon with the commander and not deviate from it. Coordination should be maintained with all brothers connected to the operation.

Note: The fictitious brother who the brothers say conceived, planned, trained, and executed the operation, should be sent away on a journey [outside the country].

UK/BM-69 TRANSLATION

Definition of Special Operations[4]:

These are operations using military means and basic security. Special operations are some of the tasks of groups specialized in intelligence and security.

Characteristics of Members that Specialize in the Special Operations:
1. Individual's physical and combat fitness (jumping, climbing, running, etc.).
2. Good training on the weapon of assassination, assault, kidnaping, and bombing (special operations).
3. Possessing cleverness, canniness, and deception.
4. Possessing intelligence, precision, and alertness.
5. Tranquility and calm personality (that allows coping with psychological traumas such as those of the operation of bloodshed, mass murder). Likewise, [the ability to withstand] reverse psychological traumas, such as killing one or all members of his group. [He should be able] to proceed with the work.
6. Special ability to keep secrets and not reveal them to anyone.
7. [Good] security sense during the interrogation.
8. Great ability to make quick decisions after altering the agreed-upon plan (proper actions in urgent situations).
9. Patience, ability to withstand, and religiousness.
10. Courage and boldness.
11. Unknown to the security apparatus.

Weapons of Special Operations:
1. Cold steel weapons (rope, knife, rod, ...).
2. Poisons
3. Pistols and rifles
4. Explosives

We note that special operations include assassinations, bombing and demolition, assault, kidnaping hostages and confiscating documents, freeing prisoners.

---

[4]Review in detail the notebook: Lessons in Special Operations.

Lesson 10 instructs al Qaeda members in how to conduct "special operations"—specifically, assassinations, bombings, and kidnappings. It also runs through the importance of such missions, as well as the "disadvantages" associated with them.

222   **APPENDIX A**

UK/BM-70 TRANSLATION

Importance of Special Operations:

1. Boosting Islamic morale and lowering that of the enemy.

2. Preparing and training new members for future tasks.

3. A form of necessary punishment.

4. Mocking the regime's admiration among the population.

5. Removing the personalities that stand in the way of the [Islamic] Da'wa [Call].

6. Agitating [the population] regarding publicized matters.

7. Rejecting compliance with and submission to the regime's practices.

8. Giving legitimacy to the Jama'a [Islamic Group].

9. Spreading fear and terror through the regime's ranks.

10. Bringing new members to the Organization's ranks.

Disadvantages of Special Operations:

1. Restraining the [Islamic] Da'wa [Call] and preachers.

2. Revealing the structure of the Military Organization.

3. Financially draining the Military Organization.

4. Use of [operations] as propaganda against the Islamic Jama'a [Group].

5. Spreading fear and terror among the population.

6. The regime's safeguards and precautions against any other operation.

7. Special operations cannot cause the fall of the regime in power.

8. Increase in failed [operation] attempts cause an increase in the regime's credibility.

9. [Operations] cause the regime to assassinate the Jama'a [Islamic Group] leaders.

UK/BM-71 TRANSLATION

10. Boosting enemy morale and lowering that of the Organization's members in case of repeated failure.

11. Members of the Organization lose faith in themselves and their leaders in case of repeatedly failed special operations. The inverse is also true.

Necessary Characteristics of Special Operations:

A successful special operation requires the following:

1. A security plan for the operation (members, weapons, apartments, documents, etc.). This requirement has been explained in detail in the security plan [lesson]. Refer to it.

2. An operational tactical plan. This requirement will be explained in this lesson in detail.

Special Operation Tactical Plan:

A special operation must have stages. These stages are integrated and inseparable, otherwise, the operation would fail. These stages are:

1. Research (reconnaissance) stage.

2. Planning stage.

3. Execution stage.

1. Research (reconnaissance) stage:

In this stage, precise information about the target is collected. The target may be a person, a place, or ...

For example, when attempting to assassinate an important target - a personality, it is necessary to gather all information related to that target, such as:
   a. His name, age, residence, social status
   b. His work
   c. Time of his departure to work
   d. Time of his return from work
   e. The routes he takes
   f. How he spends his free time
   g. His friends and their addresses
   h. The car he drives

UK/BM-78 TRANSLATION

Though scholars have disagreed about the interpretation of that
tradition, it is possible - though Allah knows best - that the Moslem
spy combines [prayers]. It is noted, however, that it is forbidden to
do the unlawful, such as drinking wine or fornicating. There is
nothing that permits those[6].

Guidelines for Beating and Killing Hostages: Religious scholars have
permitted beating. They use a tradition explained in Imam Mosallem's
manuscript, who quotes Thabit Ibn Ans that Allah's prophet - Allah
bless and keep him - sought counsel when he was informed about Abou
Soufian's arrival. Abou Bakr and Omar spoke, yet he [the prophet] did
not listen. Saad Ibn Ibada said, "Do you want us, O Allah's prophet,
who controls my life? If you order us to subdue the camel we would do
it, or beat and follow them to Al-Ghimad lakes (5-day trip beyond
Mecca), we would do it, too." The prophet - Allah bless and keep him
- called on the people, who then descended on Badr. They were met by
Kureish camels carrying water. Among their takers was a young black
[slave] man belonging to the Al-Hajjaj clan. They took him [as
hostage]. The companions of the prophet - Allah bless and keep him -
started asking him about Abou Sofian and his companions. He first
said, "I know nothing about Abou Soufian but I know about Abou Jahl,
Atba, Sheiba, and Omaya Ibn Khalaf." But when they beat him he said,
"O yes, I will tell you. This is the news of Abou Soufian ..."
Meanwhile, the prophet - Allah bless and

---
[6] Al-Morabitoun Magazine, Issue No. 6

In discussing espionage, the al Qaeda manual even offers these "Guidelines on
Beating and Killing Hostages," which invoke Muslim "religious scholars" to justify
murder.

keep him -, who was praying, started to depart saying, "Strike him if
he tells you the truth and release him if he lies." Then he said,
"That is the death of someone [the hostage]." He said that in the
presence of his companions and while moving his hand on the ground.

In this tradition, we find permission to interrogate the hostage for
the purpose of obtaining information. It is permitted to strike the
nonbeliever who has no covenant until he reveals the news,
information, and secrets of his people.

The religious scholars have also permitted the killing of a hostage if
he insists on withholding information from Moslems. They permitted
his killing so that he would not inform his people of what he learned
about the Muslim condition, number, and secrets. In the Honein
attack, after one of the spies learned about the Muslims kindness and
weakness then fled, the prophet - Allah bless and keep him - permitted
[shedding] his blood and said, "Find and kill him." Salma Ibn Al-
Akwaa followed, caught, and killed him.

The scholars have also permitted the exchange of hostages for money,
services, and expertise, as well as secrets of the enemy's army,
plans, and numbers. After the Badr attack, the prophet - Allah bless
and keep him - showed favor to some hostages, like the poet Abou Izza,
by exchanging most of them for money. The rest were released for
providing services and expertise to the Muslims[7].

Importance of Information:

1.   Based on the enemy's up-to-date information, his capabilities,
      and plans, the Organization's command can design good-quality and
      secure plans.

---

[7] Abdullah Ali Al-Salama: Military Espionage in Islam, pp. 253-
258.

UK/BM-102 TRANSLATION

5- A regular letter is written with a ballpoint pen and not with
secret ink.
6- The quill or pen should be washed before and after use, and not
used with any other ink.

How to Write on Paper with Secret Ink: An innocent-looking letter
(family-personal-greeting) is written with a ballpoint pen, but within
the letter, between the lines, write the message with secret ink.

Both ciphers and code are considered important means of conveying
information without anyone other than the party to which it is sent
being able to determine its contents. Ciphers differ from code.

Ciphers: A letter, number, or symbol takes the place of another
letter, number, or symbol. The number (1), the letter (H), or the
symbol (_) could take the place of the number (3), the letter (D), the
symbol (□), or any other number, symbol, or letter. Notice that in
simple ciphers that the same number or symbol always replaces the same
letter, while in complicated ciphers, which are currently in use, the
same symbol and number replace a different letter each time.

Code: It consists of symbols, words, or groups of letters chosen to
represent or express other words. One word could have several
meanings, or could represent a complete sentence, or could be a long
paragraph according to the system used.
Scientists have proved that the ancient Egyptians, Jews, Greeks

As vicious as these killers are, do not make the mistake of thinking of them as unso-
phisticated. The entire manual, 180 pages in total, reveals how deeply experienced
they are in everything from espionage to assassination to guerrilla warfare to other
military tactics. The manual contains 14 pages on ciphers and codes alone, including
these pages, which offer a historical overview of encryption.

UK/BM-103 TRANSLATION

and Romans used ciphers and code. [They were also used] during the
Middle Ages, simple though they may have been, like simply putting
every letter in the place of the letter that followed it in a specific
arrangement of the alphabet. Specific letters only might have been
substituted. Secret writing developed and took on more complicated
forms. America entered World War II because of a secret message that
fell into the hands of British Intelligence in 1937, which was sent by
the German Foreign Minister (Zimmermann) to the German Ambassador to
Mexico. The British learned from the deciphered letter that the
Germans were planning to wage all-out submarine warfare using. The
letter contained a proposal that Mexico enter the war on the side of
the Germans, with the provision that after the victory, Mexico would
acquire Texas, Arizona, and New Mexico. The British Foreign Minister
(Balfour) turned the letter over to the American Ambassador in London,
who in turn passed it on to the White House, which confirmed the
authenticity of the letter [by checking] the [original] ciphered
letter and correlating it with the code. Consequently, America entered
the war against Germany.
Both Roosevelt and Churchill escaped death because of a German
translator's ignorance. He was deciphering an enciphered message in
Spanish. Both Roosevelt and Churchill had agreed to meet in Casablanca
in 1943. Spanish spies in Washington learned of the news, and they
sent this in an enciphered message to Hitler. The German translator
received it for deciphering, and he read the name as two words:
(Casa), which means (house), and (Blanca), which means (white). So he
translated the message

UK/BM-104 TRANSLATION

that Churchill and Roosevelt were going to meet in the White House. German aircraft were not able to penetrate American air space, and both Churchill and Roosevelt escaped.

<u>Types of Ciphers and Codes</u>: 1. Enciphering with coordinates. 2. Enciphering with symbols and words. 3. Enciphering books, newspapers, and magazines.

Secret writing must have two important elements without which it is not a true cipher. They are:

The First Element: It must have a general system on which the sender and receivers agree, and it is normally a fixed [system].

The Second Element: There must be a special key which changes from time to time. The cipher key may be composed of a number or group of numbers. It could also be composed of a word, an expression, or a sentence according to what was agreed upon among the correspondents. This key is used to decode the cipher, and is what dictates the steps required to encipher any secret letter. There are a few other elements which secret writing must have, though less important than the two previously mentioned elements.

The message must be short, sharply delineated, and understandable. The key must be changed periodically, so that the enemy does not obtain it and [thereby be able to] read all the messages.

<u>Types of Ciphers and Codes and How to Use Them</u>:

The Numeric Method: There are 28 letters in the Arabic language; they are found in this verse:

((ABJD ?W; HUI KLMN S"FX QR:T COZ VYG))

Examples of Types of Assassinations:

Elementary Operations: Crossing the Street:
1- The target is on his way to work via public transportation.
2- The moment he crosses the street to get to the bus stop or to the
main thoroughfare, the assassins, "two people" riding a motorcycle,
open fire on the target and get away quickly in the opposite direction
of the traffic.

An Actual Example of an Assassination when the Target is Crossing the
Street
This operation took place on 3/22/1948 AD in Egypt. Al-Khazander, a
puppet judge who viewed the English presence in Egypt as legal, was
the person assassinated. Al-Khazander had been issuing severe
sentences against personnel in the covert branch of the Muslim
Brotherhood [Al-Akhwan Al-Muslimin] who were involved in bombing
operations. The "Al-Khazander Assassination" operation [occurred]
during the Christmas bombings.
1- The choice fell to both Hassan Abdel Hafez and Mahmoud Saeid to
assassinate Al-Khazander. They were from the covert branch of the Al-
Akhwan Al-Muslimin, which at that time was headed by Abdel Rahman Al-
Sandi.
2- Al-Khazander was surveyed for a period days, and it was learned
that he went to the court at Bab Al-Khalaq in Cairo and returned to
Helwan via public transportation. They went ahead to the railroad
station in Helwan, [and took] the train from Hulwan to Bab Al-Khalaq
and then other public transportation.
3- They made the plan as follows:

The al Qaeda manual devotes three full chapters to instructions on assassinations.
The lesson on "Kidnapping and Assassinations Using Rifles and Pistols" covers the
history of the weapons, their advantages and disadvantages, even the proper way to
hold the guns. And the concluding section, shown here, outlines numerous types of
assassinations and how to pull them off.

UK/BM-133 TRANSLATION

The assassins, Abdul Hafez and Mahmoud Saeid, were waiting for Al-Khazander when he was leaving his house, and Hassan assassinated him with a pistol while Mahmoud was standing guard and protecting him with a pistol and percussion bombs as he got away. They escaped to the home of Abdul Rahman Al-Sandi, the chief of the organization.
After Al-Khazander left his house, walking resolutely, Hassan Abdul Hafez approached him and fired several rounds which did not hit Al-Khazander. When Mahmoud Saeid saw that, he left his place, approached Al-Khazander, seized him, threw him to the ground, and emptied several rounds into him. He and his companion left [the victim] and departed. Hassan Abdul Hafez and Mahmoud Saeid were caught because of several mistakes.

The Errors which Hassan and Mahmoud Committed were as follows:
1- There was no car or motorcycle with which to flee after executing the operation.
2- They did not anticipate the possibility of a chase after the operation. They didn't notice that the operation was carried out near the Helwan Police Department.
3- They had no training with the pistol, as evidenced by Hassan's inability to kill Al-Khazander in spite of his proximity to him.
4- The agreement to meet after executing the operation at the home of the chief of the Covert Branch of the Brotherhood was a fatal error.
5- After police cars began pursuing them, the brothers fled to the mountain [called] "Al-Muqattam" Mountain, which was not suitable for evading [pursuit].

UK/BM-134 TRANSLATION

The Second Operation: Blocking the way of the Target's Car
1- The target goes to work in his own automobile, which comes to get
him in the morning and brings him back after work is over. A driver
operates the car and the target's bodyguard sits beside the driver.
2- The group of assassins, composed of three or four people, wait for
the target's car. The waiting place should allow the assassins' car
freedom of movement at any time.
3- The assassins' car departs upon sighting the target's car and
proceeds slowly until it comes to a spot which would allow it to block
the way in front of the target's car. It then immediately stops,
blocking the target's car.
4- At the instant the assassins' car stops, the personnel in charge of
killing or kidnaping the target get out, kill the bodyguard and the
driver, and then execute their mission.
5- This operation requires the utmost speed within a short time to
avoid any one pursuing the assassins' car or seeing any of the
brothers.

Observations:
1- It is best that one of the brothers participating in the
assassination or kidnaping fire at the automobile's tires so that it
can not evade or run away.
2- Most of the brothers participating in the operation should be very
skilled drivers to avoid problems if the driver is wounded or killed.

An Actual Example of an Assassination by Blocking the Target's Path:
Members of the Egyptian Revolution Organization* decided to
assassinate a high-ranking Israeli living in Cairo.

*The Egyptian Revolution Organization: An Organization, which followed
Nasser ([and which he] Jamal Abdel Nasser deified), executed its first
assassination in 1984 and the last in 1987. It undertook four
assassinations of Jews or Americans in Cairo, and Egyptian Security as
well as Israeli and American intelligence were not able to....
[TN: The rest of this page is cut off.]

UK/BM-135 TRANSLATION

2- Surveillance of the target was carried out for a period of time. The exits and entrances to the theater of operations were studied. The time was set to execute the operation at eight am 8/20/85, when the Israeli target would leave for work at the Israeli embassy in Cairo.

3- A car was purchased for use in the operation. Someone's identification was purchased indirectly, the photo was removed, and that of one of the organization's members was put [in its place.]

4- The organization members participating in the operation (there were four of them) rode in a car belonging to one of them. They put their weapons in the car (they had hidden their weapons in tennis racket covers.) Before arriving at the theater of operations, they left that car and got into the operations vehicle, which was close to the site of the operation.

5- After riding in the car, it became apparent the car was not in good running order, and had leaked a lot of oil, so they decided to delay the operation.

6- While they were returning in the car in poor condition, they saw a man from the Israeli Mosad, and the operation leader decided to kill him. The Israeli Mosad man was riding in a car with two Israeli women with him.

7- The Assassins' car drove behind the Israeli target's car, which noticed the surveillance in the rear view mirror, but the driver of the assassins' car was able to choke off the Mosad man's car and he wasn't able to escape. They blocked his way and forced him over by the curb.

8. One of the four personnel got out of the car and emptied the magazine of his American rifle in the direction of the Mosad man. The second one got out on the other side and emptied his bullets, and the third did likewise. After executing the operation, they fled to the other car, and left the operations car on the street.

9. After a period of time, the police force came and found the car with traces of blood.

[It was not] known that the crime was committed by the organization until one of its members (the brother of the organization's leader) turned himself in to the American Embassy and disclosed all the secrets of the operation which the Egyptian Revolution Organization undertook.

UK/BM-136 TRANSLATION

Positive [Aspects]
1- The assassins killed an Israeli person they found on the way back.
2- The purchase of a car just for the operation and a counterfeit identification.
3- Concealing the weapons in tennis racket covers.
4- Choosing a good method to stop the Israeli Mosad man's car.

Negative [Aspects]
1- Failure to inspect the car prepared for the operation with sufficient time before the execution.
2- Undertaking the operation even though the car was malfunctioning, which could have broken down and failed to run after executing the operation.
3- Failure to remove the traces of blood found on the car.

The Third Operation: The Entrance to a Building:
1- The Assassins' car is parked in a location near to the target's building.
2- When the target gets out of the car or exits from the building, the assassins open fire upon him, the bodyguard, and the driver who is opening the car door for him.
3- Run away immediately or ride the car or motorcycle which is prepared for an immediate get away.

An Actual Example of an Assassination at the Entrance to a Building (Assassination Attempt on the Former Minister of the Interior, Hassan Abu Basha):
1- A group from the Islamic organization called "[Those who have] escaped the Fire" composed of

three people waited for the previous Minister of the Interior, Hassan
Abu Basha's car in a location near the entrance to the building.
When Abu Basha arrived, and as soon as he got out of the car, two of
the brothers opened fire on him over the cabin of their vehicle (pick-
up).
3- Abu Basha threw himself between his car and another car parked
nearby as soon as they opened fire. As a result of this incident, the
minister was paralyzed in half [of his body].
4- The brothers fled after the incident took place, and they took
their car in the opposite direction of the flow of traffic.

Important Observations:
When the brothers went to the location near Abu Basha, they hadn't
gone to kill him but to do reconnaissance (gather information on him).
1- One of the brothers was bearded while doing the reconnaissance.
2- The brothers were armed while gathering information about the
minister.
3- There was no established plan for the assassination.

The Fourth Operation: While Going To or From Work:
1- The target is going to work in his own car, and he has a driver and
a bodyguard.
2- The assassins lie in wait for the target in a certain place while
he is going to or from work.
3- When the assassins see the target's car approaching, they take
their places.
4- The car's tires, the bodyguard, driver, and target are hit.

An Actual Example of an Assassination While the Target is Going to
Work: (The Assassination of Rif'at El-Mahgoub))

UK/BM-138 TRANSLATION

1- The brothers began surveillance of all the Interior Minister -
Abdul Halim Mousa's movements, from his departing his house until
entering the ministry. The surveillance lasted several weeks.
2- Friday morning was set for the execution of the operation where the
minister heads to work.
3- Exactly at ten in the morning the brothers were fully prepared. An
observer was going to give a signal to the brothers when the
minister's car departed from his house.
4- When the convoy reached the specified location of the operation
(the operations stage), bullets were sprayed from all directions on
the private car in front of him and on the escort vehicle.
5- The brothers approached the car after firing at the tires to
confirm that the minister was dead, The brothers did not find the
Minister of the Interior, but they did find Rif'at El-Mahgoub, Head of
the People's Assembly, dead inside the car. [TN: Similar to our
Speaker of the House].
6- This was an startling situation. The two convoys (the Interior
Minister's convoy and that of the Head of the People's Assembly) were
separated by only about seven minutes. After about seven minutes the
Minister of the Interior arrived at the location of the incident.
7- The brothers who were participating in the operation (four brothers
to execute the assassination and two to drive the motorcade) had only
two motorcycles (three people to each motorcycle), and after executing
the operation, one of the two motorcycles fled and the other broke
down, and after a moment they left that motorcycle behind.
8- When the motorcycle broke down, one of the brothers fled on foot,
carrying his weapon in the opposite direction of the cars. He stopped
a taxi and threatened the driver with his weapon, and then rode with
him. During the drive, a police officer (a general in the police
force) stopped the car, supposing that the armed man was just a thief.
He opened the door to arrest him, but the brother put the rifle to his
chest and emptied a burst of rounds into it and the officer fell to
the ground like a slain bull. It came to light afterwards, that this
officer was one of the criminals who used to torture the brothers in
some neighborhoods of Cairo.

UK/BM-152 TRANSLATION

Examples of Assassination Operations Using Explosives:
1- Blowing up a building or motorcade using a car bomb, whereby the driver of the car loaded with explosives blows up his [illegible-possibly car].

An Actual Example:
Some of the brothers in Egypt tried to blow up the motorcade of the former Minister of the Interior's vehicle (Z I B) by putting 200 kilograms of TNT in a pick-up truck. When the minister's car was seen, the brother approached in his car and blew up the car.
However, it didn't cause an explosion in the car, and it was confirmed afterward that the explosives didn't go off because no catalyst was placed with the large quantity of explosives. The explosives ignited but they did not explode.

2- Throwing one or more bombs into a group of enemy personnel or into the target's car:

An Actual Example:
Personnel from the Covert Branch of the Muslim Brotherhood threw some bombs into [some] stores and bars on the evening of January 7, 1947 at 11:00 pm.

3- Blowing up a location or car with a time bomb.

Some Palestinians were able to place a time bomb inside an aircraft's radio, and after the aircraft took off it blew up in the air.

It is also possible to explode a time bomb using the timer from a washing machine or any other device (a fan, etc.); at a specified time, the two wires make contact and the charge explodes.

Lesson 15 describes various explosive devices, how to prepare them, and how to detonate them. It looks at slow fuses and fast fuses, explosive chain reactions, blasting caps, booby traps, car bombs, time bombs using alarm clocks, and much more. This, the final page of the chapter, recounts actual assassinations that terrorists have carried out.

Assassinations Using Cold Steel:
A- Assassinating with a knife: When undertaking any assassination
using a knife, the enemy must be struck in one of these lethal spots:
From the Front: 1- Anywhere in the rib cage.
                2- Both or one eye.
                3- The pelvis (under target's navel)
                4- The area directly above the genitals.
From Behind: 1- The axon (back of the head).
                2- The end of the spinal column directly above
the person's buttocks.
B- Assassination with a Blunt Object: A blow with a club must be in
lethal areas.
From the front:
1- The two eyes.
2- Where the veins and arteries converge in the neck.
3- Top of the stomach, with the end of the stick.
4- Above the genitals, with the end of the club.
5- The area of the tongue.
6- Choke the neck with the stick, like in a hanging.
From the rear: 1- The area of the left ear.
2- The back of the head (axon).
[TN: Blunt object, stick, and club were all the same word in Arabic;
different choices were made to show range of meaning.]
Assassination with a Rope: 1- Choking (Neck area). There is no other
area besides the neck.
Assassination using Hands: 1- Choking. 2- Poking the fingers into one
or both eyes and gouging them.

Terrorists are thinking about *every* way they can kill us. As these instructions reveal, al Qaeda's sophisticated assassins can develop dangerous, difficult-to-detect poisons just as easily as they can use brute force ("Assassinations Using Cold Steel") to kill us.

UK/BM-155 TRANSLATION

3- Grab the testicles by the hand and twist and squeeze.
4- Grab the rib cage with both hands and squeeze.

Assassinations with Poison: We will limit [the discussion] to poisons
that the holy warrior can prepare and use without endangering his
health.
First- Herbal Poisons: A- Castor Beans
The substance Ricin, an extract from Castor Beans, is considered one
of the most deadly poisons. .035 milligrams is enough to kill someone
by inhaling or by injecting in a vein. However, though considered less
poisonous if taken through the digestive system, chewing some Castor
Beans could be fatal. It is a simple operation to extract Ricin, and
Castor Beans themselves can be obtained from nurseries throughout the
country.
Symptoms: Need to vomit - diarrhea - unawareness of surroundings - the
skin turns blue, leading to failure of blood circulation [sic] and
finally ... death.
                          B- Precatory Beans
The herbal poison Abrin, extracted from Precatory Beans, is very
similar to Ricin. The seeds of this plant are red and black and are
used in prayer beads [TN: like a Rosary]. Prepare a very dark ink or
refine some normal ink to

be as fine as possible while keeping it strong enough to penetrate the
shell of Precatory Beans. Put on a pair of leather gloves and very
carefully bore about twelve holes in each of the prayer beads. After
completing that, spray the prayer beads with DMSO (Dimehtyl
Sulfoxide). The Abrin will kill your victim slowly, but relentlessly.

Extracting Abrin and Ricin

In order to facilitate removing the shells of these seeds, soak 3.2
ounces (an ounce = 31.1 milligrams) of castor-oil plant seeds in about
10 ounces of water, adding two teaspoons of 1yo [sic, maybe meant lye]
or an alkaline (a substance extracted from soap powder). You need to
submerge the seeds in the water, so cover them with clean gravel or
use marble. Let them soak for an hour, then take out the seeds, clean
them, and let the shells dry. They can be easily removed after that.
Put the shelled seeds in a mixture four times their weight of acetone,
until they completely harden. Then put them in a covered glass
container, and leave them for 72 hours. After that, transfer them to
another container through a coffee filter. Put on surgical gloves and
a mask, and squeeze out as much of the acetone as possible. Then add
fresh acetone and repeat

UK/BM-158 TRANSLATION

the procedure of leaving them for 72 hours and straining them through a coffee filter two more times. The final result will be pure Eysein [PH] or Abrin.

C- The Water Hemlock Plant

A lethal dose is 3.2 grams. It has a palatable taste, and is very similar to another plant, parsnip.

Symptoms: Nervous spasms within 15 to 60 minutes, including severe locking and clenching of the jaw to the extent that the tongue could be cut off.

D- The Tanj Oil Tree

Second- Semi-alkaline substances: They are highly solvent in alcohol.

A- Tobacco

There is enough nicotine in three cigarettes to kill a person. Sixty to 70 milligrams of pure nicotine will kill a person within an hour if eaten.

B- Potato Sprout

The potato sprout (both rotten and green) contains Solanine.

How to Extract Poisonous Alkaline

Chop up the leaves finely. It is preferable to make a mixture, and then put it in a drip coffee maker, through which the boiling water can penetrate the coffee gradually.

UK/BM-159 TRANSLATION

Fill a metal pot with about 1/3 rubbing (isopropy[l]), alcohol mixed
with Isopropyl. Let it strain and percolate for an hour. During the
first half hour, add alcohol as needed, and during the second half
hour, let it boil until you have two ounces left in the container.
These [two] ounces or [could be] less are alcohol mixed with poison
alkaline. Put this amount on a plate, and let the alcohol evaporate.
The remainder on the plate will be very pure poison. There is another
method which is not as good, but it doesn't require the drip coffee
maker. It is simply heating the minced and mixed plants with the
alcohol [we had] before over a low flame. Its symptoms will appear in
160 days.

Poisoning from Eating Spoiled Food

Since .000028 grams will kill a person, this poison is absolutely
lethal. After consumption, the symptoms appear in 12 to 36 hours. They
include dizziness, headaches, constipation, difficulty swallowing and
speaking, fluids coming from the nose and mouth, and lack of muscle
coordination. It results in death from respiratory failure. If it is
received in the blood stream, death is very swift and almost without
symptoms.

How to Prepare Spoiled Food:

Fill a pot with corn and green beans. Put in a small piece of meat and
about two spoonfuls of fresh excrement. Pour the water into

242

APPENDIX A

UK/BM-160 TRANSLATION

into the pot until there is surface tension at the lip of the pot.
Cover the pot tightly. If you do that correctly, there will be no air
trapped in the pot. Leave the pot in a dark, moderately warm room for
15 days. At the end of that period, you will notice a substance on the
edge of the pot and a small amount of rottenness. These are known
bacteria colonies, which secrete their external poison as a result of
the process of bacterial digestion. You can make three or four pots at
the same time.
During the time of the destroyer, Jamal Abdul Nasser, someone who was
being severely tortured in prison (he had no connection with Islam),
ate some feces after losing sanity from the severity of the torture. A
few hours after he ate the feces, he was found dead.

UK/BM-180 TRANSLATION

THE IMPORTANCE OF TEAM WORK:

1. Team work is the only translation of God's command, as well as that of the prophet, to unite and not to disunite. Almighty God says, "And hold fast, all together, by the Rope which Allah (stretches out for you), and be not divided among yourselves." In "Sahih Muslim," it was reported by Abu Horairah, may Allah look kindly upon him, that the prophet, may Allah's peace and greetings be upon him, said: "Allah approves three [things] for you and disapproves three [things]: He approves that you worship him, that you do not disbelieve in Him, and that you hold fast, all together, by the Rope which Allah, and be not divided among yourselves. He disapproves of three: gossip, asking too much [for help], and squandering money."

2. Abandoning "team work" for individual and haphazard work means disobeying that orders of God and the prophet and falling victim to disunity.

3. Team work is conducive to cooperation in righteousness and piety.

4. Upholding religion, which God has ordered us by His saying, "Uphold religion," will necessarily require an all out confrontation against all our enemies, who want to recreate darkness. In addition, it is imperative to stand against darkness in all arenas: the media, education, [religious] guidance, and counseling, as well as others. This will make it necessary for us to move on numerous fields so as to enable the Islamic movement to confront ignorance and achieve victory against it in the battle to uphold religion. All these vital goals can not be adequately achieved without organized team work. Therefore, team work becomes a necessity, in accordance with the fundamental rule, "Duty cannot be accomplished without it, and it is a requirement." This way, team work is achieved through mustering and organizing the ranks, while putting the Amir (the Prince) before them, and the right man in the right place, making plans for action, organizing work, and obtaining facets of power . . . .

Al Qaeda's training manual concludes with this reminder about the "importance of team work." But the text makes clear that "team work" means staying united in order to fulfill their duty before God, which demands "an all out confrontation against all our enemies."

APPENDIX B

The Nature of the Threat

We have a ton of problems we need to fix as we fight the War on Terror. Understanding the nature of the threat—really getting it—is the first thing we have to do. So far our government hasn't gotten it, but if we push them, our leaders will figure it out.

Fortunately we have some people in government, in intelligence, in the military, and in the private sector who are pushing to get things right. In the pages that follow you'll find excerpts from government briefings on the nature of the threat we face. With these briefings, people who get it—who understand how our enemy operates—are spreading the word to those in Washington who don't get it.

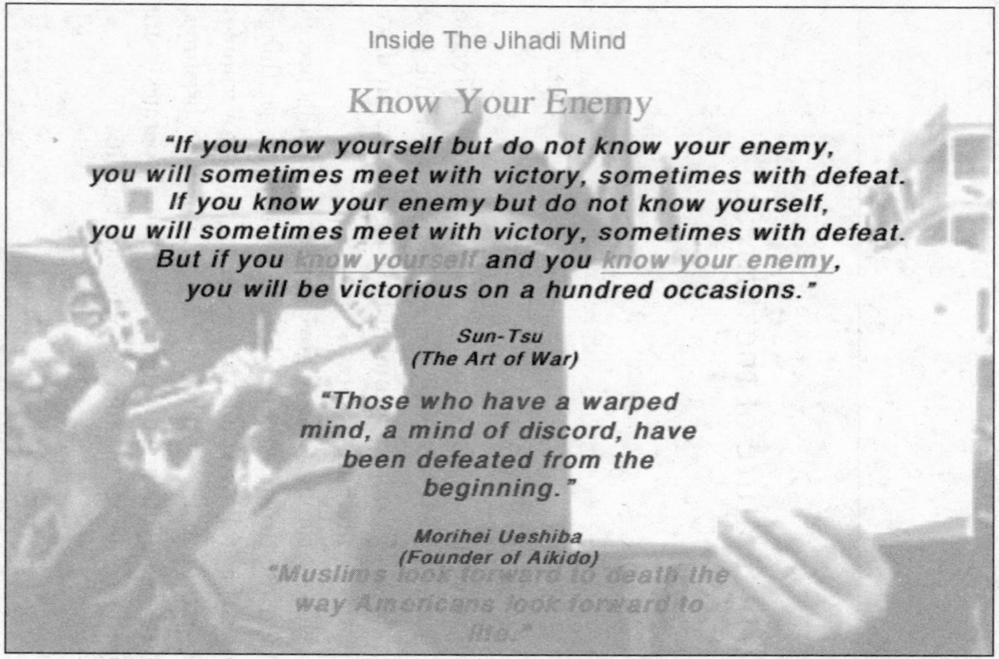

Inside The Jihadi Mind

Know Your Enemy

"If you know yourself but do not know your enemy,
you will sometimes meet with victory, sometimes with defeat.
If you know your enemy but do not know yourself,
you will sometimes meet with victory, sometimes with defeat.
But if you know yourself and you know your enemy,
you will be victorious on a hundred occasions."

Sun-Tsu
(The Art of War)

"Those who have a warped
mind, a mind of discord, have
been defeated from the
beginning."

Morihei Ueshiba
(Founder of Aikido)

"Muslims look forward to death the
way Americans look forward to
life."

In this unclassified briefing, a U.S. military terrorism expert goes "Inside the Jihadi Mind" to show what motivates the Islamic extremists who are out to kill us. The pages shown here, which come out of a much longer presentation, address the critical issue of what motivates these killers. They also highlight the need to "know your enemy."

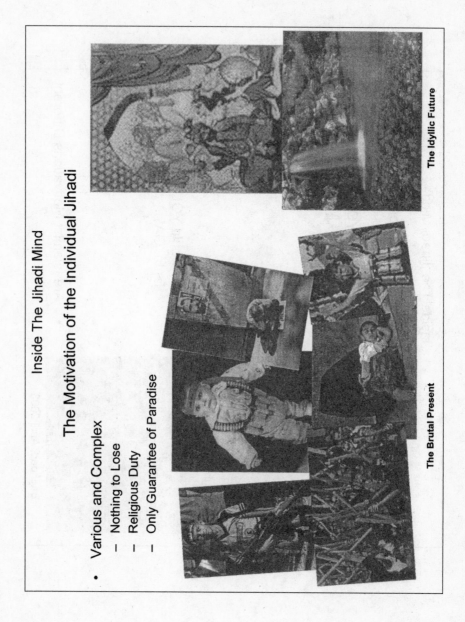

Inside The Jihadi Mind

The Motivation of the Individual Jihadi

- Various and Complex
  - Nothing to Lose
  - Religious Duty
  - Only Guarantee of Paradise

The Idyllic Future

The Brutal Present

Inside The Jihadi Mind

Islamist Perceptions & Motivations...?

• How would YOU feel if this was Kansas City, MO.?

Baghdad, April 2003

• How would YOU feel if this was Atlanta, GA?

Baghdad, April 2003

• Are Islamist Motivations Different From Ours...?

ZAKAT

> *"Take from their wealth a portion for charity,*
> *in order to clean them thereby, and sanctify them."*
> *Quran*

- Zakat is the form of alms given by Muslims for the benefit of the poor or needy and the teaching of Islam.

- The Quran requires Muslims each year to give 2.5% of the value of their wealth and assets above what they themselves need.

- Zakat is given by the beginning of the month of Muharram marking the lunar new year.

- Zakat is one of the Five Pillars of Islam. Zakat is considered the primary method for creating social justice and prosperity in the Muslim world.

Giving Bread and Milk

Ukrainian mosque
Built with Zakat funds

Unclassified

Understanding what motivates the terrorists is not enough; we need to know how they operate and where they get their money. The trouble is, terrorist organizations receive huge influxes of cash from a variety of sources, most of which are difficult to monitor. This unclassified U.S. Army briefing identifies key sources of funding for Islamic terrorists—*Zakat, Hawala,* and money laundering.

Zakat Collection and Distribution

• Saudi Arabia collects Zakat by government agency (similar to our IRS) and distributes to recognized charities. Saudi collections are estimated to exceed $10 Billion. (Saudi Ministry of Finance and National Economy)

• Most other countries, both Muslim and non-Muslim do not collect or control where Zakat money goes..

• Charities around the globe are rarely checked or audited by government oversight agencies to see how the monies are spent. The US is a notable exception.

• The Internet has numerous Islamic charity sites asking believers to pay the Zakat to them promising to apply it on their behalf.

• The giver of Zakat knows only to whom they gave their money, for what they believe will be the building of schools, mosques and to help the poor. Once given however, the giver has no further control if the funds are diverted or a portion is skimmed off for the purchase of weapons, explosives and operating terror training camps.

"If beneficiaries had used assistance for evil acts, that is not our responsibility at all"
Prince Salman, Governor of Riyadh, Saudi Arabia, Nov. 2002

Unclassified

Islamic Banking

- Many Muslims send their Zakat through Islamic banks. This process is legal but there is no assurance they have funded a legitimate charity vice a terrorist group.

- The Islamic banking system has been a mystery to most in the West. Islamic Banks cannot charge interest on loans. This requires that the Islamic Bank make its money on its investments. Western style accounting and auditing practices to monitor and track what those investments truly involve have only recently been implemented and then only under international pressure since the attacks on the US.

- Zakat funds deposited in Islamic banks are taken off the books and "disappear" because they are not considered part of the banks assets nor its liabilities and are not reported. The bank has served only as a collection agent. The Zakat can then be transferred, without regulation, to worthy charities as directed by the givers, to any worthy recipient or have some or all of it skimmed off to Islamic radicals.

- Some of the largest Islamic banks have their headquarters in Switzerland. The Swiss banking philosophy and governmental regulation, adds a second layer of secrecy yet gives the banks connectivity with world banking in general.

Unclassified

Money Movement by Hawala

HAWALA IS ILLEGAL DON'T RISK IT!

US tells India to regularize hawala transactions

Western Union Ad Warning Potential Hawala Users

- Hawala is the best known *Informal Funds Transfer* (IFT) system. Interpol estimates India alone to have $680 Billion in transactions annually.

- The process uses both legal and illegal means to move money in a way that avoids:
  - Record keeping of transmitters and receivers
  - Taxes
  - Customs duties

- It is secure, trust-based, paperless and generally untraceable.

- Hawala came into public interest after the 2001 attacks on the US when it was revealed that much of the money funding the attackers was transferred by Hawala.

- It has no formal limitations on amounts but does have practical limits. It is well suited for terror operations that cost $50-$70K to fund and complete in a short period of time.

- It is illegal in many countries including the US, yet many banks in both Islamic and Western countries utilize this system.

Unclassified

Money Laundering

- Money laundering is not just big business, it is global and large scale.

- International Monetary Fund (IMF) estimates that it accounts for 2 to 5 % of the Worlds GDP (gross domestic product) with a value of as much as 2 trillion US dollars in today's market.

- A significant portion of laundered money actually serves as a positive influence in local economies.
  - It does pay people legitimate salaries even when the business or other entity is only a "legit" cover for other activities.
  - It even pays taxes when channeled through legitimate businesses.

- When accomplished through smuggling or other criminal enterprise it pays no taxes, duties or fees.

- Bottom line – it often pays terrors bills when these groups use laundering as a method to move large sums of money or in related barter/in kind transactions.

Unclassified

Conclusions

- Terrorists and extremists around the world will continue to use multiple means to transfer monies to operatives. Whether the means are legal or illegal is of no concern so long as the process supports their operations.

- These four key methods will continue to be exploited as long as government oversight is not present or is ineffective in policing the systems.

- Zakat is a positive contribution to the Islamic world being abused by those who see it as a means to fund terrors criminal element. Only a small percentage of funds given in compliance with Zakat are intended by a knowing giver for the purpose of terror. That small percentage is enough to allow the spread of terror and end lives around the world. Just the opposite of Zakats' intended use.

- Islamic banking must continue to become mainstream in their methodology and accountability in order to be recognized as trustworthy institutions. Failing that, they will remain a secretive grouping that raises suspicions as much as they attract business.

- Hawala was originally benign in its historical intent but is now consistently misused by those who take advantage of its efficiencies. It will remain as a cultural alternative to regulated banking but certainly will continue to adapt further to accommodate the modern world. The fact that it is being made illegal in more and more countries will not end the practice in the near term.

- Money laundering will continue to face pressures from authorities. Like Hawala, it will remain as a working part of the criminal enterprise system. Increased regulation in the traditional business environment will make laundering more difficult but will not carry it to extinction.

- Nations and organizations around the world are becoming more involved in the effort to track the in and out flows of terrors money through legislation and regulation. Regulatory efforts will serve to plug more of the financial holes that terror employs. However, as with all areas of crime, laws and regulations apply to all people and entities in a given jurisdiction but are only implemented and followed by those willing to be regulated.

Unclassified

In late summer 2004, the Department of Homeland Security produced this unclassified briefing on how terrorist groups use the Internet to disseminate information. The report notes that "analysts have long suspected that speeches, images, and videos, released by the Al Qaeda group, have contained coded messages or commands for its followers." Sometimes the messages are not subtle.

Sheik Ahmed Yassin - HAMAS Leader killed by Israelis, March 2004

Abdel Aziz Rantisi - Successor to Sheik Yassin, killed by Israelis, April 2004

Al Khattab - Arab Chechen Commander - killed by Russians 2002

Omar Abdel Rachman - Imprisoned in USA 1995

911 Hijacker from Martyrdom video

Abdullah Azzam - Afghan Commander - killed by car bomb in Pakistan, 1989

"Did you notice...something in Sheikh (bin Laden's) interview with ABC when he announced the formation of the new organization?" "He sat in front of a map of Africa with Kenya and Tanzania behind his shoulders. That was his message to the Americans, but they did not get it. They are stupid." *(Abu Anas, "Masterminds of Terror.")*

(Three months after the ABC NEWS interview, explosions rocked the U.S. Embassies in Nairobi, Kenya and Dar el Salaam, Tanzania)

What does this photograph suggest???

Source: (9-11 Hijacker) Said al-Ghamdi martyrdom tape

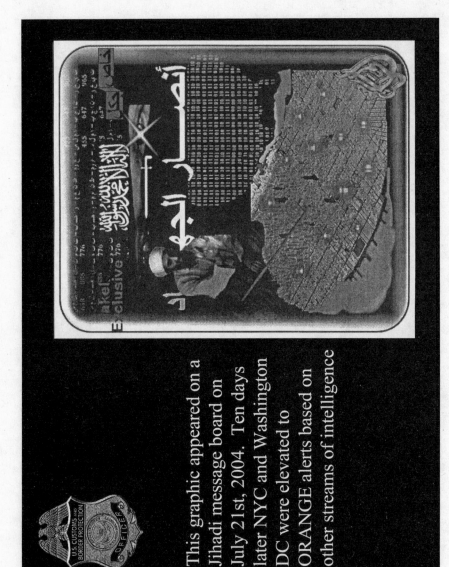

This graphic appeared on a Jihadi message board on July 21st, 2004. Ten days later NYC and Washington DC were elevated to ORANGE alerts based on other streams of intelligence

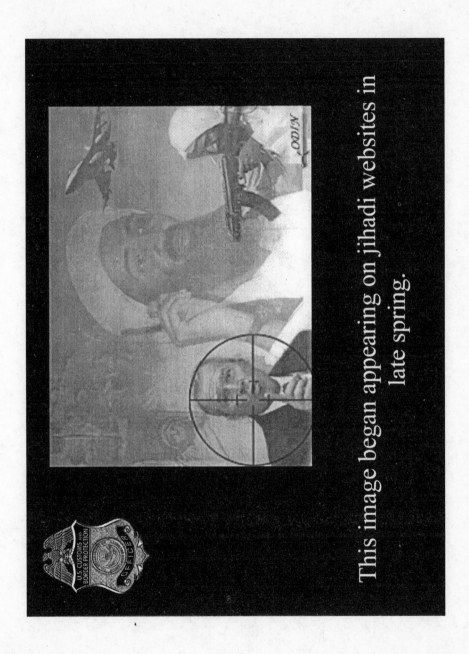

This image began appearing on jihadi websites in late spring.

ACKNOWLEDGMENTS

This is my first book, and it wouldn't have been possible without the efforts of many people besides myself. First, I would like to thank Roger Ailes and the Fox News Channel for offering me the opportunity to voice my opinions and insights on the War on Terror. I also thank my friend Bill O'Reilly, who encouraged me to write this book. My agent, Eric Simonoff, did a masterful job of guiding a first-time author through the process of developing a book idea and presenting it to publishers. I'm pleased that he led me to Crown Forum and editor Jed Donahue, who made chicken soup out of chicken s---.

In addition, I am grateful to Christine Hunsinger and Kathie Hackett for all their time spent reviewing the manuscript and making corrections when necessary. This is a better book for their input. Of course, any mistakes that remain are my own fault, not anyone else's.

Perhaps most important, I want to thank my family for making me the person I am. Some of these people, sadly, are no longer with me, but they shaped my life from the beginning. My dad was a soldier, athlete, altar boy, bouncer, political operative, and overall hero to his sons. My mother was a beautiful, sensitive, complicated, and loving woman. My two brothers were great guys who died too young—one killed in Vietnam at age twenty-one, the other killed in a car accident at twenty-three.

Every day I am grateful for the family I do have with me. I am father to three amazing guys: Jason, a micro-geneticist in Alaska who has a great mind and is a world-class outdoorsman, mountain rescue member, and skier; Evan, an athlete and writer; and Ryan, the youngest, who is fourteen going on forty, an accomplished student and athlete, and a chick magnet. All three are the best of what I am; the worst I kept for myself. I am also fortunate to have such a terrific sister in Kathleen. And of course, I count my blessings that I am married to the most beautiful, talented woman on the planet. Angela is a five-foot-ten-inch dark-eyed Italian beauty who, for whatever reason, has stayed with me for twenty years.

Finally, I want to thank all the brave men and women whom I served with in my twenty-nine years of service to this country. I am a soldier and proud of it. And I am just as proud of all the men and women who continue to protect us in the War on Terror. It is for them that I have written this book.

INDEX

COLONEL DAVID HUNT, U.S. Army (Ret.), has extensive operational experience in counterterrorism, special operations, and intelligence operations. He is a designated terrorism expert in federal court, testifying at many major terrorist trials, and has lectured at the CIA, the FBI, the National Security Agency, and Harvard University. A military analyst for the Fox News Channel, he frequently provides commentary on radio programs hosted by Bill O'Reilly, Sean Hannity, Alan Colmes, Michael Savage, Monica Crowley, and others. Colonel Hunt, a senior research fellow at Harvard's John F. Kennedy School of Government, lives in Maine with his family.